Wordsworth & Coleridge
Lyrical Ballads and Other Poems

Wordsworth & Coleridge

Lyrical Ballads

and Other Poems

with an Introduction and Notes by
MARTIN SCOFIELD

Wordsworth Poetry Library

In loving memory of

MICHAEL TRAYLER

the founder of Wordsworth Editions

2

Readers who are interested in other titles from
Wordsworth Editions are invited to visit our website at
www.wordsworth-editions.com

For our latest list and a full mail-order service, contact
Bibliophile Books, 5 Thomas Road, London e14 7bn
tel: +44 (0)20 7515 9222 fax: +44 (0)20 7538 4115
e-mail: orders@bibliophilebooks.com

First published 2003 by Wordsworth Editions Limited
8B East Street, Ware, Hertfordshire sg12 9hj

Typeset in Great Britain by Antony Gray
Printed and bound by Clays Ltd, St Ives plc

INTRODUCTION

I *Lyrical Ballads, 1798 and 1800: Wordsworth*

Sometime in mid-November 1797, William Wordsworth, his sister
Dorothy and their friend Samuel Taylor Coleridge set off on a walking
tour through the Quantock Hills in Somerset. 'As our united funds were
very small,' Wordsworth wrote later, 'we agreed to defray the expence of
our tour by writing a poem to be sent to the New Monthly Magazine.'[1]
The poem was 'The Rime of the Ancient Mariner'. In the following
months the project grew, and 'we began to talk of a volume'. Wordsworth
then wrote, as he recalled, 'The Idiot Boy', 'The Mad Mother', 'We Are
Seven' and 'The Thorn', 'and some others'. With the addition of three
more poems by Coleridge, and other poems which Wordsworth had
written earlier, *Lyrical Ballads with a Few Other Poems* appeared in the
autumn of 1798.

This small volume, so quietly and matter-of-factly conceived, was to
become a landmark in the history of English literature. Wordsworth had
published two long poems, 'The Evening Walk' and 'Descriptive
Sketches', in 1792, and Coleridge had published a few poems in the
magazines. But with *Lyrical Ballads* their poetry made its first, and
perhaps its most decisive mark, amounting to nothing less than an
unobtrusive literary revolution. It was unobtrusive at the time because
in subject matter it was not so different from much of the poetry
currently being published in the magazines. Poems about the rural
poor, beggars, deserted mothers and the like, often using the form of
the ballad, and also blank verse poems of reverie and meditation upon
scenes of natural beauty were commonplace.[2] What was new in *Lyrical
Ballads* was the depth of moral and psychological complexity with
which these subjects were treated, and also the overt experimentalism
of the language and style, an experimentalism which challenged a whole
prevailing literary aesthetic and ideology.

---

1 Wordsworth's note to Isabella Fenwick on 'The Thorn'; Butler and Green (eds)
   p. 347. For full details of this and all other references to books by or about
   Wordsworth and Coleridge, see the Bibliography at the end of this Introduction.
2 See, for example, Robert Mayo.

The 'Advertisement' at the beginning of the volume of 1798 was an immediate provocation to conventional taste. 'The majority of the following poems are to be considered as experiments,' wrote Wordsworth. 'They were written chiefly with a view to ascertain how far the language of conversation in the middle and lower classes of society is adapted to the purposes of poetic pleasure.' This was a frank challenge to the view that the language of literature was that of the educated upper classes. The reviewer in *The Monthly Review* quoted the statement, and commented: 'Though we have been extremely entertained with the fancy, the facility, and (in general) the sentiments, of these pieces, we cannot regard them as *poetry*, of a class to be cultivated at the expense of a higher species of versification . . . '[3] Other reviews were by no means universally hostile, but this claim by Wordsworth to be redefining the nature of the language of poetry was more far-reaching than it at first seemed, and its challenge was compounded in the more detailed treatment of the topic in his Preface to the second edition of 1800.

In the 1800 Preface, Wordsworth made the poetically revolutionary claim that the lives of the lower classes were better suited to the exploration of 'the primary laws of our nature' and that their language 'is a more permanent, and a far more philosophical language, than that which is frequently substituted for it by Poets'. The claim aroused a forthright refutation from the leading critic of *The Edinburgh Review*, Thomas Jeffrey. In a review of Southey's *Thalaba* in 1802, he attacked (clearly with *Lyrical Ballads* very much in mind) a new '*sect* of poets', 'dissenters from the established systems in poetry and criticism', who 'constitute, at present, the most formidable conspiracy against sound judgement in matters poetical'.[4] Jeffrey was aware that the Preface of 1800 was 'a kind of manifesto' for a linguistic radicalism; and he saw it as characterising poets distinguished by 'a splenetic and idle discontent with the existing conditions of society'.

The modern reader needs to remember that this period was one agitated by acute fears (and in some cases hopes) of political revolution. The French Revolution of 1789 had aroused a wave of anxiety throughout Europe. In England, the writings and activities of writers like Thomas Paine, author of *The Rights of Man* (1791–2), and John Thelwall, the political activist and friend of Wordsworth and Coleridge,

3   *The Monthly Review*, Vol. xxix, June 1799; reprinted in Brett and Jones (eds), p. 321

4   *The Edinburgh Review*, I, Oct. 1802; cited in Gill, p. 244

were a stimulus to radicals and a source of alarm for conservatives. *Lyrical Ballads* of 1798 and 1800 did not preach political revolution, but the attitudes of mind that they embodied radically questioned an existing social structure and dominant sensibility: they were subversive volumes. England did not undergo a political revolution, but *Lyrical Ballads* contributed to a revolution in taste which had wide social implications.

To consider first Wordsworth's contribution to the 1798 volume (nineteen out of the twenty-three poems), the challenge of poems like 'Simon Lee' or 'Old Man Travelling' or 'The Idiot Boy' or 'The Last of the Flock' is that they focus attention not so much on new social areas, but on a human significance within those areas neglected or even unperceived in the poetry of the preceding century. (Only William Blake, in his very different *Songs of Innocence and of Experience* of 1794, approaches the subject of poverty, dispossession and the radical weaknesses of conventional thinking with anything like a comparable depth of insight.)[5] If one compares, say, a poem like 'The Beggar's Petition' from *The Gentleman's Magazine* of 1791 with 'The Last of the Flock' one can see the difference between a poem which appeals to an easy sentimental compassion for the poor, one which does not challenge fundamental social preconceptions, and a poem which ponders deeply the nature of human dignity and independence and which implicitly challenges accepted social policies of the day. 'The Beggar's Petition' adopts the fiction of speaking with the voice of the beggar, but takes a conventional stance of direct (and plaintive) moral address to the ruling class, appealing in a simple way to the reader's charity:

> Pity the sorrows of a poor old man,
> Whose trembling limbs have borne him to your door;
> Whose days are dwindled to a single span:–
> Oh, give relief, and Heav'n will bless your store!

Wordsworth's 'The Last of the Flock', on the other hand, is told initially in the third person, and is an actual encounter 'in the broad highway' with a man carrying a lamb in his arms and weeping. The man tells his story to the poet, and Wordsworth is more concerned with understanding the inner motivation of the man, as a way of understanding his plight, than with arousing a stock moral response. The poem conveys the way

5   For a penetrating comparison of Blake and Wordsworth in this respect, see Heather Glen.

the man's life is bound up (and not just financially) with his livelihood, the way his springs of feeling, his sense of achievement, his pride, his love of his wife and children are closely involved with his work and his property.

> Sir! 'twas a precious flock to me,
> As dear as my own children be;
> For daily with my growing store
> I loved my children more and more.
> Alas! It was an evil time;
> God cursed me in my sore distress,
> I prayed, yet every day I thought
> I loved my children less;
> And every week, and every day,
> My flock it seemed to melt away.

This is a real man in a real place, speaking an authentic language, as opposed to the moralist's mouthpiece of the magazine poem. Wordsworth's poem draws no conclusion and neither the poet nor the shepherd exhort the reader to action: the poem is left to do its more fundamental work of impressing us with an actual case, the actual workings of the mind undergoing suffering. And implicitly the poem challenges a view of social relations which relies on the condescending charity of the rich, from their position of assured social superiority, with a view which sees human need more deeply, and how that need is bound up with the need for self-respect and independence.

Throughout these poems, Wordsworth is challenging what he calls in the Advertisement, 'that most dreadful enemy to our pleasures, our own pre-established codes of decision' – the habits which the mind forms, and which prevent it from seeing and feeling. It is also notable how persistently Wordsworth associates his moral preoccupations with the idea of pleasure, 'the grand elementary principle of pleasure, by which [man] knows, and feels, and lives, and moves':[6] the moral value of poetry is bound up inextricably with the pleasure it gives.

Adult reason and logic, and the 'polite' social and intellectual assumptions which lie, for instance, behind the eighteenth-century assurances of Pope's famous 'Essay on Man', are other elements of our 'codes of decision' which are challenged by Lyrical Ballads. And here

---

6   Preface to Lyrical Ballads (see p. 388); see also 'Lines Written in Early Spring'.

Wordsworth shows a vein of subtle humour with which he is not always credited. In 'Anecdote for Fathers', the over-insistent adult speaker is shown up as comically insensitive in his demands for adult reasoning and explanation from the child as to why he prefers one place to another ('And five times did I say to him, / "Why? Edward, tell me why?"'). Again in 'We Are Seven' a real philosophical problem as to the nature of death and the nature of 'being' is raised by the little girl's insistence, in the face of the adult's confident and conventional reasoning and religious explanation, that ' "Nay, we are seven!" ' There is a famous cartoon by Max Beerbohm showing an elderly man (though Wordsworth was only twenty-eight in 1798) solemnly lecturing a small and bewildered-looking girl, with the caption, 'William Wordsworth in the Lake District, at cross purposes'.[7] Beerbohm was making fun of Wordsworth's solemnity and the philosophic importance he attaches to children: but Wordsworth has anticipated the joke. The repetitions of the poem accentuate the uncomprehending exasperation and self-certainty with which his poetic persona lectures his infant interlocutors.

In 'The Idiot Boy' and 'The Mad Mother', Wordsworth challenges conventional feelings and notions connected with madness. In the face of characteristically rigid eighteenth-century categorisations of mad and sane, his poems arouse a deeper awareness which sees the elements of sanity in 'madness' and those common elements of human experience which link the two. (Here he could be compared to a thinker of our own time, R. D. Laing.)[8] Wordsworth was deeply interested in extreme psychological states: during the months Lyrical Ballads were being written he asked to be sent a copy of Erasmus Darwin's recently published Zoonomia, a study of the laws of organic life, from which he took the story of obsessive, psychosomatic guilt, 'Goody Blake and Harry Gill'. In 'The Mad Mother', Wordsworth shows how the woman's madness, caused, it is implied, by her abandonment by her lover, is given shape and form by her love for her child: the love is an obsession which colours and distorts her perception of the outside world, but it also provides a vein of persisting vitality and feeling which remains as a spiritual value in the midst of her suffering. In 'The Idiot Boy', he aims for a kind of wild and sublime humour which conveys both the absurdity and value of the

7   Max Beerbohm, The Poet's Corner, Penguin Books, London and New York 1943
8   See, for example, The Divided Self, Tavistock Publications, London 1960.

mother's love and the boy's mad heroism. There is disagreement among critics as to whether the poem's effort to dispel our discomfort with the subject 'works', but Donald Davie praised its 'Dionysian' energies. Wordsworth himself said, 'I never wrote anything with so much glee,' and that quality seems to be at the heart of the poem. It is at once comic, heroic and mysterious: it plays with the awkwardness of literary language and popular metres (the repetition of 'in a sad quandary' at line 181), has moments of high farce – a kind of farcical joyousness – ('She darts as with a torrent's force, / She almost has o'erturned the horse' [ll. 384–5]), and moments of ghostly mystery (e.g., ll. 87–91); and all elements are present in the concluding stanza, with Johnny's mad but mysterious refrain (like something from *King Lear*), '"The cocks did crow to-whoo, to-whoo, / And the sun did shine so cold"', so that, as the concluding line's 'that was all' is both throwaway ('that was all it was') and heroically affirmatory, the 'glory' is both ironic and genuine:

> – Thus answered Johnny in his glory,
> And that was all his travel's story.

The poem is both simple and complex, and thus demonstrates a very Wordsworthian kind of wit.

II   Coleridge: 'The Rime of the Ancient Mariner'

In the fourteenth chapter of his *Biographia Literaria*, Coleridge gives his account of how he and Wordsworth agreed to divide up the subject matter of *Lyrical Ballads* into poems of the 'supernatural' and those of 'ordinary life':[9]

The thought suggested itself (to which of us I do not recollect) that a series of poems might be composed of two sorts. In the one, the incidents and agents were to be, in part at least, supernatural; and the excellence aimed at was to consist in the interesting of the affections in the dramatic truth of such emotions, as would naturally accompany such situations, supposing them real. And real in *this* sense they have been to every human being who, from whatever source of delusion, has at any time believed himself under supernatural agency. For the second class, subjects were to be chosen from ordinary life; the characters and incidents were to be such, as will be found in every village and its vicinity, where there is a meditative and feeling mind to seek after them, or to notice them, when they present themselves.

In this idea originated the plan of the 'Lyrical Ballads'; in which it was agreed that my labours should be directed to persons and characters supernatural, or at least romantic; yet so as to transfer from our inward nature a human interest and a semblance of truth sufficient to procure for these shadows of imagination that willing suspension of disbelief for the moment which constitutes poetic faith. Mr Wordsworth, on the other hand, was to propose to himself as his object, to give the charm of novelty to things of everyday, and to excite a feeling analogous to the supernatural, by awakening the mind's attention from the lethargy of custom, and directing it to the loveliness and the wonders of the world before us; an inexhaustible treasure, but for which, in consequence of the film of familiarity and selfish solicitude, we have eyes, yet see not, ears that hear not, and hearts that neither feel nor understand.

This division of labour was not entirely adhered to, since Wordsworth included the potentially or ambiguously supernatural poems 'The Thorn' and 'Goody Blake and Harry Gill' among his contributions; and three out of the four poems by Coleridge ('The Foster-Mother's Tale', 'The Nightingale' and 'The Dungeon') are about 'everyday' subjects. But the subject of Coleridge's major poem of 1798, and the poem from which the whole project of *Lyrical Ballads* grew, was certainly supernatural – indeed it is the most famous supernatural poem in the English language.

'The Rime of the Ancient Mariner' defies interpretation, but of course will always solicit it. Despite its affinities with the old English ballad and the sources of its various elements in Coleridge's reading, it seems to come from nowhere, not even from any obvious source in Coleridge's psychological experience.[10] But one interesting fact may be noted about it at the outset: it is a poem about guilt and penance, or crime and punishment. As such it is associated with a strong preoccupation in *Lyrical Ballads*, and in Wordsworth's and Coleridge's poetry as a whole, with these elements of experience. Wordsworth's 'Goody Blake and Harry Gill' and 'The Thorn' in 1798 and 'Hart-Leap Well' and 'Nutting' in 1800, the episodes of bird-stealing and boat-stealing in Book II of *The*

---

10 For the literary sources of the poem, see Livingstone Lowes, *The Road to Xanadu*.

Prelude, together with Coleridge's 'Christabel' and 'The Three Graves', as well as the 'Ancient Mariner', are all about feelings of guilt, sometimes more sometimes less explicable. And the notable thing about the 'Ancient Mariner' is that the guilt arises from a casual and seemingly slight act of destruction or transgression ('Nutting' and the *Prelude* scenes are comparable here). One does not imagine that the killing of albatrosses aroused such terrible guilt and met with such terrible consequences on most early voyages of exploration or trade. 'The Rime of the Ancient Mariner' is a nightmare exploration of the seemingly irrational workings of guilt, a voyage into a fantasy world that compels its readers' imaginative assent. As a tale of irrational but compelling guilt it has resonances, for the modern reader, with the world Kafka's *The Trial* or his short story 'The Knock at the Manor Gate'.

'The Rime of the Ancient Mariner' holds a unique place in English literature as *the* exemplary poem of the Romantic period which explores a world of unreason, fantasy (even perhaps madness), in a way that makes this world seem not a case of aberrant pathology (which is how a typical eighteenth-century mind would have seen it and how many contemporary reviewers did see it) but something like a universal parable. The Ancient Mariner has no name, no distinct 'character' (as Wordsworth pointed out), but stands as a mythic or emblematic figure for the mysteries of unmotivated crime and the unfathomable workings of a moral universe. He is hardly 'Everyman', and yet every reader finds an element of recognition in the tale. Through a created world of imagination, Coleridge explores the psychological state of madness caused by guilt and isolation: we can call it an irrational world, but as in Kafka, there is always the suspicion that we call it that only because we cannot understand it.

The poem is one in which the external world becomes the theatre for a state of mind. Another way of describing this is to say that Coleridge is, with Blake, one of the first modern poets of the symbol. 'In looking at objects of Nature while I am thinking,' Coleridge wrote in his Notebooks,[11]

> as at yonder moon dim-glimmering through the dewy window-pane, I seem rather to be seeking, as it were *asking* for, a symbolical language for something within me that already and for ever exists, than observing anything new. Even when that latter is the case, yet

11 *Anima Poetae*, entry for 14 April 1805, *The Nonesuch Coleridge*, p. 175

still I have always an obscure feeling as if that new phenomena were the dim awaking of a forgotten or hidden truth of my inner nature.

So in the 'Ancient Mariner', the moon and sun, the wind, the mist, all seem to be equivalents of inner states, or at least to play their part in the Mariner's moments of psychological transformation. We do not need to make these objects of nature into an allegory (with, say, the sun and moon standing for Coleridge's much later distinction between understanding and fancy), as some mid-twentieth-century critics did,[12] but the poem does work through an interpenetration of inner and outer. The sun and moon are both malign and beneficent presences at different points in the poem. And winds and breezes have always a potential suggestion of the inner movement of the spirit (just as the 'blessing' of the 'gentle breeze' at the opening of Wordsworth's *Prelude* (1805) points forward to the internal 'corresponding mild creative breeze' of line 43 of that poem). The 'roaring wind' (l. 309) that the Mariner hears after he has blessed the water snakes and the rain has come, and that 'shook the sails' but 'did not come anear' – suggests a power and energy audible but remote, something the Mariner can sense but not fully experience (compare 'Dejection: An Ode', 276: 'I see, not feel, how beautiful they are'). And the 'loud wind' which 'never reached the ship / Yet now the ship moved on' (ll. 327–8) suggests a power still outside the range of effectiveness, but which is replaced by another power moving the ship from beneath, as we learn at line 376. In Part VI, however, after the spell of the curse of his fellow-mariners' eyes is 'snapped' (l. 443),

> But soon there breathed a wind on me,
> Nor sound nor motion made:
> Its path was not upon the sea,
> In ripple or in shade.   [ll. 452–5]

This wind acts uniquely on the Mariner, and as such is surely an image of the effect of a spiritual grace. Inner and outer states sometimes combine in harmony and sometimes act separately, but there is a feeling of 'one life' working through them both, an idea which we shall see at work in other of Coleridge's (and Wordsworth's) poems.

The Ancient Mariner holds us with his glittering eye, just as he held the wedding guest: the enigma of the poem, its driving ballad rhythm

12 Humphry House discusses some of these views, pp. 92–113.

and its extraordinary descriptive vividness grip our imaginations beyond any attempt we may make to interpret it. No other poem in English conveys so compellingly a world of fantasy and nightmare, but it is one which at the same time is rooted in a plausibly created quasi-historical setting of a sixteenth-century voyage. Its tactile imagery of horror ('Yea, slimy things did crawl with legs / Upon a slimy sea') is, again, also an imagery of inner obsession. And its supernatural imagery (like the figure of 'DEATH' and the 'Nightmare LIFE-IN-DEATH') comes from deep psychological fears as well as from traditional emblems (death as a skeleton, the whore of Babylon).

The meaning of the poem certainly goes beyond the rather simplistic 'moral' ('He prayeth best who loveth best,' etc., lines 614–17) which the Mariner utters at the end. Indeed, Coleridge commented later, in response to the criticism that the poem had 'no moral', that on the contrary, 'the only, or chief fault . . . was the obtrusion of the moral sentiment so openly on the reader as a principle or cause of action in a work of such pure imagination'.[13] And yet even this explicit moral has a dramatic rightness and plays a part in the whole: it looks back to the crucial moment when the Mariner blesses the water snakes and is suddenly able to pray (l. 288); and its very naïvety expresses the Mariner's exhausted falling back into simple conventional belief (just as he finds it 'sweeter than the marriage-feast' 'To walk together to the kirk / With goodly company!' (ll. 603–4) after his extreme and harrowing experience.

Of Coleridge's other 1798 poems, 'The Nightingale', with its successful development of a conversational blank verse, will be discussed below. 'The Foster-Mother's Tale', an excerpt from Coleridge's play Osorio, is written in a mode of narrative dialogue that Wordsworth was to develop more successfully in 'The Brothers'. And in 'The Dungeon', Coleridge shows a sympathy for the criminal which shocked a number of contemporary reviewers, but which is surely related to the theme of 'The Ancient Mariner'. It is the counterpart of Wordsworth's similar but formally (in its awkward metre) less successful 'The Convict' (omitted in the 1800 edition); and more significantly it is part of a recurring concern with understanding the experience of the outcast, criminalised and dispossessed, which characterises both poets.

13 'Table Talk', *The Nonesuch Coleridge*, p. 488

III Wordsworth's Lyrical Ballads of 1800

It is not known which of the two poets first suggested the term 'Lyrical Ballads', nor precisely what they intended by it:[14] but it has been suggested that the term combines the idea of the objective story-telling of the traditional ballad, with that of the subjective element of the personal lyric: a union, perhaps, of impersonality and personality, of objective quasi-historical truth and subjective perception. This certainly fits well the nature of a poem like 'Simon Lee' or 'The Thorn', where an anecdote or tale is infused with a subtle or impassioned subjective response. Sometimes a poem tends towards one pole, sometimes the other, but the twin impulse is always there, its two elements in harmony or in tension.

Poems of 1798 like 'Lines Written in Early Spring', 'Expostulation and Reply' and 'The Tables Turned' tend towards the subjective or philosophical pole, though they still have an element of narrative, the relation of an incident or event ('I heard a thousand blended notes / While in a grove I sate reclined', etc.). In Wordsworth's poems from the 1800 volume onwards this subjective element grows more predominant, as he more searchingly interrogates the bases of his vision, and questions (as Heather Glen has suggested)[15] the assurances and optimism of 'Tintern Abbey'. Wordsworth's famous faith in 'Nature' is complex and shifting: a matter of repeated encounters and renegotiations with experience rather than a fixed 'philosophy'.

In particular there is a growing feeling that there may be a disjunction between the self and the natural world, a sense of human egoism and destructiveness, and a sense that the impersonal laws of nature are ultimately at odds with human desire. The poem 'Nutting' suggests, through a biographical anecdote, the way in which a triumphant appropriation of the natural world can lead to destruction and an ensuing sense of guilt. The ballad-like 'Hart-Leap Well' relates a similar story in a legendary, medieval setting. 'Michael' explores the tragic way a life of domestic happiness in the heart of 'nature', in which human love and natural beauty seem to exist in unbreakable harmony, is undermined by human weakness, time and change. Michael's 'pleasurable feeling of blind love / The pleasure which there is in life itself' for the woods and fields is compounded and strengthened by his love for his son, who

14 For a discussion of this issue, see Jordan, Chapter 8.
15 Glen, p. 261

prompts feelings which are (in a beautiful phrase) 'light to the sun and music to the wind' (l. 212). But love and human continuity are not assured; the son's briefly narrated dereliction leaves Michael with the unfinished sheepfold, the fact and symbol of an unrealised future:

> . . . many and many a day he thither went
> And never lifted up a single stone.   [ll. 474–5]

These poems and many others express in a simple language, which is the distillation of deep thought and long contemplation, what Wordsworth in his 1800 Preface called 'the primary laws of our nature', the elemental facts of love, desire and death. And it is above all for their distinctive rendering of these primary laws of the human condition that Wordsworth's poems retain their special value.

One group of poems that explores this condition in a particularly personal, subtle and elusive way – with an elusiveness which has led to great differences of opinion as to their success – is that group known as the 'Lucy' poems: 'Strange fits of passion', 'She dwelt among th' untrodden ways' and 'A slumber did my spirit seal'. These poems attempt, one might say, to express the inexpressible, to evoke a sense of the nature of love and its relation to death which registers the extra-linguistic reality of both in a language that is as transparent as possible. Matthew Arnold once famously (or notoriously) said of Wordsworth, to suggest the quality of his greatness, that he has 'no style', that 'Nature herself seems, I say, to take the pen out of his hand and to write for him with her own bare, sheer, penetrating power'.[16] Arnold was wrong, of course (Wordsworth's 'style' – or styles – with its limpid simplicities, its grandeurs, its awkwardnesses, its loquacities and pomposities, is always recognisable), but Arnold's rhetorical flourish (and he only says 'seems') has a rich suggestiveness: it bespeaks the effort *towards* naked simplicity, the profound effort of clarity of thought, which lies behind all of Wordsworth's best poems. There is a fine passage in Wordsworth's 'Essay on Epitaphs', which deserves to be known as well as more famous pronouncements from the 1800 Preface, in which he speaks of the dangerous power of language:[17]

> Words are too awful an instrument for good and evil, to be trifled
> with; they hold above all other external powers a dominion over

16 Introduction to *Poems of Wordsworth* (1879), in McMaster (ed.), p. 233
17 'Essay on Epitaphs', III (1810), in Zall (ed.), p. 125

thoughts. If words be not . . . an incarnation of the thought, but only a clothing for it, then surely will they prove an ill gift; such a one as those possessed vestments, read of in the stories of superstitious times, which had the power to consume and to alienate from his right mind the victim who put them on. Language, if it do not uphold, and feed, and leave in quiet, like the power of gravitation or the air we breathe, is counter-spirit, unremittingly and noiselessly at work, to subvert, to lay waste, to vitiate, and to dissolve.

The effort of Wordsworth's simple (as opposed to his Miltonic) style is, one might say, to find a language which upholds, feeds and leaves in quiet; and such a language is nowhere better exemplified than in the 'Lucy' poems.

'Strange fits of passion I have known' – the first line seems to promise some extraordinary and extreme experience, but the poem that follows is about a seemingly commonplace and random thought. The simple ballad stanzas lead us into an artless-seeming love poem with its conventional properties (the 'rose in June', the cottage, the moon, the 'sweet dreams'). Like the lover on his steadily clopping horse the reader is lulled into a romantic dream, each stanza keeping our eye on the descending moon. And then in the penultimate stanza, at the point at which we are most mesmerisingly lulled by the horse's motion, the moon suddenly disappears; and the 'fond and wayward' thought slides into the lover's head –' "If Lucy should be dead!" ' Why is this thought 'fond' (foolish) and 'wayward'? Why is the experience a 'strange fit[] of passion'? It is foolish and strange, and induces a reaction of guilt (' "O mercy!" ') because it reveals to the lover the unawareness, the unthinkingness, of his 'sweet dream[]'. The lover's mind is solipsistic: it assimilates everything, including the reality of the beloved, to its own happiness. This tendency of the imagination – particularly perhaps the poetic imagination – was one which Wordsworth was aware of both as a strength and as a weakness. (Keats caught the paradox brilliantly in his characterisation of the Wordsworthian mode as 'the egotistical sublime').[18] The imagination of the lover (or the poet) has created a world in which Lucy's separate identity is occluded. The sudden awareness of her mortality, induced by the disappearing moon (that index of time and change), brings a pang of anxiety which has an element of guilt

---

18 in a letter to Woodhouse, 27 October 1818 (*Letters of John Keats*, World's Classics, Oxford, 1965, p. 172)

since it offends against the beneficence of the setting, and the mind could even be seen to collude in the thought of her death. No less than in 'Nutting' or 'Hart-Leap Well', but with a new and remarkable subtlety since it finds its instance in the most casual movement of the mind, Wordsworth has shown the seductiveness and destructiveness of the human assimilation of the outside world to itself.

'She dwelt among th' untrodden ways' explores further the implications of Lucy's death (now imagined as actual) and the poet's relation to it. Lucy barely existed in the public world: her significance is distinct but elusive. F. W. Bateson pointed out many years ago how the internal paradoxes ('untrodden ways', 'none to praise / And very few to love', 'unknown, and few could know') seem simultaneously to assert and deny Lucy's existence in a social world.[19] She is delicately beautiful but half-hidden, her beauty is ethereal, outside the world. It is as if she existed for the poet alone, and his last exclamation, 'The difference to me', has something (is meant to have something) egoistic about it (the poet, or lover, can only think about her significance for *him*), as well as affirming her overwhelming meaning for him. The poem reveals the lover's sense of delicate beauty and almost ineffable significance, but also his inevitable selfishness (which is why the poem is so open to parody). But in 'A slumber did my spirit seal' the poet awakens from his selfishness in a movement of profound realism. The spirit-sealing slumber of the first stanza was fine, beautiful, but also stultifying: it turned Lucy into something immortal, but also into a 'thing'; the poet 'had no human fears', but in this state he was less than human. The second stanza reveals his disillusioned, awakened state. It asserts the utter finality of Lucy's death, her real becoming of a 'thing': but it also affirms the grandeur as well as the passivity of her being-dead, her assimilation to and continued existence with the great impersonal material universe. It contradicts, but in its truthfulness it also confirms and outdoes, the wishful claim to immortality of the first stanza. The whole poem is one of the greatest moments of Wordsworth's philosophic poetry, in a style that combines the plainest ('rocks and stones and trees') and the most exact scientific language (the Latinate and learned 'diurnal'). It is 'simple' only because it is exact: it penetrates to essentials.

19 Bateson, pp. 31–5

IV   *Coleridge: the supernatural, the conversational and the psychological*

Coleridge's 'Christabel' was originally intended for publication in the second volume of *Lyrical Ballads,* but it was finally omitted, perhaps because it was too long or because it did not fit in with the tenor of the volume.[20] Perhaps Coleridge also lost faith in it to some extent, because it was never finished. As it stands it is incomplete, oddly compelling in many ways, but baffling. The overall story, which Coleridge sketched out to his son Derwent and to Edward Gilman, is undiscernible in the poem as we have it.[21] Christabel is supposed to be tormented by Geraldine (an evil spirit in one account of the plot, and good spirit in another), as a kind of vicarious suffering to protect her lover 'that's far away'. But what emerges in the unfinished, published poem is the presence of a mysterious woman who seems far from benign, haunting Christabel and stirring up division between her and her father, Sir Leoline. There are suggestions of snake-like evil in Geraldine (l. 459 and ll. 583–5, and in Bard Bracy's dream of the snake and the dove, ll. 527–59), and a strong suggestion too of homoerotic passion, as in the passage where Geraldine undresses, lies down beside Christabel and takes her in her arms. Geraldine seems here to be an example of the figure of the predatory female intruder who wins the confidence of a family and then proceeds to seduce and corrupt them. Geraldine claims to be the wronged daughter of a friend of Sir Leoline, but the latter seems to respond to her with more than fatherly interest (ll. 399–402), and as she 'roll[s] her large bright eyes divine / Wildly upon Sir Leoline' (ll. 595–6), Christabel sees only 'a serpent's eye' and pleads with her father to send Geraldine away. For Hazlitt, in his review of 1816, there was 'something disgusting at the bottom of his subject, which is but ill-glossed over by a veil of Della Cruscan sentiment and fine writing – like moonbeams playing upon a charnel house, or flowers strewed on a dead body'.[22] There does seem something dark and transgressive in this poem, though we may be less censorious of this quality than Hazlitt was – and from its unfinished state its final nature can only be guessed at: it may have been working its way to a harmonious resolution and a

20 See *The Complete Poems,* ed. Keach, pp. 505–6.
21 See, for example, House, pp. 126–8.
22 Reprinted in Jones and Tydeman (eds), pp. 62–5. 'Della Cruscan' refers to a
     school of poets at the end of the eighteenth century, led by Robert Merry, who
     wrote sentimental and affected verse.

benevolent view of Geraldine. The poem's form, with its insistent and incantatory varied metre and rhyme, seems to complement this sense of Gothic horror and the irrational, and it looks forward to a poetry of incantation in Poe, Mallarmé and parts of Eliot, where the imagery and music have a suggestiveness that goes beyond articulable meaning.

If 'Christabel' is clearly unfinished, 'Kubla Khan', despite Coleridge's prefatory note to the contrary, is whole and entire – a perfect symbolic statement and evocation of the workings of the poetic imagination. It embodies in poetic form the idea of the imagination which Coleridge put forward later more obscurely and metaphysically in Chapter XIII of *Biographia Literaria*: 'The primary IMAGINATION I hold to be the living Power and prime Agent of all human Perception, and as a repetition in the finite mind of the eternal act of creation in the infinite I AM.'[23] Like the Judaeo-Christian God, the mythical king Kubla Khan decrees the original act of creation of a walled garden (a paradise) which contains both an ordered and a wild landscape: 'twice five miles of fertile ground' on one hand, and on the other 'caverns measureless to man' and an irruptive 'mighty fountain'. It also contains erotic passion (the association of the 'woman wailing for her demon lover') and prophecies of war. The 'dome of pleasure' represents art, which echoes with the sound of birth (the fountain) and death (the caves). In the final stanza the poet speaks of repeating Kubla's original act of creation, through his memory of the Abyssinian maid's song of Mount Abora (another mythical location of paradise): 'I would build that dome in air'. 'Kubla Khan' is not a precise allegory – it retains the element of mystery – but in its basic structure it approaches one. It stands as a great poetic symbol of the imagination.

In other poetic moods Coleridge was not the wild bard of 'Kubla Khan', with 'flashing eyes and floating hair', but the 'man speaking to men' of Wordsworth's Preface. With reference to his 'Conversation' poems – 'The Nightingale', 'Reflections on Having Left a Place of Retirement', 'This Lime-Tree Bower My Prison', 'Frost at Midnight' and others – Coleridge spoke of wanting to capture the casual effect of what he called 'the divine chit-chat of Cowper'.[24] William Cowper's long poem *The Task* (1785) had shown what could be done with an iambic pentameter blank verse which avoided the sonority and Latinate syntax of the Miltonic style and aimed at an easy, reflective

23 *Biographia Literaria*, op. cit., Vol. I, p. 202
24 cited in House, p. 72

measure suitable for reflecting variously on common rather than heroic experience. Both Wordsworth and Coleridge are to some extent his heirs in their blank verse poems, but Wordsworth, in his tendencies to elevation and sublimity, in *The Prelude* and even in places in 'Tintern Abbey', still often ascends into the Miltonic tone; and one feels that Coleridge assimilated Cowper more fully, and indeed passed that influence on to Wordsworth (at least three of Coleridge's conversation poems, including 'This Lime-Tree Bower My Prison' were written before 'Tintern Abbey'). 'The Nightingale' in the 1798 volume shows the straightforward syntax and relaxed reflectiveness, the domestic setting and affections mingled with the precise observation of nature, and the elements of educational theory ('And I deem it wise / To make him [Coleridge's baby son, Hartley] Nature's playmate') which we shall see more fully developed in the other conversation poems.

Perhaps the finest of these is 'Frost at Midnight'. If 'Kubla Khan' was a brilliant, visionary statement of the poetic imagination, 'Frost at Midnight' is a quiet meditation on the nature of the same, a structure of wandering thought in the language and setting of everyday life. Coleridge is sitting at night beside his sleeping baby son, aware of the surrounding sea, wood, hill and village, the 'extreme silentness' of the night and the frost performing 'its secret ministry'. The floating film of ash on the grate takes his mind back to memories of sitting in school dreaming of the future; this brings him back to the present and the child at his side, and this in turn leads him to think of his child's future, and how he will try to raise him in the midst of the natural world so that he will 'see and hear / The lovely shapes and sounds intelligible / Of that eternal language, which thy God / Utters'. This movement between present, past and future, and between the inner and outer world, is an instance of the workings of all human thought, which builds our conscious sense of identity and our moments of creativity out of this movement. In this it is similar to the movement in 'Tintern Abbey': the present scene recalling the past, leading to a statement of what passes away and what persists in consciousness as faith and belief, and ending with an anticipation of the future. The process is partly dependent on conscious will, but is also partly an involuntary one, in which our half-aware sense of the uncontrollable workings of the outer world plays its part. So the poem ends with the beautiful lines which gather together all the seasons, present winter, past summer and future spring. Coleridge looks to his son's future while returning us to the present and to the first line of the poem, to 'the secret ministry of frost' which produces its handiwork by a mysterious and unseen process, just as the poetic imagination has produced the completed poem:

> Therefore all seasons shall be sweet to thee,
> Whether the summer clothe the general earth
> With greenness, or the redbreast sit and sing
> Betwixt the tufts of snow on the bare branch
> Of mossy apple-tree, while the nigh thatch
> Smokes in the sun thaw; whether the eave-drops fall
> Heard only in the trances of the blast,
> Or if the secret ministry of frost
> Shall hang them up in quiet icicles,
> Quietly shining to the quiet moon.

V Wordsworth after 1802

Wordsworth's poems of first-person experience (as opposed to third-person narrative poems like 'Michael' or 'The Ruined Cottage', though even these usually make some explicit reference to the poet's own reaction, to the poetic 'I') might be divided into two main classes: those in which he analyses his own mind, and through it 'the mind of man, 'My haunt, and the main region of my song' (the 'Prospectus' to *The Excursion*, l. 41); and those in which he encounters another person who brings about a distinct change in his sense of being. In the first category would come poems like 'Lines Written in Early Spring', 'Tintern Abbey', 'Nutting' and 'There was a Boy'; in the second, poems like 'Anecdote for Fathers', 'Simon Lee', 'Old Man Travelling', 'The Last of the Flock', 'Stepping Westward', or the encounters with the discharged soldier in *The Prelude,* in which the poet is a man listening as well as 'speaking to men'.[25] The two categories correspond to the two major tendencies in Wordsworth's imagination: the first (and the stronger) directed inward towards the solitary self, and the second, pulling against this, outward towards a world of community. The greatest of his poems (like the Lucy poems already examined) directly confront this tension and opposition, in poems which dramatise a self tending to solipsism but held back from it by a strong sense of objective fact. Both kinds of poems can be found at all stages of Wordsworth's career, but

25 Preface to *Lyrical Ballads* (see p. 13)

the sharper conflicts between the two sides tend to come in poems after those of 1798.

In 'Elegiac Stanzas Suggested by a Picture of Peele Castle', composed in 1806 after the news of the death of his brother John, Wordsworth explores with a strong reflective clarity the difference between his youthful faith and vision when he first saw the actual Peele Castle, and his more sober sense of human weakness and mortality which came to him in later years and which is imaged for him in the painting (by George Beaumont) of the castle in a storm. In the past, to reflect its 'perfect calm', he would have painted it 'Beside a sea that could not cease to smile', adding from his imagination 'The light that never was, on sea or land, / the consecration, and the Poet's dream'. Now 'this fond illusion' is no longer possible:

> A power is gone, which nothing can restore;
> A deep distress hath humanised my Soul,

and he is glad to see this painting of it under duress, 'Cased in the unfeeling armour of old time'. The significant 'encounter' here, the shock of his brother's death, is only alluded to in the poem, and what is focused on is the resulting state of mind.

Another and greater poem recording a sense of loss and the effort to hold on to a faith in life is the famous 'Ode: Intimations of Immortality from Recollections of Early Childhood'. If 'Tintern Abbey' is Wordsworth's first great ode to poetic faith (he did not call that poem an ode, but said he was aiming at something of the effect of one, with its 'transitions' and 'impassioned music'),[26] and one which aims at unshaken affirmation, this is his second, where the emphasis is by contrast on a lament for lost poetic vision. 'There was a time. . . /. . . It is not now as it has been of yore'. The music of the first stanza (in which the language is utterly simple) is plangent and passionate: re-reading it can still bring unexpected tears to the eyes. (Philip Larkin once said that hearing the poem by chance on the car radio while he was driving on the M1 'was almost the price of me'.)[27] The Ode also aims at a more bravura performance than 'Tintern Abbey' (the distinguished American critic Lionel Trilling, comparing it to the more sober blank verse movement of the earlier poem, once called it, with admiring

26 cited in Haydon (ed.), *Poems*, Vol. I, p. 954
27 Philip Larkin, *Required Writing*, Faber and Faber, London 1973, p. 53

irony, 'flashy').[28] In places the language dazzles with its baroque splendour: 'trailing clouds of glory do we come'; 'The winds come to me from the fields of sleep'; 'Though nothing can bring back the hour / Of splendour in the grass and glory in the flower'. But this is combined with a simplicity of statement that carries sober conviction:

> We will grieve not, rather find
> Strength in what remains behind.

The whole performance, with its dynamic use of the rhythms, the long and short lines of the Pindaric ode (what has been described as 'the alternate accumulation and discharge of metrical energy'),[29] and its combination of elevated and simple language, is a unique success, unlike anything Wordsworth achieved elsewhere.

The Immortality Ode celebrates the intensely idealistic, visionary and even solipsistic experience of Wordsworth's earliest years, the drama of the solitary mind. Another poem published in 1807, 'Resolution and Independence', is perhaps more typical of his style and complex sensibility, and explores in a characteristic narrative form that tension between solitary experience and the awareness of other lives of which I spoke above. The poem begins with a characteristic mood of joy in the natural world, but this is followed in Stanza IV by a sudden plunge into 'dejection' (that equally characteristic opposite of the former mood, in both Wordsworth and Coleridge). The poet thinks of the possibility of 'Solitude, pain of heart, distress and poverty', and of the suicide of the poet Thomas Chatterton. Suddenly he encounters an old man. In his interpretation of the poem in a letter, Wordsworth spoke of the setting as 'A lonely place, a pond' 'by which an old man *was* . . . not stood, not sat, but *was*' (his emphases) – a striking instance of his elemental preoccupation with *being* and his fondness for the verb 'to be'. In the poem he elaborates with the similes of the stone and the sea-beast, which place the man half-way between animate and inanimate life, between human mortality and the permanence of rock. The man strikes Wordsworth as an instance of that combination of the two which he frequently finds, and indeed seeks, in the figures of his imagination (like 'Old Man Travelling'). In

28 in a seminar at the University of Oxford, 1964
29 Mark van Doren, *John Dryden: A Study of his Poetry*, Indiana University Press, Bloomington 1960, p. 189

this poem, the leech-gatherer comes as an admonition, an emblem of persistence and suffering.

What the poem achieves (as W. W. Robson showed in a fine essay) is a fusion of the sublime and the everyday, the world of imagination and fact. The old man is both a mysterious figure in the poet's imagination, and an ordinary, courteous, hardworking man. Stanzas XIII to XIX show a narrative dialectic of these two qualities: Wordsworth asks what the old man does for a living, and 'He told, that to these waters he had come / To gather leeches, being old and poor' (XV). But Wordsworth hardly hears his reply:

> But now his voice to me was as a stream
> Scarce heard; nor word from word could I divide;
> And the whole body of the Man did seem
> Like one whom I had met with in a dream.

Then his 'former thoughts' and anxieties return, and he (like his counterpart in Lewis Carroll's penetrating parody of the poem, 'You are Old, Father William', and like the poet in other poems of encounter like 'Anecdote for Fathers' or 'We Are Seven'), locked in his solipsistic world, once again does not listen. Then, 'He with a smile did then his words repeat': the leech-gatherer's smile is the finest stroke of the poem. Wordsworth, lost in a dream of imaginative vision and personal anxiety, is recalled to actuality by that smile – and recalled to the irony that in this conversation with the old man it is he himself who is being absent-minded. The grandeur of the old man in the poet's imagination is not annulled, but it is fused with his sense of him as a human being existing independently of the poet's fantasies about him, 'a moral discovery of the greatest importance' (Robson). The old man is a figure who shows 'courtesy' (that often overlooked Wordsworthian value that we find also in 'Stepping Westward') and deserves it in return, as well as the response of poetic dreaming and wonder which returns again in Stanza XIX: 'In my mind's eye I seemed to see him pace / About the weary moors continually'. The 'apt admonishment' that Wordsworth receives from the leech-gather's 'so firm a mind' (XX) is at once that of the latter's almost mythic heroism (as the poet dreams it), his moral courage and his quite ordinary human awareness of others.

Wordsworth's poetry springs from the intense, and usually solitary, emotional and visionary experiences of his earliest years, but what turns it into great poetry is its encounter with loss and death and the different centres of self of others. The encounter was clearly hard, and the cost of an often obscure personal suffering was high. Wordsworth's nature, as Shelley brilliantly and wittily described it in 'Peter Bell the Third', was self-absorbed, or rather it absorbed everything into itself ('All things that Peter saw and felt / . . . seemed to melt / Like cloud to cloud, into him.' ll. 273–7). In later life, indeed from around 1810 onwards, he continued to write prolifically, but the verse too often falls back on conventional pieties and sustaining sympathies which very rarely approach the imaginative heights and chasms of the great period of 1798–1807. Wordsworth also had little sympathy for the urban, industrial developments of the new Victorian era. When Thomas Carlyle met Wordsworth in 1840, he commented: 'His face bore the marks of much, not always peaceful meditation; the look of it not bland or benevolent, but close, impregnable and hard'.[30]

But among the banal poems after 1810 – poems about small domestic or literary occurrences (with their unenticing titles : 'To the Spade of a Friend', 'Desultory Stanzas on Receiving the Preceding Sheets from the Press'), about places visited, or the interminable collection of the Ecclesiastical Sonnets – there are exceptions, some of which are included in this volume: 'The Duddon Sonnets' (1806–20), with their intermittent fine imaginative touches (two of these sonnets are selected here); the poignant access of memory in the sonnet 'Surprised by Joy' (1813); the strongly-versed lament, at once tender and stern, for the death of fellow-poets, 'Extempore Effusion on the Death of James Hogg':

> Like clouds that rake the mountain-summits
> Or waves that own no curbing hand,
> How fast has brother followed brother,
> From sunshine to the sunless land!

– or the firm artistry of the 'Ode to Lycoris' and the 'Vernal Ode' (both of 1817).[31] The latter poem shows that Wordsworth could still sustain a vision of nature at once grand and minute, albeit now with more classical and literary stage-properties, but at times with an almost scientific precision, 'metaphysical' concentration and sense of paradox, as in the description of the bee:

---

30 Thomas Carlyle, *Reminiscences,* ed. C.E. Norton, Everyman Library, J. M. Dent, London 1972, p. 259

31 For an interesting discussion of the 'Vernal Ode' and other later poems by Wordsworth, see John Jones, pp. 177–92.

> Observe each wing! — a tiny van!
> The structure of her laden thigh,
> How fragile! yet of ancestry
> Mysteriously remote and high.

And generally these poems show the strength and resource of a literary technique, and a sense of the power of artifice (already there in the virtuosity of the Immortality Ode) as a sustaining force when the power of sheer inspiration or vision fades. As the 'Ode to Lycoris' puts it:

> But something whispers to my heart
> That, as we downward tend,
> Lycoris! life requires an *art*
> To which our souls must bend.

VI   *Wordsworth and Coleridge: poetry and philosophy*

Wordsworth and Coleridge were ideal collaborators in 1798 because of their differences as much as their similarities, and the differences were to grow as the years passed. Coleridge was in the early years more concerned than Wordsworth about religious orthodoxy, as the exclamatory piety of 'Hymn before Sunrise, in the Vale of Chamonix' and the apologetic final verse-paragraph of 'The Eolian Harp' testify.[32] His mind also tended more to the abstract, the conceptual and the speculative. It was he who encouraged Wordsworth in the idea of a long philosophic poem, of which the first part was to become *The Prelude* (on 'the growth of the poet's mind'), the second the now little-read *Excursion* and the third the barely begun *Recluse*. But Wordsworth was soon to realise that the nature of his poetry tended too much towards the specific experience and the particular incident to be able to carry out this large philosophic scheme. Coleridge wrote in Chapter XXII of his *Biographia Literaria* of what he saw as the 'beauties' and 'defects' of Wordsworth's poetry: and among the 'defects' he instanced the quality of 'matter-of-factness', which he defined as firstly 'a laborious minuteness and fidelity in the representation of objects' and secondly *'accidentality'* or 'the insertion of accidental circumstances in order to [give] the full explanation of his living characters' (Vol. 2, p. 101). But this 'matter-of-

---

32 In this connection it is interesting to compare Wordsworth's 'Simplon Pass' with Coleridge's 'Hymn before Sunrise, in the Vale of Chamonix': Wordsworth writes of 'Eternity' and 'Apocalypse', but not 'God'.

factness' was, as we have seen in several instances above, essential to Wordsworth's poetry. It constitutes the element in his mental constitution which is balanced against the tendency to ideality, the sublime; the tendency that, as he says in his note on the Immortality Ode, often made him doubt the existence of external things: 'Many times while going to school have I grasped at a wall or tree to recall myself from this abyss of idealism.'

Wordsworth countered a tendency to idealism by holding on to a world of facts and particular experiences. Coleridge too had a fine sense of the objective details of the natural world (as in the descriptive passages of 'This Lime Tree Bower My Prison'). But his tendency was to stress the transforming power of the imagination (Wordsworth probably derived a great deal of his language in the more philosophic parts of *The Prelude* from Coleridge), and also to render his ideas in systematic and conceptual terms. Keats saw this as a lack of the 'Negative Capability' of the true poet, an 'irritable searching after fact and reason': 'Coleridge, for instance, would let go by a fine isolated verisimilitude, caught from the penetralium of mystery, from being incapable of being content with half-knowledge.'[33]   At any rate, Coleridge's poetic output is much smaller than Wordsworth's, even in the great years of 1796–1800; and after 1805 his mind, always wonderfully wide ranging, tended to find its outlet – and often to dissipate itself – in unrealised projects, fragmentary if often brilliant speculation and mesmerising conversation.

Behind the different tendencies of Coleridge's and Wordsworth's minds lay a fundamental difference in their attitudes to language. Is language founded on things or ideas? Wordsworth would have had some sympathy with William Carlos Williams's dictum: 'No ideas but in things.' He wrote in his 1800 Preface of men in rustic life being in touch with 'the best objects from which the best parts of language originally derive' (see p. 7). There is some dispute about what he meant by 'best objects' (some critics say 'natural objects', others cite the later phrase about 'the great and Universal passions of men'): but there is certainly something of the former meaning in it. Things, objects, the external world: these things have a reality about them which is salutary and corrective, and which can be in some sense, known. They may be

---

33 Letter of 21 Dec. 1817: *Letters,* op. cit., p. 53. Keats may however have been thinking of the *Biographia* or Coleridge's lectures rather than, say, 'The Ancient Mariner' or 'Frost at Midnight'.

shaped by our concepts, but they are not simply products of the mind. Coleridge, on the other hand, later took strong exception to this idea of 'the best parts of language': for him 'the best part of human language, properly so-called, is derived from reflection on the acts of the mind itself':[34] in other words it is philosophical.

This fundamental difference has been recast in our own time as a conflict between a view of language that could be called broadly 'realist' – that sees language reflecting an existing reality, and one which sees it as constitutive of reality, with words (as a recent critic of Wordsworth puts it) taking 'their meaning from other words, without reference to an external world at all'.[35] This is not the place to elaborate on that great divide and its ensuing theory-wars (though it is difficult to see how such an extreme position as this last is tenable). But however much (or little) we may follow the deconstructive tendency of modern critical thought, Wordsworth's remarks on the important discipline for the poet of keeping his 'eye on the object' will never, presumably, become otiose. Wordsworth's defence of detailed criticism might also apply to poetry itself: it teaches 'the art of bringing words rigorously to the test of thoughts; and these again to a comparison with things'.[36]

Beyond the controversies about language and the language of poetry which divide Wordsworth and Coleridge, it would be better to close on a note which emphasises their extraordinarily close sympathy and the wonderful fruitfulness of their collaboration. They were, for a time at least, at one in their understanding of 'the one Life within us and abroad' as Coleridge called it in lines added to 'The Eolian Harp' in 1816,

> Which meets all motion and becomes its soul,
> A light in sound, a sound-like power in light,
> Rhythm in all thought, and joyance everywhere.

Or as Wordsworth described it in the more famous passage in 'Tintern Abbey': 'A motion and a spirit that impels / All thinking things, all objects of all thought / And rolls through all things.' At the same time, their other poetry often tested and challenged that affirmative vision, Coleridge most strikingly in 'The Rime of the Ancient Mariner' and 'Dejection: An Ode' and Wordsworth in a host of varied and searching

34 *Biographia Literaria,* pp. 39–40
35 Paul Hamilton, p. 6
36 Zall (ed.), p. 116

poems between 1798 and 1807. Poetry for both (though particularly and more consciously perhaps for Wordsworth) was a matter of the fluctuations of experience, of bringing beliefs into contact with particular experiences and instances. Coleridge would also, I think, have subscribed to the great central statements about poetry which Wordsworth added to his 1800 Preface in 1802. And however wary as modern readers we may be about claims to 'universal' truth, we too, I think, need have no reservations about seeing the centrality, the classic nature of these statements:

> Its [poetry's] object is truth, not individual and local, but general, and operative; not standing upon external testimony, but carried alive into the heart by passion; truth which is its own testimony . . .
>
> [p. 15]

> Poetry is the breath and finer spirit of all knowledge; it is the impassioned expression which is the countenance of all science.
>
> [p. 16]

And of the poet:

> He is a man speaking to men.[37]   [p. 13]

> He is the rock of defence of human nature; an upholder and preserver, carrying everywhere with him relationship and love. In spite of difference of soil and climate, of language and manners, of laws and customs, in spite of things silently gone out of mind and things violently destroyed, the Poet binds together by passion and knowledge the vast empire of human society, as it is spread over the whole earth, and over all time.   [p. 16]

MARTIN SCOFIELD
University of Kent at Canterbury

---

37 Wordsworth is of course using 'man' and 'men' in the generic sense of 'human being(s)'. Cf. the same usage elsewhere in the Preface (e.g., p. 15).

SELECT BIBLIOGRAPHY

Note: Dates in brackets, placed after the date of an edition, are those of first publication

WORDSWORTH & COLERIDGE

Editions of Lyrical Ballads

Lyrical Ballads: The text of the 1798 edition with the additional 1800 poems and the Prefaces, edited by R. L. Brett and A. R. Jones, Methuen, London 1965

Lyrical Ballads, edited by Michael Mason, Longman Annotated Texts, Longman, London and New York 1992

Lyrical Ballads and Other Poems, 1797–1800, edited by James Butler and Karen Green, The Cornell Wordsworth, Cornell University Press, Ithaca and London 1992

Critical Studies of Lyrical Ballads

Robert Mayo, 'The Contemporaneity of Lyrical Ballads', PMLA, 69, 1954

Alun R. Jones and William Tydeman (eds), Wordsworth, Lyrical Ballads, Casebook Series, Macmillan, London 1972

Stephen Prickett, Wordsworth and Coleridge: The Lyrical Ballads, Edward Arnold, London 1973

Stephen Maxfield Parrish, The Art of the Lyrical Ballads, Harvard University Press, Cambridge, Mass. 1973

John E. Jordan, Why the Lyrical Ballads?, University of California Press, Berkeley, Los Angeles and London 1976

Mary Jacobus, Tradition and Experiment in Wordsworth's Lyrical Ballads (1798), Oxford University Press, Oxford 1976

Patrick Campbell, Wordsworth and Coleridge, Lyrical Ballads: Critical Perspectives, Macmillan 1991

Books about Wordsworth and Coleridge

H. M. Margoliouth, Wordsworth and Coleridge, 1795–1834, Oxford University Press, London and New York 1953

Stephen Prickett, *Wordsworth and Coleridge and the Poetry of Growth,* Cambridge University Press, Cambridge 1970

G. H. Hartman (ed.), *New Perspectives on Wordsworth and Coleridge,* Columbia University Press, New York 1972

T. McFarland, *Romanticism and the Forms of Ruin: Wordsworth and Coleridge and the Moralities of Fragmentation,* Princeton University Press, New Haven 1981

Lucy Newlyn, *Coleridge, Wordsworth and the Language of Allusion,* Oxford University Press, Oxford 1986

Paul Magnuson, *Wordsworth and Coleridge: A Lyrical Dialogue,* Princeton University Press, Princeton, NJ 1988

Nicholas Roe, *Wordsworth and Coleridge: The Radical Years,* Oxford University Press, Oxford 1988

A. S. Byatt, *Unruly Times: Wordsworth and Coleridge in Their Time,* Hogarth Press, London 1989

Gene Ruoff, *Wordsworth and Coleridge: The Making of the Major Lyrics, 1802–4,* Harvester Wheatsheaf Press, London 1989

WORDSWORTH

Editions

The Poetical Works, edited by Ernest de Selincourt and Helen Darbishire, 5 vols, Oxford University Press, Oxford 1940–9

The Cornell Wordsworth, General Editor Stephen Parrish, 16 vols, Cornell University Press, Ithaca and London 1975–99

The Poems, edited by John O. Hayden, 2 vols, Penguin, Harmondsworth 1977

Literary Criticism of William Wordsworth, edited by Paul M. Zall, University of Nebraska Press, Lincoln 1966

Biographies

Mary Moorman, *William Wordsworth, A Biography,* Vol. I: *The Early Years, 1770–1803,* Vol. II: *The Later Years,* Oxford University Press, Oxford 1957, 1965

Stephen Gill, *William Wordsworth: A Life,* Oxford University Press, Oxford 1989

John Williams, *William Wordsworth: A Literary Life,* Macmillan, London 1996

Juliet Barker, *Wordsworth: A Life,* Viking Press, London 2000

Critical Studies of the Poetry

John Jones, *The Egotistical Sublime: A History of Wordsworth's Imagination,* Chatto & Windus, London 1954

F. W. Bateson, *Wordsworth: A Reinterpretation,* Longmans Green, London and New York 1956

David Ferry, *The Limits of Mortality: An Essay on Wordsworth's Major Poems,* Wesleyan University Press, 1959

John Danby, *The Simplicity of Wordsworth: Studies in the Poetry 1797–1807,* Routledge and Kegan Paul, London 1960

Colin Clarke, *Romantic Paradox: An Essay on the Poetry of Wordsworth,* Routledge and Kegan Paul, London 1962

Geoffrey Hartman, *Wordsworth's Poetry 1787–1814,* Yale University Press, New Haven 1964

Christopher Salvesen, *Wordsworth and the Landscape of Memory,* Edward Arnold, London 1965

W. W. Robson, 'Wordsworth's "Resolution and Independence" ', in *Critical Essays,* Routledge and Kegan Paul, London 1966

Geoffrey Durrant, *William Wordsworth,* Cambridge University Press, Cambridge 1969

Donald Davie, 'Dionysus in *Lyrical Ballads',* in A. W. Thompson (ed.), *Wordsworth's Mind and Art,* Oliver & Boyd, Edinburgh 1969

Graham McMaster (ed.), *Wordsworth,* Penguin Critical Anthologies, Penguin, Harmondsworth 1972

M. H. Abrams (ed.), *Wordsworth: A Collection of Critical Essays,* Twentieth-Century Views, Prentice-Hall, Englewood Cliffs, New Jersey 1972

Frances Ferguson, *Wordsworth: Language as Counter-Spirit,* Yale University Press, New Haven 1977

James H. Averill, *Wordsworth and the Poetry of Human Suffering,* Cornell University Press, Ithaca and London 1980

John Purkis, *A Preface to Wordsworth,* Longman, London 1982

Jonathan Wordsworth, *William Wordsworth: The Borders of Vision,* Oxford University Press, Oxford 1982

Heather Glen, *Vision and Disenchantment: Blake's Songs and Wordsworth's Lyrical Ballads,* Cambridge University Press, Cambridge 1983

Paul Hamilton, *Wordsworth,* Harvester New Readings, Harvester, Brighton 1986

John Williams (ed.), *Wordsworth,* New Casebooks, Macmillan, London 1993

COLERIDGE

Editions of the Poetry and Prose

The Poems of Samuel Taylor Coleridge, edited by E. H. Coleridge, Oxford University Press, Oxford 1912

Select Poetry and Prose, edited by Stephen Potter, Nonesuch Press, London 1962 (1933)

Coleridge's Verse: A Selection, edited by William Empson and David Pirie, Faber and Faber, London 1972

Poems, edited by John Beer, Everyman Library, J. M. Dent, London 1973

The Complete Poems, edited by William Keach, Penguin, Harmondsworth 1997

Collected Works, Vol. 16, Part I, Poems, Reading Text; Part II, Variorum Text; edited by J. C. C. Mays, Bollinger Foundation, Princeton 2001–2

Biographia Literaria, 2 vols, edited by J. Shawcross, Oxford University Press, Oxford 1965 (1907)

Biographies

Walter Jackson Bate, *Coleridge*, Macmillan, Toronto 1968

Richard Holmes, *Coleridge: Early Visions,* Hodder & Stoughton, London 1989

Richard Holmes, *Coleridge: Darker Reflections,* HarperCollins, London 1998

Critical Studies of the Poetry and General Studies

John Livingstone Lowes, *The Road to Xanadu: A Study in the Ways of the Imagination,* Houghton Mifflin, Boston 1964 (1926)

Humphry House, *Coleridge*, Rupert Hart-Davis, London 1967 (1953)

John Beer, *Coleridge the Visionary*, Chatto & Windus, London 1959

George Watson, *Coleridge the Poet,* Routledge and Kegan Paul, London 1966

Kathleen Coburn (ed.), *Coleridge*, Twentieth-Century Views, Prentice-Hall, Englewood Cliffs, New Jersey 1967

William Walsh, *Coleridge: The Work and the Relevance,* Chatto & Windus, London 1967

A. Grant, *A Preface to Coleridge,* Longman, London 1972

Alun R. Jones and William Tydeman (eds), *The Rime of the Ancient Mariner and Other Poems*, Casebook Series, Macmillan, London 1973

Kelvin Everest, *Coleridge's Secret Ministry: The Context of the Conversation Poems*, Harvester, Brighton 1979

K. M. Wheeler, *The Creative Mind in Coleridge's Poetry,* Heinemann, London 1981

Richard Holmes, *Coleridge*, Past Masters, Oxford University Press, Oxford 1982

Paul Hamilton, *Coleridge's Poetics,* Blackwell, Oxford 1983

Harold Bloom (ed.), *Samuel Taylor Coleridge,* Chelsea House, London 1986

Harold Bloom (ed.), *The Rime of the Ancient Mariner: Modern Interpretations*, Chelsea House, London 1986

Leonard Orr (ed.), *Critical Essays on Samuel Taylor Coleridge,* G. K. Hall, Boston 1994

Peter J. Kitson, *Coleridge, Keats and Shelley,* New Casebooks, Macmillan, London 1996

Stephen Bygrave, *Samuel Taylor Coleridge,* Writers and Their Work, Northcote House (in association with the British Council), London 1997

CONTENTS

WILLIAM WORDSWORTH

WILLIAM WORDSWORTH

1 Advertisement to *Lyrical Ballads* (1798)

It is the honourable characteristic of Poetry that its materials are to be found in every subject which can interest the human mind. The evidence of this fact is to be sought, not in the writings of Critics, but in those of Poets themselves.

The majority of the following poems are to be considered as experiments. They were written chiefly with a view to ascertain how far the language of conversation in the middle and lower classes of society is adapted to the purposes of poetic pleasure. Readers accustomed to the gaudiness and inane phraseology of many modern writers,[1] if they persist in reading this book to its conclusion, will perhaps frequently have to struggle with feelings of strangeness and awkwardness: they will look round for poetry, and will be induced to enquire by what species of courtesy these attempts can be permitted to assume that title. It is desirable that such readers, for their own sakes, should not suffer the solitary word Poetry, a word of very disputed meaning, to stand in the way of their gratification; but that, while they are perusing this book, they should ask themselves if it contains a natural delineation of human passions, human characters, and human incidents; and if the answer be favorable to the author's wishes, that they should consent to be pleased in spite of that most dreadful enemy to our pleasures, our own pre-established codes of decision.

Readers of superior judgment may disapprove of the style in which many of these pieces are executed. It must be expected that many lines and phrases will not exactly suit their taste. It will perhaps appear to them, that wishing to avoid the prevalent fault of the day, the author has sometimes descended too low, and that many of his expressions are too familiar, and not of sufficient dignity. It is apprehended, that the more conversant the reader is with our elder writers, and with those in modern times who have been the most successful in painting manners and passions,[2] the fewer complaints of this kind will he have to make.

An accurate taste in poetry, and in all the other arts, Sir Joshua Reynolds has observed, is an acquired talent, which can only be produced by severe thought, and a long continued intercourse with the best models of compositions.[3] This is mentioned not with so ridiculous a purpose as to prevent the most inexperienced reader from judging for himself; but merely to temper the rashness of decision, and to suggest that if poetry be a subject on which much time has not been bestowed, the judgment may be erroneous, and that in many cases it necessarily will be so.

The tale of Goody Blake and Harry Gill is founded on a well-authenticated fact which happened in Warwickshire.[4] Of the other poems in the collection, it may be proper to say that they are either absolute inventions of the author, or facts which took place within his personal observation or that of his friends. The poem of The Thorn, as the reader will soon discover, is not supposed to be spoken in the author's own person: the character of the loquacious narrator will sufficiently shew itself in the course of the story. The Rime of the Ancyent Marinere was professedly written in imitation of the *style*, as well as of the spirit of the elder poets,[5] but with a few exceptions, the Author believes that the language adopted in it has been equally intelligible for these three last centuries. The lines entitled Expostulation and Reply, and those which follow, arose out of conversation with a friend[6] who was somewhat unreasonably attached to modern books of moral philosophy.

The first Volume of these Poems has already been submitted to general perusal. It was published, as an experiment, which, I hoped, might be of some use to ascertain, how far, by fitting to metrical arrangement a selection of the real language of men in a state of vivid sensation, that sort of pleasure and that quantity of pleasure may be imparted, which a Poet may rationally endeavour to impart.

I had formed no very inaccurate estimate of the probable effect of those Poems: I flattered myself that they who should be pleased with them would read them with more than common pleasure: and, on the other hand, I was well aware that by those who should dislike them they would be read with more than common dislike. The result has differed from my expectation in this only, that I have pleased a greater number than I ventured to hope I should please.

For the sake of variety, and from a consciousness of my own weakness, I was induced to request the assistance of a Friend,[2] who furnished me with the Poems of the ANCIENT MARINER, the FOSTER-MOTHER'S TALE, the NIGHTINGALE, and the Poem entitled LOVE.[3] I should not, however, have requested this assistance, had I not believed that the Poems of my Friend would in a great measure have the same tendency as my own, and that, though there would be found a difference, there would be found no discordance in the colours of our style; as our opinions on the subject of poetry do almost entirely coincide.

Several of my Friends[4] are anxious for the success of these Poems from a belief, that, if the views with which they were composed were indeed realised, a class of Poetry would be produced, well adapted to interest mankind permanently, and not unimportant in the multiplicity, and in the quality of its moral relations: and on this account they have advised me to prefix a systematic defence of the theory upon which the poems were written. But I was unwilling to undertake the task, because I knew that on this occasion the Reader would look coldly upon my arguments, since I might be suspected of having been principally influenced by the selfish and foolish hope of *reasoning* him into an approbation of these particular Poems: and I was still more unwilling to undertake the task, because, adequately to display my opinions, and fully to enforce my arguments, would require a space wholly disproportionate to the nature of a preface. For to treat the subject with the clearness and coherence, of which I believe it susceptible, it would be necessary to give a full account of the present state of the public taste in this country, and to determine how far this taste is healthy or depraved; which, again, could not be determined, without pointing out in what manner language and the human mind act and react on each other, and without retracing the revolutions, not of literature alone, but likewise of society itself. I have therefore altogether declined to enter regularly upon this defence; yet I am sensible that there would be some impropriety in abruptly obtruding upon the Public, without a few words of introduction, Poems so materially different from those upon which general approbation is at present bestowed.

It is supposed, that by the act of writing in verse an Author makes a formal engagement that he will gratify certain known habits of association; that he not only thus apprises the Reader that certain classes of ideas and expressions will be found in his book, but that others will be carefully excluded. This exponent or symbol held forth by metrical language must in different eras of literature have excited very different expectations: for example, in the age of Catullus, Terence and Lucretius, and that of Statius or Claudian;[5] and in our own country, in the age of Shakespeare and Beaumont and Fletcher, and that of Donne and Cowley, or Dryden, or Pope.[6] I will not take upon me to determine the exact import of the promise which by the act of writing in verse an Author, in the present day, makes to his Reader; but I am certain it will appear to many persons that I have not fulfilled the terms of an engagement thus voluntarily contracted. They who have been accustomed to the gaudiness and inane phraseology of many modern writers,[7] if they persist in reading this book to its conclusion, will, no doubt, frequently have to struggle with feelings of strangeness and awkwardness: they will look round for poetry, and will be induced to inquire by what species of courtesy these attempts can be permitted to assume that title. I hope therefore the Reader will not censure me, if I attempt to state what I have proposed to myself to perform; and also (as far as the limits of a preface will permit) to explain some of the chief reasons which have determined me in the choice of my purpose: that at least he may be spared any unpleasant feeling of disappointment, and that I myself may be protected from the most dishonourable accusation which can be brought against an Author, namely, that of an indolence which prevents him from endeavouring to ascertain what is his duty, or, when his duty is ascertained, prevents him from performing it.

The principal object, then, which I proposed to myself in these Poems was to choose incidents and situations from common life, and to relate or describe them, throughout, as far as was possible, in a selection of language really used by men; and, at the same time, to throw over them a certain colouring of imagination, whereby ordinary things should be presented to the mind in an unusual way; and, further, and above all, to make these incidents and situations interesting by tracing in them, truly though not ostentatiously, the primary laws of our nature: chiefly, as far as regards the manner in which we associate ideas in a state of excitement.

Low and rustic life was generally chosen, because in that condition, the essential passions of the heart find a better soil in which they can attain their maturity, are less under restraint, and speak a plainer and more emphatic language; because in that condition of life our elementary feelings co-exist in a state of greater simplicity, and, consequently, may be more accurately contemplated, and more forcibly communicated; because the manners of rural life germinate from those elementary feelings; and, from the necessary character of rural occupations, are more easily comprehended; and are more durable; and lastly, because in that condition the passions of men are incorporated with the beautiful and permanent forms of nature. The language, too, of these men is adopted (purified indeed from what appear to be its real defects, from all lasting and rational causes of dislike or disgust) because such men hourly communicate with the best objects from which the best part of language is originally derived; and because, from their rank in society and the sameness and narrow circle of their intercourse, being less under the influence of social vanity they convey their feelings and notions in simple and unelaborated expressions. Accordingly, such a language, arising out of repeated experience and regular feelings, is a more permanent and a far more philosophical language than that which is frequently substituted for it by Poets, who think that they are conferring honour upon themselves and their art, in proportion as they separate themselves from the sympathies of men, and indulge in arbitrary and capricious habits of expression, in order to furnish food for fickle tastes, and fickle appetites, of their own creation.*

I cannot, however, be insensible of the present outcry against the triviality and meanness, both of thought and language, which some of my contemporaries have occasionally introduced into their metrical compositions; and I acknowledge that this defect, where it exists, is more

---

* It is worth while here to observe that the affecting parts of Chaucer are almost always expressed in language pure and universally intelligible even to this day.
(Wordsworth's footnote)

dishonourable to the Writer's own character than false refinement or arbitrary innovation, though I should contend at the same time that it is far less pernicious in the sum of its consequences. From such verses the Poems in these volumes will be found distinguished at least by one mark of difference, that each of them has a worthy *purpose*. Not that I mean to say, that I always began to write with a distinct purpose formally conceived; but I believe that my habits of meditation have so formed my feelings, as that my descriptions of such objects as strongly excite those feelings, will be found to carry along with them a *purpose*. If in this opinion I am mistaken, I can have little right to the name of a Poet. For all good poetry is the spontaneous overflow of powerful feelings: but though this be true, Poems to which any value can be attached, were never produced on any variety of subjects but by a man, who being possessed of more than usual organic sensibility, had also thought long and deeply. For our continued influxes of feeling are modified and directed by our thoughts, which are indeed the representatives of all our past feelings; and, as by contemplating the relation of these general representatives to each other we discover what is really important to men, so, by the repetition and continuance of this act, our feelings will be connected with important subjects, till at length, if we be originally possessed of much sensibility, such habits of mind will be produced, that, by obeying blindly and mechanically the impulses of those habits, we shall describe objects, and utter sentiments, of such a nature and in such connection with each other, that the understanding of the being to whom we address ourselves, if he be in a healthful state of association, must necessarily be in some degree enlightened, and his affections ameliorated.

I have said that each of these poems has a purpose. I have also informed my Reader what this purpose will be found principally to be: namely, to illustrate the manner in which our feelings and ideas are associated in a state of excitement. But, speaking in language somewhat more appropriate, it is to follow the fluxes and refluxes of the mind when agitated by the great and simple affections of our nature. This object I have endeavoured in these short essays to attain by various means; by tracing the maternal passion through many of its more subtile windings, as in the poems of THE IDIOT BOY and THE MAD MOTHER; by accompanying the last struggles of a human being, at the approach of death, cleaving in solitude to life and society, as in the Poem of THE FORSAKEN INDIAN; by showing, as in the Stanzas entitled WE ARE SEVEN, the perplexity and obscurity which in childhood attend our notion of death, or rather our utter inability to admit that notion; or by displaying the strength of fraternal, or to speak more philosophically, of moral attachment when early associated with the great and beautiful objects of nature, as in THE BROTHERS; or, as in the incident of SIMON LEE, by placing my Reader in the way of receiving from ordinary moral sensations another and more salutary impression than we are accustomed to receive from them. It has also been part of my general purpose to attempt to sketch characters under the influence of less impassioned feelings, as in the TWO APRIL MORNINGS, THE FOUNTAIN, THE OLD MAN TRAVELLING, THE TWO THIEVES, etc., characters of which the elements are simple, belonging rather to nature than to manners, such as exist now, and will probably always exist, and which from their constitution may be distinctly and profitably contemplated. I will not abuse the indulgence of my Reader by dwelling longer upon this subject; but it is proper that I should mention one other circumstance which distinguishes these Poems from the popular Poetry of the day; it is this, that the feeling therein developed gives importance to the action and situation, and not the action and situation to the feeling. My meaning will be rendered perfectly intelligible by referring my Reader to the Poems entitled POOR SUSAN and the CHILDLESS FATHER, particularly to the last Stanza of the latter Poem.

I will not suffer a sense of false modesty to prevent me from asserting that I point my Reader's attention to this mark of distinction far less for the sake of these particular Poems than from the general importance of the subject. The subject is indeed important! For the human mind is capable of being excited without the application of gross and violent stimulants; and he must have a very faint perception of its beauty and dignity who does not know this, and who does not further know, that one being is elevated above another, in proportion as he possesses this capability. It has therefore appeared to me, that to endeavour to produce or enlarge this capability is one of the best services in which, at any period, a Writer can be engaged; but this service, excellent at all times, is especially so at the present day. For a multitude of causes, unknown to former times, are now acting with a combined force to blunt the discriminating powers of the mind, and unfitting it for all voluntary exertion to reduce it to a state of almost savage torpor. The most effective of these causes are the great national events[8] which are daily taking place, and the increasing accumulation of men in cities, where the uniformity of their occupations produces a craving for extraordinary incident, which the rapid communication of intelligence hourly gratifies. To this tendency of life and manners the literature and theatrical exhibitions of the country have conformed themselves. The invaluable works of our elder writers, I had almost said the works of Shakespeare and Milton, are driven into neglect by frantic novels, sickly and stupid German Tragedies,[9] and deluges of idle and extravagant stories in verse. – When I think upon this degrading thirst after outrageous stimulation, I am almost ashamed to have spoken of the feeble effort with which I have endeavoured to counteract it; and, reflecting upon the magnitude of the general evil, I should be oppressed with no dishonorable melancholy, had I not a deep impression of certain inherent and indestructible qualities of the human mind, and likewise of certain powers in the great and permanent objects that act upon it, which are equally inherent and indestructible; and did I not further add to this impression a belief that the time is approaching when the evil will be systematically opposed, by men of greater powers, and with far more distinguished success.

Having dwelt thus long on the subjects and aim of these Poems, I shall request the Reader's permission to apprise him of a few circumstances relating to their *style*, in order, among other reasons, that I may not be censured for not having performed what I never attempted. The Reader will find that personifications of abstract ideas rarely occur in these volumes; and, I hope, are utterly rejected as an ordinary device to elevate the style, and raise it above prose. I have proposed to myself to imitate, and, as far as is possible, to adopt the very language of men; and assuredly such personifications do not make any natural or regular part of that language. They are, indeed, a figure of speech occasionally prompted by passion, and I have made use of them as such; but I have endeavoured utterly to reject them as a mechanical device of style, or as a family language which Writers in metre seem to lay claim to by prescription. I have wished to keep my Reader in the company of flesh and blood, persuaded that by so doing I shall interest him. I am, however, well aware that others who pursue a different track may interest him likewise; I do not interfere with their claim, I only wish to prefer a different claim of my own. There will also be found in these volumes little of what is usually called poetic diction; I have taken as much pains to avoid it as others ordinarily take to produce it; this I have done for the reason already alleged, to bring my language near to the language of men, and further, because the pleasure which I have proposed to myself to impart is of a kind very different from that which is supposed by many persons to be the proper object of poetry. I do not know how, without being culpably particular, I can give my Reader a more exact notion of the style in which I wished these poems to be written than by informing him that I have at all times endeavoured to look steadily at my subject; consequently, I hope that there is in these Poems little falsehood of description, and that my ideas are expressed in language fitted to their respective importance. Something I must have gained by this practice, as it is friendly to one property of all good poetry, namely good sense; but it has necessarily cut me off from a large portion of phrases and figures of speech which from father to son have long been regarded as the common inheritance of Poets. I have also thought it expedient to restrict myself still further, having abstained from the use of many expressions, in themselves proper and beautiful, but which have been foolishly repeated by bad Poets, till such feelings of disgust are connected with them as it is scarcely possible by any art of association to overpower.

If in a poem there should be found a series of lines, or even a single line, in which the language, though naturally arranged, and according to the strict laws of metre, does not differ from that of prose, there is a numerous class of critics, who, when they stumble upon these prosaisms, as they call them, imagine that they have made a notable discovery, and exult over the Poet as over a man ignorant of his own profession. Now these men would establish a canon of criticism which the Reader will conclude he must utterly reject, if he wishes to be pleased with these volumes. And it would be a most easy task to prove to him, that not only the language of a large portion of every good poem, even of the most elevated character, must necessarily, except with reference to the metre, in no respect differ from that of good prose, but likewise that some of the most interesting parts of the best poems will be found to be strictly the language of prose, when prose is well written. The truth of this assertion might be demonstrated by innumerable passages from almost all the poetical writings, even of Milton himself. I have not space for much quotation; but, to illustrate the subject in a general manner, I will here adduce a short composition of Gray,[10] who was at the head of those who, by their reasonings, have attempted to widen the space of separation betwixt Prose and Metrical composition, and was more than any other man curiously elaborate in the structure of his own poetic diction.

> In vain to me the smiling mornings shine,
> And reddening Phoebus lifts his golden fire:
> The birds in vain their amorous descant join,
> Or cheerful fields resume their green attire.
> These ears, alas! for other notes repine;
> *A different object do these eyes require;*
> *My lonely anguish melts no heart but mine;*
> *And in my breast the imperfect joys expire;*
> Yet morning smiles the busy race to cheer,
> And new-born pleasure brings to happier men;
> The fields to all their wonted tribute bear;

> To warm their little loves the birds complain.
> *I fruitless mourn to him that cannot hear,*
> *And weep the more because I weep in vain.*

It will easily be perceived that the only part of this Sonnet which is of any value is the lines printed in Italics: it is equally obvious, that, except in the rhyme, and in the use of the single word 'fruitless' for fruitlessly, which is so far a defect, the language of these lines does in no respect differ from that of prose.

By the foregoing quotation I have shown that the language of Prose may yet be well adapted to Poetry; and I have previously asserted that a large portion of the language of every good poem can in no respect differ from that of good Prose. I will go further. I do not doubt that it may be safely affirmed that there neither is, nor can be, any essential difference between the language of prose and metrical composition. We are fond of tracing the resemblance between Poetry and Painting, and, accordingly, we call them Sisters: but where shall we find bonds of connection sufficiently strict to typify the affinity betwixt metrical and prose composition? They both speak by and to the same organs; the bodies in which both of them are clothed may be said to be of the same substance, their affections are kindred, and almost identical, not necessarily differing even in degree; Poetry sheds no tears 'such as Angels weep',[11] but natural and human tears; she can boast of no celestial Ichor[12] that distinguishes her vital juices from those of prose; the same human blood circulates through the veins of them both.

If it be affirmed that rhyme and metrical arrangement of themselves constitute a distinction which overturns what I have been saying on the strict affinity of metrical language with that of prose, and paves the way for other artificial distinctions which the mind voluntarily admits, I answer that the language of such Poetry as I am recommending[13] is, as far as is possible, a selection of the language really spoken by men; that this selection, wherever it is made with true taste and feeling, will of itself form a distinction far greater than would at first be imagined, and will entirely separate the composition from the vulgarity and meanness of ordinary life; and, if metre be superadded thereto, I believe that a dissimilitude will be produced altogether sufficient for the gratification of a rational mind. What other distinction would we have? Whence is it to come? And where is it to exist? Not, surely, where the Poet speaks through the mouths of his characters: it cannot be necessary here, either for elevation of style, or any of its supposed ornaments; for, if the Poet's subject be judiciously chosen, it will naturally, and upon fit occasion, lead him to passions the language of which, if selected truly and judiciously, must necessarily be dignified and variegated, and alive with metaphors and figures. I forbear to speak of an incongruity which would shock the intelligent Reader, should the Poet interweave any foreign splendour of his own with that which the passion naturally suggests: it is sufficient to say that such addition is unnecessary. And, surely, it is more probable that those passages, which with propriety abound with metaphors and figures, will have their due effect, if, upon other occasions where the passions are of a milder character, the style also be subdued and temperate.

But, as the pleasure which I hope to give by the Poems I now present to the Reader must depend entirely on just notions upon this subject, and, as it is in itself of the highest importance to our taste and moral feelings, I cannot content myself with these detached remarks. And if, in what I am about to say, it shall appear to some that my labour is unnecessary, and that I am like a man fighting a battle without enemies, I would remind such persons that, whatever may be the language outwardly holden by men, a practical faith in the opinions which I am wishing to establish is almost unknown. If my conclusions are admitted, and carried as far as they must be carried if admitted at all, our judgments concerning the works of the greatest Poets both ancient and modern will be far different from what they are at present, both when we praise, and when we censure: and our moral feelings influencing, and influenced by these judgments will, I believe, be corrected and purified.

Taking up the subject, then, upon general grounds, I ask what is meant by the word Poet? What is a Poet? To whom does he address himself? And what language is to be expected from him? He is a man speaking to men:[14] a man, it is true, endued with more lively sensibility, more enthusiasm and tenderness, who has a greater knowledge of human nature, and a more comprehensive soul, than are supposed to be common among mankind; a man pleased with his own passions and volitions, and who rejoices more than other men in the spirit of life that is in him; delighting to contemplate similar volitions and passions as manifested in the goings-on of the Universe, and habitually impelled to create them where he does not find them. To these qualities he has added a disposition to be affected more than other men by absent things as if they were present; an ability of conjuring up in himself passions, which are indeed far from being the same as those produced by real events, yet (especially in those parts of the general sympathy which are pleasing and delightful) do more nearly resemble the passions produced by real events, than anything which, from the motions of their own minds merely, other men are accustomed to feel in themselves; whence, and from practice, he has acquired a greater readiness and power in expressing what he thinks and feels, and especially those thoughts and feelings which, by his own choice, or from the structure of his own mind, arise in him without immediate external excitement.

But, whatever portion of this faculty we may suppose even the greatest Poet to possess, there cannot be a doubt but that the language which it will suggest to him must, in liveliness and truth, fall far short of that which is uttered by men in real life, under the actual pressure of those passions, certain shadows of which the Poet thus produces, or feels to be produced, in himself. However exalted a notion we would wish to cherish of the character of a Poet, it is obvious, that, while he describes and imitates passions, his situation is altogether slavish and mechanical, compared with the freedom and power of real and substantial action and suffering. So that it will be the wish of the Poet to bring his feelings near to those of the persons whose feelings he describes, nay, for short spaces of time perhaps, to let himself slip into an entire delusion, and even confound and identify his own feelings with theirs; modifying only the language which is thus suggested to him, by a consideration that he describes for a particular purpose, that of giving pleasure. Here, then, he will apply the principle on which I have so much insisted, namely, that of selection; on this he will depend for removing what would otherwise be painful or disgusting in the passion; he will feel that there is no necessity to trick out or to elevate nature: and, the more industriously he applies this principle, the deeper will be his faith that no words, which his fancy or imagination can suggest, will be to be compared with those which are the emanations of reality and truth.

But it may be said by those who do not object to the general spirit of these remarks, that, as it is impossible for the Poet to produce upon all occasions language as exquisitely fitted for the passion as that which the real passion itself suggests, it is proper that he should consider himself as in the situation of a translator, who deems himself justified when he substitutes excellences of another kind for those which are unattainable by him; and endeavours occasionally to surpass his original, in order to make some amends for the general inferiority to which he feels that he must submit. But this would be to encourage idleness and unmanly despair. Further, it is the language of men who speak of what they do not understand; who talk of Poetry as of a matter of amusement and idle pleasure; who will converse with us as gravely about a *taste* for Poetry, as they express it, as if it were a thing as indifferent as a taste for Rope-dancing, or Frontiniac[15] or Sherry. Aristotle, I have been told, hath said, that Poetry is the most philosophic of all writing:[16] it is so: its object is truth, not individual and local, but general, and operative; not standing upon external testimony, but carried alive into the heart by passion; truth which is its own testimony, which gives strength and divinity to the tribunal to which it appeals, and receives them from the same tribunal. Poetry is the image of man and nature. The obstacles which stand in the way of the fidelity of the Biographer and Historian, and of their consequent utility, are incalculably greater than those which are to be encountered by the Poet who has an adequate notion of the dignity of his art. The Poet writes under one restriction only, namely, that of the necessity of giving immediate pleasure to a human Being possessed of that information which may be expected from him, not as a lawyer, a physician, a mariner, an astronomer or a natural philosopher, but as a Man.[17] Except this one restriction, there is no object standing between the Poet and the image of things; between this, and the Biographer and Historian there are a thousand.

Nor let this necessity of producing immediate pleasure be considered as a degradation of the Poet's art. It is far otherwise. It is an acknowledgment of the beauty of the universe, an acknowledgment the more sincere, because it is not formal, but indirect; it is a task light and easy to him who looks at the world in the spirit of love: further, it is a homage paid to the native and naked dignity of man, to the grand elementary principle of pleasure, by which he knows, and feels, and lives, and moves. We have no sympathy but what is propagated by pleasure: I would not be misunderstood; but wherever we sympathise with pain it will be found that the sympathy is produced and carried on by subtle combinations with pleasure. We have no knowledge, that is, no general principles drawn from the contemplation of particular facts, but what has been built up by pleasure, and exists in us by pleasure alone. The Man of Science, the Chemist and Mathematician, whatever difficulties and disgusts they may have had to struggle with, know and feel this. However painful may be the objects with which the Anatomist's knowledge is connected, he feels that his knowledge is pleasure; and where he has no pleasure he has no knowledge. What then does the Poet? He considers man and the objects that surround him as acting and reacting upon each other, so as to produce an infinite complexity of pain and pleasure; he considers man in his own nature and in his ordinary life as contemplating this with a certain quantity of immediate knowledge, with certain convictions, intuitions, and deductions which by habit become of the nature of intuitions; he considers him as looking upon this complex scene of ideas and sensations, and finding everywhere objects that immediately excite in him sympathies which, from the necessities of his nature, are accompanied by an overbalance of enjoyment.

To this knowledge which all men carry about with them, and to these sympathies in which without any other discipline than that of our daily life we are fitted to take delight, the Poet principally directs his attention. He considers man and nature as essentially adapted to each other, and the mind of man as naturally the mirror of the fairest and most interesting qualities of nature. And thus the Poet, prompted by this feeling of pleasure which accompanies him through the whole course of his studies, converses with general nature with affections akin to those, which, through labour and length of time, the Man of Science has raised up in himself, by conversing with those particular parts of nature which are the objects of his studies. The knowledge both of the Poet and the Man of Science is pleasure; but the knowledge of the one cleaves to us as a necessary part of our existence, our natural and unalienable inheritance; the other is a personal and individual acquisition, slow to come to us, and by no habitual and direct sympathy connecting us with our fellow-beings. The Man of Science seeks truth as a remote and unknown benefactor; he cherishes and loves it in his solitude: the Poet, singing a song in which all human beings join with him, rejoices in the presence of truth as our visible friend and hourly companion. Poetry is the breath and finer spirit of all knowledge; it is the impassioned expression which is in the countenance of all Science. Emphatically may it be said of the Poet, as Shakespeare hath said of man, 'that he looks before and after'.[18] He is the rock of defence of human nature; an upholder and preserver, carrying everywhere with him relationship and love. In spite of difference of soil and climate, of language and manners, of laws and customs, in spite of things silently gone out of mind and things violently destroyed, the Poet binds together by passion and knowledge the vast empire of human society, as it is spread over the whole earth, and over all time. The objects of the Poet's thoughts are everywhere; though the eyes and senses of man are, it is true, his favourite guides, yet he will follow wheresoever he can find an atmosphere of sensation in which to move his wings. Poetry is the first and last of all knowledge – it is as immortal as the heart of man. If the labours of Men of Science should ever create any material revolution, direct or indirect, in our condition, and in the impressions which we habitually receive, the Poet will sleep then no more than at present, but he will be ready to follow the steps of the Man of Science, not only in those general indirect effects, but he will be at his side, carrying sensation into the midst of the objects of the Science itself. The remotest discoveries of the Chemist, the Botanist, or Mineralogist, will be as proper objects of the Poet's art as any upon which it can be employed, if the time should ever come when these things shall be familiar to us, and the relations under which they are contemplated by the followers of these respective Sciences shall be manifestly and palpably material to us as enjoying and suffering beings. If the time should ever come when what is now called Science, thus familiarised to men, shall be ready to put on, as it were, a form of flesh and blood, the Poet will lend his divine spirit to aid the transfiguration, and will welcome the Being thus produced, as a dear and genuine inmate of the household of man. – It is not, then, to be supposed that anyone, who holds that sublime notion of Poetry which I have attempted to convey, will break in upon the sanctity and truth of his pictures by transitory and accidental ornaments, and endeavour to excite admiration of himself by arts, the necessity of which must manifestly depend upon the assumed meanness of his subject.

What I have thus far said applies to Poetry in general; but especially to those parts of composition where the Poet speaks through the mouths of his characters; and upon this point it appears to have such weight that I will conclude there are few persons of good sense who would not allow that the dramatic parts of composition are defective, in proportion as they deviate from the real language of nature, and are coloured by a diction of the Poet's own, either peculiar to him as an individual Poet, or belonging simply to Poets in general, to a body of men who, from the circumstance of their compositions being in metre, it is expected will employ a particular language.

It is not, then, in the dramatic parts of composition that we look for this distinction of language; but still it may be proper and necessary where the Poet speaks to us in his own person and character. To this I answer by referring my Reader to the description which I have before given of a Poet. Among the qualities which I have enumerated as principally conducing to form a Poet is implied nothing differing in kind from other men, but only in degree. The sum of what I have there said is, that the Poet is chiefly distinguished from other men by a greater promptness to think and feel without immediate external excitement, and a greater power in expressing such thoughts and feelings as are produced in him in that manner. But these passions and thoughts and feelings are the general passions and thoughts and feelings of men. And with what are they connected? Undoubtedly with our moral sentiments and animal sensations, and with the causes which excite these; with the operations of the elements and the appearances of the visible universe; with storm and sunshine, with the revolutions of the seasons, with cold and heat, with loss of friends and kindred, with injuries and resentments, gratitude and hope, with fear and sorrow. These, and the like, are the sensations and objects which the Poet describes, as they are the sensations of other men, and the objects which interest them. The Poet thinks and feels in the spirit of the passions of men. How, then, can his language differ in any material degree from that of all other men who feel vividly and see clearly? It might be *proved* that it is impossible. But supposing that this were not the case, the Poet might then be allowed to use a peculiar language when expressing his feelings for his own gratification, or that of men like himself. But Poets do not write for Poets alone, but for men. Unless therefore we are advocates for that admiration which depends upon ignorance, and that pleasure which arises from hearing what we do not understand, the Poet must descend from this supposed height, and, in order to excite rational sympathy, he must express himself as other men express themselves. To this it may be added that while he is only selecting from the real language of men, or, which amounts to the same thing, composing accurately in the spirit of such selection, he is treading upon safe ground, and we know what we are to expect from him. Our feelings are the same with respect to metre; for, as it may be proper to remind the Reader,[19] the distinction of metre is regular and uniform, and not like that which is produced by what is usually called poetic diction, arbitrary, and subject to infinite caprices upon which no calculation whatever can be made. In the one case, the Reader is utterly at the mercy of the Poet respecting what imagery or diction he may choose to connect with the passion, whereas, in the other, the metre obeys certain laws, to which the Poet and Reader both willingly submit because they are certain, and because no interference is made by them with the passion but such as the concurring testimony of ages has shown to heighten and improve the pleasure which co-exists with it.

It will now be proper to answer an obvious question, namely, Why, professing these opinions, have I written in verse? To this, in addition to such answer as is included in what I have already said, I reply in the first place, Because, however I may have restricted myself, there is still left open to me what confessedly constitutes the most valuable object of all writing, whether in prose or verse, the great and universal passions of men, the most general and interesting of their occupations, and the entire world of nature, from which I am at liberty to supply myself with endless combinations of forms and imagery. Now, supposing for a moment that whatever is interesting in these objects may be as vividly described in prose, why am I to be condemned if to such description I have endeavoured to superadd the charm which, by the consent of all nations, is acknowledged to exist in metrical language? To this, by such as are unconvinced by what I have already said, it may be answered, that a very small part of the pleasure given by Poetry depends upon the metre, and that it is injudicious to write in metre, unless it be accompanied with the other artificial distinctions of style with which metre is usually accompanied, and that by such deviation more will be lost from the shock which will be thereby given to the Reader's associations, than will be counterbalanced by any pleasure which he can derive from the general power of numbers. In answer to those who still contend for the necessity of accompanying metre with certain appropriate colours of style in order to the accomplishment of its appropriate end, and who also, in my opinion, greatly under-rate the power of metre in itself, it might perhaps, as far as relates to these Poems, have been almost sufficient to observe, that poems are extant,[20] written upon more humble subjects, and in a more naked and simple style than I have aimed at, which poems have continued to give pleasure from generation to generation. Now, if nakedness and simplicity be a defect, the fact here mentioned affords a strong presumption that poems somewhat less naked and simple are capable of affording pleasure at the present day; and, what I wished *chiefly* to attempt, at present, was to justify myself for having written under the impression of this belief.

But I might point out various causes why, when the style is manly, and the subject of some importance, words metrically arranged will long continue to impart such a pleasure to mankind as he who is sensible of the extent of that pleasure will be desirous to impart. The end of Poetry is to produce excitement in co-existence with an over-balance of pleasure. Now, by the supposition, excitement is an unusual and irregular state of the mind; ideas and feelings do not in that state succeed each other in accustomed order. But, if the words by which this excitement is produced are in themselves powerful, or the images and feelings have an undue proportion of pain connected with them, there is some danger that the excitement may be carried beyond its proper bounds. Now the co-presence of something regular, something to which the mind has been accustomed in various moods and in a less excited state, cannot but have great efficacy in tempering and restraining the passion by an intertexture of ordinary feeling, and of feeling not strictly and necessarily connected with the passion. This is unquestionably true, and hence, though the opinion will at first appear paradoxical, from the tendency of metre to divest language in a certain degree of its reality, and thus to throw a sort of half consciousness

of unsubstantial existence over the whole composition, there can be little
doubt but that more pathetic situations and sentiments, that is, those
which have a greater proportion of pain connected with them, may be
endured in metrical composition, especially in rhyme, than in prose. The
metre of the old ballads is very artless; yet they contain many passages
which would illustrate this opinion, and, I hope, if the following Poems be
attentively perused, similar instances will be found in them. This opinion
may be further illustrated by appealing to the Reader's own experience of
the reluctance with which he comes to the re-perusal of the distressful parts
of Clarissa Harlowe, or the Gamester.[21] While Shakespeare's writings, in the
most pathetic scenes, never act upon us as pathetic beyond the bounds of
pleasure – an effect which, in a much greater degree than might at first be
imagined, is to be ascribed to small, but continual and regular impulses of
pleasurable surprise from the metrical arrangement. – On the other hand
(what it must be allowed will much more frequently happen) if the Poet's
words should be incommensurate with the passion, and inadequate to raise
the Reader to a height of desirable excitement, then (unless the Poet's
choice of his metre has been grossly injudicious), in the feelings of pleasure
which the Reader has been accustomed to connect with metre in general,
and in the feeling, whether cheerful or melancholy, which he has been
accustomed to connect with that particular movement of metre, there will
be found something which will greatly contribute to impart passion to the
words, and to effect the complex end which the Poet proposes to himself.

If I had undertaken a systematic defence of the theory upon which these
poems are written, it would have been my duty to develop the various
causes upon which the pleasure received from metrical language depends.
Among the chief of these causes is to be reckoned a principle which must
be well known to those who have made any of the Arts the object of
accurate reflection; I mean the pleasure which the mind derives from the
perception of similitude in dissimilitude. This principle is the great spring
of the activity of our minds, and their chief feeder. From this principle the
direction of the sexual appetite, and all the passions connected with it, take
their origin: it is the life of our ordinary conversation; and upon the
accuracy with which similitude in dissimilitude, and dissimilitude in
similitude are perceived, depend our taste and our moral feelings. It would
not have been a useless employment to have applied this principle to the
consideration of metre, and to have shown that metre is hence enabled to
afford much pleasure, and to have pointed out in what manner that
pleasure is produced. But my limits will not permit me to enter upon this
subject, and I must content myself with a general summary.

I have said that Poetry is the spontaneous overflow of powerful feelings: it takes its origin from emotion recollected in tranquillity: the emotion is contemplated till by a species of reaction the tranquillity gradually disappears, and an emotion, kindred to that which was before the subject of contemplation, is gradually produced, and does itself actually exist in the mind. In this mood successful composition generally begins, and in a mood similar to this it is carried on; but the emotion, of whatever kind and in whatever degree, from various causes is qualified by various pleasures, so that in describing any passions whatsoever, which are voluntarily described, the mind will upon the whole be in a state of enjoyment. Now, if Nature be thus cautious in preserving in a state of enjoyment a being thus employed, the Poet ought to profit by the lesson thus held forth to him, and ought especially to take care that whatever passions he communicates to his Reader, those passions, if his Reader's mind be sound and vigorous, should always be accompanied with an overbalance of pleasure. Now the music of harmonious metrical language, the sense of difficulty overcome, and the blind association of pleasure which has been previously received from works of rhyme or metre of the same or similar construction, an indistinct perception perpetually renewed of language closely resembling that of real life, and yet, in the circumstance of metre, differing from it so widely, all these imperceptibly make up a complex feeling of delight, which is of the most important use in tempering the painful feeling which will always be found intermingled with powerful descriptions of the deeper passions. This effect is always produced in pathetic and impassioned poetry; while, in lighter compositions, the ease and gracefulness with which the Poet manages his numbers are themselves confessedly a principal source of the gratification of the Reader. I might perhaps include all which it is *necessary* to say upon this subject by affirming, what few persons will deny that, of two descriptions, either of passions, manners, or characters, each of them equally well executed, the one in prose and the other in verse, the verse will be read a hundred times where the prose is read once. We see that Pope, by the power of verse alone, has contrived to render the plainest common sense interesting, and even frequently to invest it with the appearance of passion. In consequence of these convictions I related in metre the tale of GOODY BLAKE AND HARRY GILL, which is one of the rudest of this collection. I wished to draw attention to the truth that the power of the human imagination is sufficient to produce such changes even in our physical nature as might almost appear miraculous. The truth is an important one; the fact (for it is a *fact*) is a valuable illustration of it. And I have the satisfaction of knowing that it has been communicated to many hundreds of people who would never have heard of it, had it not been narrated as a Ballad, and in a more impressive metre than is usual in Ballads.

Having thus explained a few of the reasons why I have written in verse, and why I have chosen subjects from common life, and endeavoured to bring my language near to the real language of men, if I have been too minute in pleading my own cause, I have at the same time been treating a subject of general interest; and it is for this reason that I request the Reader's permission to add a few words with reference solely to these particular poems, and to some defects which will probably be found in them. I am sensible that my associations must have sometimes been particular instead of general, and that, consequently, giving to things a false importance, sometimes from diseased impulses I may have written upon unworthy subjects; but I am less apprehensive on this account than that my language may frequently have suffered from those arbitrary connections of feelings and ideas with particular words and phrases from which no man can altogether protect himself. Hence I have no doubt that, in some instances, feelings even of the ludicrous may be given to my Readers by expressions which appeared to me tender and pathetic. Such faulty expressions, were I convinced they were faulty at present, and that they must necessarily continue to be so, I would willingly take all reasonable pains to correct. But it is dangerous to make these alterations on the simple authority of a few individuals, or even of certain classes of men; for where the understanding of an Author is not convinced, or his feelings altered, this cannot be done without great injury to himself: for his own feelings are his stay and support, and, if he sets them aside in one instance, he may be induced to repeat this act till his mind loses all confidence in itself, and becomes utterly debilitated. To this it may be added that the Reader ought never to forget that he is himself exposed to the same errors as the Poet, and perhaps in a much greater degree: for there can be no presumption in saying that it is not probable he will be so well acquainted with the various stages of meaning through which words have passed, or with the fickleness or stability of the relations of particular ideas to each other; and above all, since he is so much less interested in the subject, he may decide lightly and carelessly.

Long as I have detained my Reader, I hope he will permit me to caution him against a mode of false criticism which has been applied to Poetry in which the language closely resembles that of life and nature. Such verses have been triumphed over in parodies of which Dr Johnson's stanza[22] is a fair specimen.

> I put my hat upon my head,
> And walk'd into the Strand,
> And there I met another man
> Whose hat was in his hand.

Immediately under these lines I will place one of the most justly admired stanzas of the 'Babes in the Wood'.[23]

> These pretty Babes with hand in hand
> Went wandering up and down;
> But never more they saw the Man
> Approaching from the Town.

In both these stanzas the words, and the order of the words, in no respect differ from the most unimpassioned conversation. There are words in both, for example, 'the Strand', and 'the Town', connected with none but the most familiar ideas; yet the one stanza we admit as admirable, and the other as a fair example of the superlatively contemptible. Whence arises this difference? Not from the metre, not from the language, not from the order of the words; but the *matter* expressed in Dr Johnson's stanza is contemptible. The proper method of treating trivial and simple verses, to which Dr Johnson's stanza would be a fair parallelism, is not to say, This is a bad kind of poetry, or This is not poetry; but This wants sense; it is neither interesting in itself, nor can *lead* to anything interesting; the images neither originate in that sane state of feeling which arises out of thought, nor can excite thought or feeling in the Reader. This is the only sensible manner of dealing with such verses. Why trouble yourself about the species till you have previously decided upon the genus? Why take pains to prove that an ape is not a Newton, when it is self-evident that he is not a man?

I have one request to make of my Reader, which is, that in judging these Poems he would decide by his own feelings genuinely, and not by reflection upon what will probably be the judgment of others. How common is it to hear a person say, 'I myself do not object to this style of composition, or this or that expression, but to such and such classes of people it will appear mean or ludicrous.' This mode of criticism, so destructive of all sound unadulterated judgment, is almost universal: I have therefore to request that the Reader would abide independently by his own feelings, and that if he finds himself affected he would not suffer such conjectures to interfere with his pleasure.

If an Author by any single composition has impressed us with respect for his talents, it is useful to consider this as affording a presumption that, on other occasions where we have been displeased, he nevertheless may not have written ill or absurdly; and, further, to give him so much credit for this one composition as may induce us to review what has displeased us with more care than we should otherwise have bestowed upon it. This is not only an act of justice, but, in our decisions upon poetry especially, may conduce in a high degree to the improvement of our own taste: for an *accurate* taste in poetry, and in all the other arts, as Sir Joshua Reynolds[24] has observed, is an *acquired* talent, which can only be produced by thought, and a long continued intercourse with the best models of composition. This is mentioned, not with so ridiculous a purpose as to prevent the most inexperienced Reader from judging for himself (I have already said that I wish him to judge for himself), but merely to temper the rashness of decision, and to suggest that if Poetry be a subject on which much time has not been bestowed the judgment may be erroneous; and that in many cases it necessarily will be so.

I know that nothing would have so effectually contributed to further the end which I have in view, as to have shown of what kind the pleasure is, and how that pleasure is produced, which is confessedly produced by metrical composition essentially different from that which I have here endeavoured to recommend: for the Reader will say that he has been pleased by such composition; and what can I do more for him? The power of any art is limited; and he will suspect that if I propose to furnish him with new friends it is only upon condition of his abandoning his old friends. Besides, as I have said, the Reader is himself conscious of the pleasure which he has received from such composition, composition to which he has peculiarly attached the endearing name of Poetry; and all men feel an habitual gratitude, and something of an honorable bigotry for the objects which have long continued to please them; we not only wish to be pleased, but to be pleased in that particular way in which we have been accustomed to be pleased. There is a host of arguments in these feelings; and I should be the less able to combat them successfully, as I am willing to allow that, in order entirely to enjoy the Poetry which I am recommending, it would be necessary to give up much of what is ordinarily enjoyed. But, would my limits have permitted me to point out how this pleasure is produced, I might have removed many obstacles, and assisted my Reader in perceiving that the powers of language are not so limited as he may suppose; and that it is possible that poetry may give other enjoyments, of a purer, more lasting, and more exquisite nature. This part of my subject I have not altogether neglected; but it has been less my present aim to prove that the interest excited by some other kinds of poetry is less vivid, and less worthy of the nobler powers of the mind, than to offer reasons for presuming that if the object which I have proposed to myself were adequately attained, a species of poetry would be produced which is genuine poetry; in its nature well adapted to interest mankind permanently, and likewise important in the multiplicity and quality of its moral relations.

From what has been said, and from a perusal of the Poems, the Reader will be able clearly to perceive the object which I have proposed to myself: he will determine how far I have attained this object; and, what is a much more important question, whether it be worth attaining: and upon the decision of these two questions will rest my claim to the approbation of the public.

Lines Left upon a Seat in a Yew-Tree

*which stands near the Lake of Esthwaite,[1] on a desolate part of
the shore, yet commanding a beautiful prospect*

– Nay, Traveller! rest. This lonely yew-tree stands
Far from all human dwelling: what if here
No sparkling rivulet spread the verdant herb;
What if these barren boughs the bee not loves;
Yet, if the wind breathe soft, the curling waves,
That break against the shore, shall lull thy mind
By one soft impulse saved from vacancy.

            Who he was
That piled these stones, and with the mossy sod
First covered o'er, and taught this aged tree,   10
Now wild, to bend its arms in circling shade,
I well remember. – He was one who own'd
No common soul. In youth, by genius nurs'd,
And big with lofty views, he to the world
Went forth, pure in his heart, against the taint
Of dissolute tongues, 'gainst jealousy, and hate,
And scorn, against all enemies prepared,
All but neglect: and so, his spirit damped
At once, with rash disdain he turned away,
And with the food of pride sustained his soul   20
In solitude. – Stranger! these gloomy boughs
Had charms for him; and here he loved to sit,
His only visitants a straggling sheep,
The stone-chat, or the glancing sandpiper;
And on these barren rocks, with juniper,
And heath, and thistle, thinly sprinkled o'er,
Fixing his downward eye, he many an hour
A morbid pleasure nourished, tracing here
An emblem of his own unfruitful life:
And lifting up his head, he then would gaze   30

On the more distant scene; how lovely 'tis
Thou seest, and he would gaze till it became
Far lovelier, and his heart could not sustain
The beauty still more beauteous. Nor, that time,
Would he forget those beings, to whose minds,
Warm from the labours of benevolence,
The world, and man himself, appeared a scene
Of kindred loveliness: then he would sigh
With mournful joy, to think that others felt
What he must never feel: and so, lost man!   40
On visionary views would fancy feed,
Till his eye streamed with tears. In this deep vale
He died, this seat his only monument.

If thou be one whose heart the holy forms
Of young imagination have kept pure,
Stranger! henceforth be warned; and know, that pride,
Howe'er disguised in its own majesty,
Is littleness; that he, who feels contempt
For any living thing, hath faculties
Which he has never used; that thought with him   50
Is in its infancy. The man, whose eye
Is ever on himself, doth look on one,
The least of nature's works, one who might move
The wise man to that scorn which wisdom holds
Unlawful, ever. O, be wiser thou!
Instructed that true knowledge leads to love,
True dignity abides with him alone
Who, in the silent hour of inward thought,
Can still suspect, and still revere himself,
In lowliness of heart.   60

The Female Vagrant

By Derwent's[1] side my Father's cottage stood
(The Woman thus her artless story told),
One field, a flock, and what the neighbouring flood
Supplied, to him were more than mines of gold.
Light was my sleep; my days in transport roll'd:
With thoughtless joy I stretch'd along the shore
My father's nets, or watched, when from the fold
High o'er the cliffs I led my fleecy store,
A dizzy depth below! his boat and twinkling oar.

My father was a good and pious man,   10
An honest man by honest parents bred,
And I believe that, soon as I began
To lisp, he made me kneel beside my bed,
And in his hearing there my prayers I said:
And afterwards, by my good father taught,
I read, and loved the books in which I read;
For books in every neighbouring house I sought,
And nothing to my mind a sweeter pleasure brought.

Can I forget what charms did once adorn
My garden, stored with pease, and mint, and thyme,   20
And rose and lilly for the sabbath morn?
The sabbath bells, and their delightful chime;
The gambols and wild freaks at shearing time;
My hen's rich nest through long grass scarce espied;
The cowslip-gathering at May's dewy prime;
The swans, that, when I sought the waterside,
From far to meet me came, spreading their snowy pride.

The staff I yet remember which upbore
The bending body of my active sire;
His seat beneath the honeyed sycamore   30
When the bees hummed, and chair by winter fire;
When market-morning came, the neat attire
With which, though bent on haste, myself I deck'd;
My watchful dog, whose starts of furious ire,
When stranger passed, so often I have check'd;
The redbreast known for years, which at my casement peck'd.

The suns of twenty summers danced along –
Ah! little marked, how fast they rolled away:
Then rose a mansion proud our woods among,
And cottage after cottage owned its sway,   40
No joy to see a neighbouring house, or stray
Through pastures not his own, the master took;
My Father dared his greedy wish gainsay;
He loved his old hereditary nook,
And ill could I the thought of such sad parting brook.

But, when he had refused the proffered gold,
To cruel injuries he became a prey,
Sore traversed in whate'er he bought and sold.
His troubles grew upon him day by day,
Till all his substance fell into decay.   50
His little range of water was denied;*
All but the bed where his old body lay,
All, all was seized, and weeping, side by side,
We sought a home where we uninjured might abide.

Can I forget that miserable hour,
When from the last hill-top, my sire surveyed,
Peering above the trees, the steeple tower
That on his marriage-day sweet music made?
Till then he hoped his bones might there be laid,
Close by my mother in their native bowers: 60
Bidding me trust in God, he stood and prayed –
I could not pray – through tears that fell in showers,
Glimmer'd our dear-loved home, alas! no longer ours!

There was a youth whom I had loved so long,
That when I loved him not I cannot say.
'Mid the green mountains many and many a song
We two had sung, like little birds in May.
When we began to tire of childish play
We seemed still more and more to prize each other:
We talked of marriage and our marriage day;   70

* Several of the Lakes in the north of England are let out to different fishermen, in
  parcels marked out by imaginary lines drawn from rock to rock.
                                                (Wordsworth's footnote)

And I in truth did love him like a brother,
For never could I hope to meet with such another.

His father said that to a distant town
He must repair, to ply the artist's trade.
What tears of bitter grief till then unknown!
What tender vows our last sad kiss delayed!
To him we turned: – we had no other aid.
Like one revived, upon his neck I wept,
And her whom he had loved in joy, he said
He well could love in grief: his faith he kept;   80
And in a quiet home once more my father slept.

Four years each day with daily bread was blest,
By constant toil and constant prayer supplied.
Three lovely infants lay upon my breast;
And often, viewing their sweet smiles, I sighed,
And knew not why. My happy father died
When sad distress reduced the children's meal:
Thrice happy! that from him the grave did hide
The empty loom, cold hearth, and silent wheel,
And tears that flowed for ills which patience could not heal.   90

'Twas a hard change, an evil time was come;
We had no hope, and no relief could gain.
But soon, with proud parade, the noisy drum
Beat round, to sweep the streets of want and pain.
My husband's arms now only served to strain
Me and his children hungering in his view:
In such dismay my prayers and tears were vain:
To join those miserable men he flew;
And now to the sea-coast, with numbers more, we drew.

There foul neglect for months and months we bore,   100
Nor yet the crowded fleet its anchor stirred.
Green fields before us and our native shore,
By fever, from polluted air incurred,
Ravage was made, for which no knell was heard.
Fondly we wished, and wished away, nor knew.
'Mid that long sickness, and those hopes deferr'd,
That happier days we never more must view:
The parting signal streamed, at last the land withdrew,

But from delay the summer calms were past.
On as we drove, the equinoctial deep   110
Ran mountains-high before the howling blast.
We gazed with terror on the gloomy sleep
Of them that perished in the whirlwind's sweep,
Untaught that soon such anguish must ensue,
Our hopes such harvest of affliction reap,
That we the mercy of the waves should rue.[2]
We reached the western world,[3] a poor, devoted[4] crew.

Oh! dreadful price of being to resign
All that is dear *in* being! better far
In Want's most lonely cave till death to pine,   120
Unseen, unheard, unwatched by any star;
Or in the streets and walks where proud men are,
Better our dying bodies to obtrude,
Than dog-like, wading at the heels of war,
Protract a curst existence, with the brood
That lap (their very nourishment!) their brother's blood.

The pains and plagues that on our heads came down,
Disease and famine, agony and fear,
In wood or wilderness, in camp or town,
It would thy brain unsettle even to hear.   130
All perished – all, in one remorseless year,
Husband and children! one by one, by sword
And ravenous plague, all perished: every tear
Dried up, despairing, desolate, on board
A British ship I waked, as from a trance restored.

Peaceful as some immeasurable plain
By the first beams of dawning light impress'd,
In the calm sunshine slept the glittering main.
The very ocean has its hour of rest,
That comes not to the human mourner's breast.   140
Remote from man, and storms of mortal care,
A heavenly silence did the waves invest;
I looked and looked along the silent air,
Until it seemed to bring a joy to my despair.

Ah! how unlike those late terrific sleeps!
And groans, that rage of racking famine spoke,
Where looks inhuman dwelt on festering heaps!
The breathing pestilence that rose like smoke!
The shriek that from the distant battle broke!
The mine's dire earthquake, and the pallid host   150
Driven by the bomb's incessant thunder-stroke
To loathsome vaults, where heart-sick anguish toss'd,
Hope died, and fear itself in agony was lost!

Yet does that burst of woe congeal my frame,
When the dark streets appeared to heave and gape,
While like a sea the storming army came,
And Fire from Hell reared his gigantic shape,
And Murder, by the ghastly gleam, and Rape
Seized their joint prey, the mother and the child!
But from these crazing thoughts my brain, escape!   160
– For weeks the balmy air breathed soft and mild,
And on the gliding vessel Heaven and Ocean smiled.

Some mighty gulf of separation past,
I seemed transported to another world: –
A thought resigned with pain, when from the mast
The impatient mariner the sail unfurl'd,
And whistling, called the wind that hardly curled
The silent sea. From the sweet thoughts of home,
And from all hope I was forever hurled.
For me – farthest from earthly port to roam   170
Was best, could I but shun the spot where man might come.

And oft, robb'd of my perfect mind, I thought
At last my feet a resting-place had found:
Here will I weep in peace (so fancy wrought),
Roaming the illimitable waters round;
Here watch, of every human friend disowned,
All day, my ready tomb the ocean-flood –
To break my dream the vessel reached its bound:
And homeless near a thousand homes I stood,
And near a thousand tables pined, and wanted food.   180

By grief enfeebled was I turned adrift,
Helpless as sailor cast on desert rock;
Nor morsel to my mouth that day did lift,
Nor dared my hand at any door to knock.
I lay, where with his drowsy mates, the cock
From the cross timber of an out-house hung;
How dismal tolled, that night, the city clock!
At morn my sick heart hunger scarcely stung,
Nor to the beggar's language could I frame my tongue.

So passed another day, and so the third: 190
Then did I try, in vain, the crowd's resort,
In deep despair by frightful wishes stirr'd,
Near the sea-side I reached a ruined fort:
There, pains which nature could no more support,
With blindness linked, did on my vitals fall;
Dizzy my brain, with interruption short
Of hideous sense; I sunk, nor step could crawl,
And thence was borne away to neighbouring hospital.

Recovery came with food: but still, my brain
Was weak, nor of the past had memory.   200
I heard my neighbours, in their beds, complain
Of many things which never troubled me;
Of feet still bustling round with busy glee,
Of looks where common kindness had no part,
Of service done with careless cruelty,
Fretting the fever round the languid heart,
And groans, which, as they said, would make a dead man start.

These things just served to stir the torpid sense,
Nor pain nor pity in my bosom raised.
Memory, though slow, returned with strength; and thence   210
Dismissed, again on open day I gazed,
At houses, men, and common light, amazed.
The lanes I sought, and as the sun retired,
Came, where beneath the trees a faggot blazed;
The wild brood saw me weep, my fate enquired,
And gave me food, and rest, more welcome, more desired.

My heart is touched to think that men like these,
The rude earth's tenants, were my first relief:
How kindly did they paint their vagrant ease!
And their long holiday that feared not grief,   220
For all belonged to all, and each was chief.
No plough their sinews strained; on grating road
No wain they drove, and yet, the yellow sheaf
In every vale for their delight was stowed:
For them, in nature's meads, the milky udder flowed.

Semblance, with straw and panniered ass, they made
Of potters wandering on from door to door:
But life of happier sort to me portrayed,
And other joys my fancy to allure;
The bagpipe dinning on the midnight moor   230
In barn uplighted, and companions boon
Well met from far with revelry secure,
In depth of forest glade, when jocund June
Rolled fast along the sky his warm and genial moon.

But ill it suited me, in journey dark
O'er moor and mountain, midnight theft to hatch;
To charm the surly house-dog's faithful bark,
Or hang on tiptoe at the lifted latch;
The gloomy lantern, and the dim blue match,
The black disguise, the warning whistle shrill,   240
And ear still busy on its nightly watch,
Were not for me, brought up in nothing ill;
Besides, on griefs so fresh my thoughts were brooding still.

What could I do, unaided and unblest?
Poor Father! gone was every friend of thine:
And kindred of dead husband are at best
Small help, and, after marriage such as mine,
With little kindness would to me incline.
Ill was I then for toil or service fit:
With tears whose course no effort could confine,   250
By highway side forgetful would I sit
Whole hours, my idle arms in moping sorrow knit.

I lived upon the mercy of the fields,
And oft of cruelty the sky accused;
On hazard, or what general bounty yields,
Now coldly given, now utterly refused.
The fields I for my bed have often used:
But, what afflicts my peace with keenest ruth
Is that I have my inner self abused,
Forgone the home delight of constant truth,   260
And clear and open soul, so prized in fearless youth.

Three years a wanderer, often have I view'd,
In tears, the sun towards that country tend
Where my poor heart lost all its fortitude:
And now across this moor my steps I bend –
Oh! tell me whither – for no earthly friend
Have I. – She ceased, and weeping turned away,
As if because her tale was at an end
She wept; – because she had no more to say
Of that perpetual weight which on her spirit lay.   270

Goody Blake, and Harry Gill,

A TRUE STORY

Oh! what's the matter? what's the matter?
What is't that ails young Harry Gill?
That evermore his teeth they chatter,
Chatter, chatter, chatter still.
Of waistcoats Harry has no lack,
Good duffle grey, and flannel fine;
He has a blanket on his back,
And coats enough to smother nine.

In March, December, and in July,
'Tis all the same with Harry Gill;   10
The neighbours tell, and tell you truly,
His teeth they chatter, chatter still.
At night, at morning, and at noon,
'Tis all the same with Harry Gill;
Beneath the sun, beneath the moon,
His teeth they chatter, chatter still.

Young Harry was a lusty drover,[1]
And who so stout of limb as he?
His cheeks were red as ruddy clover,
His voice was like the voice of three.   20
Auld Goody Blake was old and poor,
Ill fed she was, and thinly clad;
And any man who pass'd her door,
Might see how poor a hut she had.

All day she spun in her poor dwelling,
And then her three hours' work at night!
Alas! 'twas hardly worth the telling,
It would not pay for candlelight.
– This woman dwelt in Dorsetshire,
Her hut was on a cold hillside,   30
And in that country coals are dear,
For they come far by wind and tide.

By the same fire to boil their pottage,
Two poor old dames, as I have known,
Will often live in one small cottage,
But she, poor woman, dwelt alone.
'Twas well enough when summer came,
The long, warm, lightsome summer-day,
Then at her door the *canty*[2] dame
Would sit, as any linnet gay.   40

But when the ice our streams did fetter,
Oh! then how her old bones would shake!
You would have said, if you had met her,
'Twas a hard time for Goody Blake.
Her evenings then were dull and dead;
Sad case it was, as you may think,
For very cold to go to bed,
And then for cold not sleep a wink.

Oh joy for her! when e'er in winter
The winds at night had made a rout,[3]   50
And scatter'd many a lusty splinter,
And many a rotten bough about.
Yet never had she, well or sick,
As every man who knew her says,
A pile before-hand, wood or stick,
Enough to warm her for three days.

Now, when the frost was past enduring,
And made her poor old bones to ache,
Could anything be more alluring,
Than an old hedge to Goody Blake?   60
And now and then, it must be said,
When her old bones were cold and chill,
She left her fire, or left her bed,
To seek the hedge of Harry Gill.

Now Harry he had long suspected
This trespass of old Goody Blake,
And vow'd that she should be detected,

And he on her would vengeance take.
And oft from his warm fire he'd go,
And to the fields his road would take,   70
And there, at night, in frost and snow,
He watch'd to seize old Goody Blake.

And once, behind a rick of barley,
Thus looking out did Harry stand;
The moon was full and shining clearly,
And crisp with frost the stubble-land.
– He hears a noise– he's all awake –
Again? – on tiptoe down the hill
He softly creeps – 'Tis Goody Blake,
She's at the hedge of Harry Gill.   80

Right glad was he when he beheld her:
Stick after stick did Goody pull,
He stood behind a bush of elder,
Till she had filled her apron full.
When with her load she turned about,
The byroad back again to take,
He started forward with a shout,
And sprang upon poor Goody Blake.

And fiercely by the arm he took her,
And by the arm he held her fast,   90
And fiercely by the arm he shook her,
And cried, 'I've caught you then at last!'
Then Goody, who had nothing said,
Her bundle from her lap let fall;
And kneeling on the sticks, she pray'd
To God that is the judge of all.

She pray'd, her wither'd hand uprearing,
While Harry held her by the arm –
'God! who art never out of hearing,
O may he never more be warm!'   100
The cold, cold moon above her head,
Thus on her knees did Goody pray,

Young Harry heard what she had said,
And icy-cold he turned away.

He went complaining all the morrow
That he was cold and very chill:
His face was gloom, his heart was sorrow,
Alas! that day for Harry Gill!
That day he wore a riding-coat,
But not a whit the warmer he: 110
Another was on Thursday brought,
And ere the Sabbath he had three.

'Twas all in vain, a useless matter,
And blankets were about him pinn'd;
Yet still his jaws and teeth they clatter,
Like a loose casement in the wind.
And Harry's flesh it fell away;
And all who see him say 'tis plain,
That, live as long as live he may,
He never will be warm again.   120

No word to any man he utters,
A-bed or up, to young or old;
But ever to himself he mutters,
'Poor Harry Gill is very cold.'
A-bed or up, by night or day;
His teeth they chatter, chatter still.
Now think, ye farmers all, I pray,
Of Goody Blake and Harry Gill.

Lines Written at a Small Distance from My House

*and sent by my little Boy to the Person
to whom they are addressed*[1]

It is the first mild day of March:
Each minute sweeter than before,
The redbreast sings from the tall larch
That stands beside our door.

There is a blessing in the air,
Which seems a sense of joy to yield
To the bare trees, and mountains bare,
And grass in the green field.

My Sister! ('tis a wish of mine)
Now that our morning meal is done,   10
Make haste, your morning task resign;
Come forth and feel the sun.

Edward will come with you, and pray,
Put on with speed your woodland dress,
And bring no book, for this one day
We'll give to idleness.

No joyless forms shall regulate
Our living Calendar:
We from today, my friend, will date
The opening of the year.   20

Love, now a universal birth,
From heart to heart is stealing,
From earth to man, from man to earth,
– It is the hour of feeling.

One moment now may give us more
Than fifty years of reason;
Our minds shall drink at every pore
The spirit of the season.

Some silent laws our hearts may make,
Which they shall long obey;
We for the year to come may take
Our temper from today.　　　　　　　　　　　　　　30

And from the blessed power that rolls
About, below, above;
We'll frame the measure of our souls,
They shall be tuned to love.

Then come, my sister! come, I pray,
With speed put on your woodland dress,
And bring no book; for this one day
We'll give to idleness.　　　　　　　　　　　　　　40

Simon Lee[1]

*the Old Huntsman, with an incident in
which he was concerned*

In the sweet shire of Cardigan,[2]
Not far from pleasant Ivor Hall,[3]
An old man dwells, a little man,
I've heard he once was tall.
Of years he has upon his back,
No doubt, a burthen weighty;
He says he is three score and ten,
But others say he's eighty.

A long blue livery-coat has he,
That's fair behind, and fair before;   10
Yet, meet him where you will, you see
At once that he is poor.
Full five and twenty years he lived
A running huntsman merry;
And, though he has but one eye left,
His cheek is like a cherry.

No man like him the horn could sound,
And no man was so full of glee;
To say the least, four counties round
Had heard of Simon Lee;   20
His master's dead, and no one now
Dwells in the hall of Ivor;
Men, dogs, and horses, all are dead;
He is the sole survivor.

His hunting feats have him bereft
Of his right eye, as you may see:
And then, what limbs those feats have left
To poor old Simon Lee!
He has no son, he has no child,
His wife, an aged woman,   30
Lives with him, near the waterfall,
Upon the village common.

And he is lean and he is sick,
His little body's half awry;
His ankles they are swoln and thick,
His legs are thin and dry.
When he was young he little knew
Of husbandry or tillage;
And now he's forced to work, though weak,
– The weakest in the village.   40

He all the country could outrun,
Could leave both man and horse behind;
And often, ere the race was done,
He reeled and was stone-blind.
And still there's something in the world
At which his heart rejoices;
For when the chiming hounds are out,
He dearly loves their voices![4]

Old Ruth works out of doors with him,
And does what Simon cannot do;   50
For she, not over stout of limb,
Is stouter of the two.
And though you with your utmost skill
From labour could not wean them,
Alas! 'tis very little, all
Which they can do between them.

Beside their moss-grown hut of clay,
Not twenty paces from the door,
A scrap of land they have, but they
Are poorest of the poor.   60
This scrap of land he from the heath
Enclosed when he was stronger;
But what avails the land to them,
Which they can till no longer?

Few months of life has he in store,
As he to you will tell,
For still, the more he works, the more
His poor old ankles swell.
My gentle reader, I perceive

How patiently you've waited,   70
And I'm afraid that you expect
Some tale will be related.

O reader! had you in your mind
Such stores as silent thought can bring,
O gentle reader! you would find
A tale in everything.
What more I have to say is short,
I hope you'll kindly take it;
It is no tale; but should you think,
Perhaps a tale you'll make it.   80

One summer-day I chanced to see
This old man doing all he could
About the root of an old tree,
A stump of rotten wood.
The mattock totter'd in his hand
So vain was his endeavour
That at the root of the old tree
He might have worked for ever.

'You're overtasked, good Simon Lee,
Give me your tool,' to him I said;   90
And at the word right gladly he
Received my proffer'd aid.
I struck, and with a single blow
The tangled root I sever'd,
At which the poor old man so long
And vainly had endeavour'd.

The tears into his eyes were brought,
And thanks and praises seemed to run
So fast out of his heart, I thought
They never would have done.   100
– I've heard of hearts unkind, kind deeds
With coldness still returning.
Alas! the gratitude of men
Has oftner left me mourning.

Anecdote for Fathers

showing how the art of lying may be taught

I have a boy[1] of five years old,
His face is fair and fresh to see;
His limbs are cast in beauty's mould,
And dearly he loves me.

One morn we stroll'd on our dry walk,
Our quiet house all full in view,
And held such intermitted talk
As we are wont to do.

My thoughts on former pleasures ran;
I thought of Kilve's[2] delightful shore,   10
My pleasant home, when spring began,
A long, long year before.

A day it was when I could bear
To think, and think, and think again;
With so much happiness to spare,
I could not feel a pain.

My boy was by my side, so slim
And graceful in his rustic dress!
And oftentimes I talked to him,
In very idleness.   20

The young lambs ran a pretty race;
The morning sun shone bright and warm;
'Kilve,' said I, 'was a pleasant place,
And so is Liswyn farm.[3]

'My little boy, which like you more,'
I said and took him by the arm –
'Our home by Kilve's delightful shore,
Or here at Liswyn farm?

'And tell me, had you rather be,'
I said and held him by the arm,   30

'At Kilve's smooth shore by the green sea,
Or here at Liswyn farm?'

In careless mood he looked at me,
While still I held him by the arm,
And said, 'At Kilve I'd rather be
Than here at Liswyn farm.'

'Now, little Edward, say why so;
My little Edward, tell me why;'
'I cannot tell, I do not know.'
'Why this is strange,' said I.   40

'For, here are woods and green-hills warm;
There surely must some reason be
Why you would change sweet Liswyn farm
For Kilve by the green sea.'

At this, my boy, so fair and slim,
Hung down his head, nor made reply;
And five times did I say to him,
'Why? Edward, tell me why?'

His head he raised – there was in sight,
It caught his eye, he saw it plain –   50
Upon the house-top, glittering bright,
A broad and gilded vane.

Then did the boy his tongue unlock,
And thus to me he made reply;
'At Kilve there was no weather-cock,
And that's the reason why.'

Oh dearest, dearest boy! my heart
For better lore would seldom yearn,
Could I but teach the hundredth part
Of what from thee I learn.   60

We Are Seven

A simple child, dear brother Jim,[1]
That lightly draws its breath,
And feels its life in every limb,
What should it know of death?

I met a little cottage girl,
She was eight years old, she said;
Her hair was thick with many a curl
That cluster'd round her head.

She had a rustic, woodland air,
And she was wildly clad;   10
Her eyes were fair, and very fair,
– Her beauty made me glad.

'Sisters and brothers, little maid,
How many may you be?'
'How many? seven in all,' she said,
And wondering looked at me.

'And where are they, I pray you tell?'
She answered, 'Seven are we,
And two of us at Conway dwell,
And two are gone to sea.'   20

'Two of us in the churchyard lie,
My sister and my brother,
And in the churchyard cottage, I
Dwell near them with my mother.'

'You say that two at Conway dwell,
And two are gone to sea,
Yet you are seven; I pray you tell
Sweet Maid, how this may be?'

Then did the little Maid reply,
'Seven boys and girls are we;

Two of us in the churchyard lie,   30
Beneath the churchyard tree.'

'You run about, my little maid,
Your limbs they are alive;
If two are in the churchyard laid,
Then ye are only five.'

'Their graves are green, they may be seen,'
The little Maid replied,
'Twelve steps or more from my mother's door,
And they are side by side.   40

'My stockings there I often knit,
My 'kerchief there I hem;
And there upon the ground I sit –
I sit and sing to them.

'And often after sunset, Sir,
When it is light and fair,
I take my little porringer,
And eat my supper there.

'The first that died was little Jane;
In bed she moaning lay,   50
Till God released her of her pain,
And then she went away.

'So in the churchyard she was laid,
And all the summer dry,
Together round her grave we played,
My brother John and I.

'And when the ground was white with snow,
And I could run and slide,
My brother John was forced to go,
And he lies by her side.'   60

'How many are you then,' said I,
'If they two are in Heaven?'
The little Maiden did reply,
'O Master! we are seven.'

'But they are dead; those two are dead!
Their spirits are in heaven!'
'Twas throwing words away; for still
The little Maid would have her will,
And said, 'Nay, we are seven!'

Lines Written in Early Spring

I heard a thousand blended notes,
While in a grove I sate reclined,
In that sweet mood when pleasant thoughts
Bring sad thoughts to the mind.

To her fair works did nature link
The human soul that through me ran;
And much it griev'd my heart to think
What man has made of man.

Through primrose-tufts, in that sweet bower,
The periwinkle trail'd its wreathes;   10
And 'tis my faith that every flower
Enjoys the air it breathes.

The birds around me hopp'd and play'd:
Their thoughts I cannot measure,
But the least motion which they made,
It seem'd a thrill of pleasure.

The budding twigs spread out their fan,
To catch the breezy air;
And I must think, do all I can,
That there was pleasure there.   20

If I these thoughts may not prevent,
If such be of my creed the plan,
Have I not reason to lament
What man has made of man?

The Thorn[1]

1

There is a thorn; it looks so old,
In truth you'd find it hard to say,
How it could ever have been young,
It looks so old and grey.
Not higher than a two-years' child,
It stands erect this aged thorn;
No leaves it has, no thorny points;
It is a mass of knotted joints,
A wretched thing forlorn.
It stands erect, and like a stone   10
With lichens it is overgrown.

2

Like rock or stone, it is o'ergrown
With lichens to the very top,
And hung with heavy tufts of moss,
A melancholy crop:
Up from the earth these mosses creep,
And this poor thorn they clasp it round
So close, you'd say that they were bent
With plain and manifest intent,
To drag it to the ground;   20
And all had joined in one endeavour
To bury this poor thorn for ever.

3

High on a mountain's highest ridge,
Where oft the stormy winter gale
Cuts like a scythe, while through the clouds
It sweeps from vale to vale;
Not five yards from the mountain-path,
This thorn you on your left espy;
And to the left, three yards beyond,
You see a little muddy pond   30
Of water, never dry;
I've measured it from side to side:
'Tis three feet long, and two feet wide.

4

And close beside this aged thorn,
There is a fresh and lovely sight,
A beauteous heap, a hill of moss,
Just half a foot in height.
All lovely colours there you see,
All colours that were ever seen,
And mossy network too is there,   40
As if by hand of lady fair
The work had woven been,
And cups, the darlings of the eye
So deep is their vermilion dye.

5

Ah me! what lovely tints are there!
Of olive-green and scarlet bright,
In spikes, in branches, and in stars,
Green, red, and pearly white.
This heap of earth o'ergrown with moss
Which close beside the thorn you see,   50
So fresh in all its beauteous dyes,
Is like an infant's grave in size
As like as like can be:
But never, never anywhere,
An infant's grave was half so fair.

6

Now would you see this aged thorn,
This pond and beauteous hill of moss,
You must take care and choose your time
The mountain when to cross.
For oft there sits, between the heap   60
That's like an infant's grave in size,
And that same pond of which I spoke,
A woman in a scarlet cloak,
And to herself she cries,
'Oh misery! oh misery!
Oh woe is me! oh misery!'

7

At all times of the day and night
This wretched woman thither goes,
And she is known to every star,
And every wind that blows;   70
And there beside the thorn she sits
When the blue daylight's in the skies,
And when the whirlwind's on the hill,
Or frosty air is keen and still,
And to herself she cries,
'Oh misery! oh misery!
Oh woe is me! oh misery!'

8

'Now wherefore thus, by day and night,
In rain, in tempest, and in snow,
Thus to the dreary mountain-top   80
Does this poor woman go?
And why sits she beside the thorn
When the blue daylight's in the sky,
Or when the whirlwind's on the hill,
Or frosty air is keen and still,
And wherefore does she cry? –
Oh wherefore? wherefore? tell me why
Does she repeat that doleful cry?'

9

I cannot tell; I wish I could;
For the true reason no one knows,   90
But if you'd gladly view the spot,
The spot to which she goes;
The heap that's like an infant's grave,
The pond – and thorn, so old and grey,
Pass by her door – 'tis seldom shut –
And if you see her in her hut,
Then to the spot away! –
I never heard of such as dare
Approach the spot when she is there.

10

'But wherefore to the mountain-top   100
Can this unhappy woman go,
Whatever star is in the skies,
Whatever wind may blow?'
Nay rack your brain – 'tis all in vain,
I'll tell you everything I know;
But to the thorn, and to the pond
Which is a little step beyond,
I wish that you would go:
Perhaps when you are at the place
You something of her tale may trace.   110

11

I'll give you the best help I can:
Before you up the mountain go,
Up to the dreary mountain-top,
I'll tell you all I know.
'Tis now some two and twenty years,
Since she (her name is Martha Ray)
Gave with a maiden's true goodwill
Her company to Stephen Hill;
And she was blithe and gay,
And she was happy, happy still   120
Whene'er she thought of Stephen Hill.

12

And they had fix'd the wedding-day,
The morning that must wed them both;
But Stephen to another maid
Had sworn another oath;
And with this other maid to church
Unthinking Stephen went –
Poor Martha! on that woeful day
A cruel, cruel fire, they say,
Into her bones was sent: 130
It dried her body like a cinder,
And almost turn'd her brain to tinder.

13

They say, full six months after this,
While yet the summer-leaves were green,
She to the mountain-top would go,
And there was often seen.
'Tis said, a child was in her womb,
As now to any eye was plain;
She was with child, and she was mad,
Yet often she was sober sad   140
From her exceeding pain.
Oh me! ten thousand times I'd rather
That he had died, that cruel father!

14

Sad case for such a brain to hold
Communion with a stirring child!
Sad case, as you may think, for one
Who had a brain so wild!
Last Christmas when we talked of this,
Old Farmer Simpson did maintain,
That in her womb the infant wrought   150
About its mother's heart, and brought
Her senses back again:
And when at last her time drew near,
Her looks were calm, her senses clear.

15

No more I know, I wish I did,
And I would tell it all to you;
For what became of this poor child
There's none that ever knew:
And if a child was born or no,
There's no one that could ever tell;   160
And if 'twas born alive or dead,
There's no one knows, as I have said,
But some remember well,
That Martha Ray about this time
Would up the mountain often climb.

16

And all that winter, when at night
The wind blew from the mountain-peak,
'Twas worth your while, though in the dark,
The churchyard path to seek:
For many a time and oft were heard   170
Cries coming from the mountain-head,
Some plainly living voices were,
And others, I've heard many swear,
Were voices of the dead:
I cannot think, whate'er they say,
They had to do with Martha Ray.

17

But that she goes to this old thorn,
The thorn which I've described to you,
And there sits in a scarlet cloak,
I will be sworn is true.   180
For one day with my telescope,
To view the ocean wide and bright,
When to this country first I came,
Ere I had heard of Martha's name,
I climbed the mountain's height:
A storm came on, and I could see
No object higher than my knee.

18

'Twas mist and rain, and storm and rain,
No screen, no fence could I discover,
And then the wind! in faith, it was   190
A wind full ten times over.
I looked around, I thought I saw
A jutting crag, and off I ran,
Head-foremost, through the driving rain,
The shelter of the crag to gain,
And, as I am a man,
Instead of jutting crag, I found
A woman seated on the ground.

19

I did not speak — I saw her face,
Her face it was enough for me;   200
I turned about and heard her cry,
'O misery! O misery!'
And there she sits, until the moon
Through half the clear blue sky will go,
And when the little breezes make
The waters of the pond to shake,
As all the country know,
She shudders and you hear her cry,
'Oh misery! oh misery!'

20

'But what's the thorn? and what's the pond?   210
And what's the hill of moss to her?
And what's the creeping breeze that comes
The little pond to stir?'
I cannot tell; but some will say
She hanged her baby on the tree,
Some say she drowned it in the pond,[8]
Which is a little step beyond,
But all and each agree,
The little babe was buried there,
Beneath that hill of moss so fair.   220

21

I've heard the scarlet moss is red
With drops of that poor infant's blood;
But kill a new-born infant thus!
I do not think she could.
Some say, if to the pond you go,
And fix on it a steady view,
The shadow of a babe you trace,
A baby and a baby's face,
And that it looks at you;
Whene'er you look on it, 'tis plain   230
The baby looks at you again.

22

And some had sworn an oath that she
Should be to public justice brought;
And for the little infant's bones
With spades they would have sought.
But then the beauteous hill of moss
Before their eyes began to stir;
And for full fifty yards around,
The grass it shook upon the ground;
But all do still aver   240
The little babe is buried there,
Beneath that hill of moss so fair.

23

I cannot tell how this may be,
But plain it is, the thorn is bound
With heavy tufts of moss, that strive
To drag it to the ground.
And this I know, full many a time,
When she was on the mountain high,
By day, and in the silent night,
When all the stars shone clear and bright,   250
That I have heard her cry,
'Oh misery! oh misery!
O woe is me! oh misery!'

The Last of the Flock

In distant countries I have been,
And yet I have not often seen
A healthy man, a man full grown,
Weep in the public roads alone.
But such a one, on English ground,
And in the broad highway, I met;
Along the broad highway he came,
His cheeks with tears were wet.
Sturdy he seemed, though he was sad;
And in his arms a lamb he had.   10

He saw me, and he turned aside,
As if he wished himself to hide:
Then with his coat he made essay
To wipe those briny tears away.
I follow'd him, and said, 'My friend
What ails you? wherefore weep you so?'
– 'Shame on me, Sir! this lusty lamb,
He makes my tears to flow.
Today I fetched him from the rock;
He is the last of all my flock.   20

'When I was young, a single man,
And after youthful follies ran,
Though little given to care and thought,
Yet, so it was, a ewe I bought;
And other sheep from her I raised,
As healthy sheep as you might see,
And then I married, and was rich
As I could wish to be;
Of sheep I number'd a full score,
And every year increas'd my store.   30

'Year after year my stock it grew,
And from this one, this single ewe,
Full fifty comely sheep I raised,
As sweet a flock as ever grazed!

Upon the mountain did they feed;
They throve, and we at home did thrive.
– This lusty lamb of all my store
Is all that is alive:
And now I care not if we die,
And perish all of poverty.   40

'Ten children, Sir! had I to feed,
Hard labour in a time of need!
My pride was tamed, and in our grief
I of the parish ask'd relief.
They said I was a wealthy man;[1]
My sheep upon the mountain fed,
And it was fit that thence I took
Whereof to buy us bread:'
'Do this; how can we give to you,'
They cried, 'what to the poor is due?   50

'I sold a sheep as they had said,
And bought my little children bread,
And they were healthy with their food;
For me it never did me good.
A woeful time it was for me,
To see the end of all my gains,
The pretty flock which I had reared
With all my care and pains,
To see it melt like snow away!
For me it was a woeful day.   60

'Another still! and still another!
A little lamb, and then its mother!
It was a vein that never stopp'd,
Like blood-drops from my heart they dropp'd.
Till thirty were not left alive
They dwindled, dwindled, one by one,
And I may say that many a time
I wished they all were gone:
They dwindled one by one away;
For me it was a woeful day.   70

'To wicked deeds I was inclined,
And wicked fancies cross'd my mind,
And every man I chanc'd to see,
I thought he knew some ill of me.
No peace, no comfort could I find,
No ease, within doors or without,
And crazily, and wearily,
I went my work about.
Oft-times I thought to run away;
For me it was a woeful day.   80

'Sir! 'twas a precious flock to me,
As dear as my own children be;
For daily with my growing store
I loved my children more and more.
Alas! it was an evil time;
God cursed me in my sore distress,
I prayed, yet every day I thought
I loved my children less;
And every week, and every day,
My flock, it seemed to melt away.   90

'They dwindled, Sir, sad sight to see!
From ten to five, from five to three,
A lamb, a wether, and a ewe;
And then at last, from three to two;
And of my fifty, yesterday
I had but only one,
And here it lies upon my arm,
Alas! and I have none;
Today I fetched it from the rock
It is the last of all my flock.'   100

The Mad Mother

Her eyes are wild, her head is bare,
The sun has burnt her coal-black hair,
Her eyebrows have a rusty stain,
And she came far from over the main.
She has a baby on her arm,
Or else she were alone;
And underneath the haystack warm,
And on the green-wood stone,
She talked and sung the woods among;
And it was in the English tongue.   10

'Sweet babe! they say that I am mad,
But nay, my heart is far too glad;
And I am happy when I sing
Full many a sad and doleful thing:
Then, lovely baby, do not fear!
I pray thee have no fear of me,
But, safe as in a cradle, here,
My lovely baby! thou shalt be,
To thee I know too much I owe;
I cannot work thee any woe.   20

'A fire was once within my brain;
And in my head a dull, dull pain;
And fiendish faces one, two, three,
Hung at my breasts, and pulled at me.
But then there came a sight of joy;
It came at once to do me good;
I waked, and saw my little boy,
My little boy of flesh and blood;
Oh joy for me that sight to see!
For he was here, and only he.   30

'Suck, little babe, oh suck again!
It cools my blood; it cools my brain;
Thy lips I feel them, baby! they
Draw from my heart the pain away.

Oh! press me with thy little hand;
It loosens something at my chest;
About that tight and deadly band
I feel thy little fingers press'd.
The breeze I see is in the tree;
It comes to cool my babe and me.   40

'Oh! love me, love me, little boy!
Thou art thy mother's only joy;
And do not dread the waves below,
When o'er the sea-rock's edge we go;
The high crag cannot work me harm,
Nor leaping torrents when they howl;
The babe I carry on my arm,
He saves for me my precious soul;
Then happy lie, for blest am I;
Without me my sweet babe would die.   50

'Then do not fear, my boy! for thee
Bold as a lion I will be;
And I will always be thy guide,
Through hollow snows and rivers wide.
I'll build an Indian bower; I know
The leaves that make the softest bed:
And if from me thou wilt not go,
But still be true 'till I am dead,
My pretty thing! then thou shalt sing,
As merry as the birds in spring.   60

'Thy father cares not for my breast,
'Tis thine, sweet baby, there to rest:
'Tis all thine own! and if its hue
Be changed, that was so fair to view,
'Tis fair enough for thee, my dove!
My beauty, little child, is flown;
But thou wilt live with me in love,
And what if my poor cheek be brown?
'Tis well for me; thou canst not see
How pale and wan it else would be.   70

'Dread not their taunts, my little life!
I am thy father's wedded wife;
And underneath the spreading tree
We two will live in honesty.
If his sweet boy he could forsake,
With me he never would have stay'd:
From him no harm my babe can take,
But he, poor man! is wretched made,
And every day we two will pray
For him that's gone and far away.   80

'I'll teach my boy the sweetest things;
I'll teach him how the owlet sings.
My little babe! thy lips are still,
And thou hast almost suck'd thy fill.
– Where art thou gone my own dear child?
What wicked looks are those I see?
Alas! alas! that look so wild,
It never, never came from me:
If thou art mad, my pretty lad,
Then I must be for ever sad.   90

'Oh! smile on me, my little lamb!
For I thy own dear mother am.
My love for thee has well been tried:
I've sought thy father far and wide.
I know the poisons of the shade,
I know the earth-nuts fit for food;
Then, pretty dear, be not afraid;
We'll find thy father in the wood.
Now laugh and be gay, to the woods away!
And there, my babe; we'll live for aye.'   100

The Idiot Boy[1]

'Tis eight o'clock – a clear March night,
The moon is up – the sky is blue,
The owlet in the moonlight air,
He shouts from nobody knows where;
He lengthens out his lonely shout,
Halloo! halloo! a long halloo!

– Why bustle thus about your door,
What means this bustle, Betty Foy?
Why are you in this mighty fret?
And why on horseback have you set   10
Him whom you love, your idiot boy?

Beneath the moon that shines so bright,
Till she is tired, let Betty Foy
With girt and stirrup fiddle-faddle;
But wherefore set upon a saddle
Him whom she loves, her idiot boy?

There's scarce a soul that's out of bed;
Good Betty! put him down again;
His lips with joy they burr at you,
But, Betty! what has he to do   20
With stirrup, saddle, or with rein?

The world will say 'tis very idle,
Bethink you of the time of night;
There's not a mother, no not one,
But when she hears what you have done,
Oh! Betty she'll be in a fright.

But Betty's bent on her intent,
For her good neighbour, Susan Gale,
Old Susan, she who dwells alone,
Is sick, and makes a piteous moan,   30
As if her very life would fail.

There's not a house within a mile,
No hand to help them in distress:
Old Susan lies abed in pain,
And sorely puzzled are the twain,
For what she ails they cannot guess.

And Betty's husband's at the wood,
Where by the week he doth abide,
A woodman in the distant vale;
There's none to help poor Susan Gale,   40
What must be done? what will betide?

And Betty from the lane has fetched
Her pony, that is mild and good,
Whether he be in joy or pain,
Feeding at will along the lane,
Or bringing faggots from the wood.

And he is all in travelling trim,
And by the moonlight, Betty Foy
Has up upon the saddle set,
The like was never heard of yet,   50
Him whom she loves, her idiot boy.

And he must post without delay
Across the bridge that's in the dale,
And by the church, and o'er the down,
To bring a doctor from the town,
Or she will die, old Susan Gale.

There is no need of boot or spur,
There is no need of whip or wand,
For Johnny has his holly-bough,
And with a hurly-burly² now   60
He shakes the green bough in his hand.

And Betty o'er and o'er has told
The boy, who is her best delight,
Both what to follow, what to shun,
What do, and what to leave undone,
How turn to left, and how to right.

And Betty's most especial charge,
Was, 'Johnny! Johnny! mind that you
Come home again, nor stop at all,
Come home again, whate'er befall,   70
My Johnny do, I pray you do.'

To this did Johnny answer make,
Both with his head, and with his hand,
And proudly shook the bridle too,
And then! his words were not a few,
Which Betty well could understand.

And now that Johnny is just going,
Though Betty's in a mighty flurry,
She gently pats the pony's side,
On which her idiot boy must ride,   80
And seems no longer in a hurry.

But when the pony moved his legs,
Oh! then for the poor idiot boy!
For joy he cannot hold the bridle,
For joy his head and heels are idle,
He's idle all for very joy.

And while the pony moves his legs,
In Johnny's left-hand you may see,
The green bough's motionless and dead;
The moon that shines above his head   90
Is not more still and mute than he.

His heart it was so full of glee,
That till full fifty yards were gone,
He quite forgot his holly whip,
And all his skill in horsemanship,
Oh! happy, happy, happy John.

And Betty's standing at the door,
And Betty's face with joy o'erflows,
Proud of herself, and proud of him,
She sees him in his travelling trim;   100
How quietly her Johnny goes.

The silence of her idiot boy,
What hopes it sends to Betty's heart!
He's at the guide-post – he turns right,
She watches till he's out of sight,
And Betty will not then depart.

Burr, burr – now Johnny's lips they burr,
As loud as any mill, or near it,
Meek as a lamb the pony moves,
And Johnny makes the noise he loves,   110
And Betty listens, glad to hear it.

Away she hies to Susan Gale:
And Johnny's in a merry tune,
The owlets hoot, the owlets curr,
And Johnny's lips they burr, burr, burr,
And on he goes beneath the moon.

His steed and he right well agree,
For of this pony there's a rumour,
That should he lose his eyes and ears,
And should he live a thousand years,   120
He never will be out of humour.

But then he is a horse that thinks!
And when he thinks his pace is slack;
Now, though he knows poor Johnny well,
Yet for his life he cannot tell
What he has got upon his back.

So through the moonlight lanes they go,
And far into the moonlight dale,
And by the church, and o'er the down,
To bring a doctor from the town,   130
To comfort poor old Susan Gale.

And Betty, now at Susan's side,
Is in the middle of her story,
What comfort Johnny soon will bring,
With many a most diverting thing,
Of Johnny's wit and Johnny's glory.

And Betty's still at Susan's side:
By this time she's not quite so flurried;
Demure with porringer[3] and plate
She sits, as if in Susan's fate   140
Her life and soul were buried.

But Betty, poor good woman! she,
You plainly in her face may read it,
Could lend out of that moment's store
Five years of happiness or more,
To any that might need it.

But yet I guess that now and then
With Betty all was not so well,
And to the road she turns her ears,
And thence full many a sound she hears,   150
Which she to Susan will not tell.

Poor Susan moans, poor Susan groans,
'As sure as there's a moon in heaven,'
Cries Betty, 'he'll be back again;
They'll both be here, 'tis almost ten,
They'll both be here before eleven.'

Poor Susan moans, poor Susan groans,
The clock gives warning for eleven;
'Tis on the stroke – 'If Johnny's near,'
Quoth Betty, 'he will soon be here,   160
As sure as there's a moon in heaven.'

The clock is on the stroke of twelve,
And Johnny is not yet in sight,
The moon's in heaven, as Betty sees,
But Betty is not quite at ease;
And Susan has a dreadful night.

And Betty, half an hour ago,
On Johnny vile reflections cast;
'A little idle sauntering thing!'
With other names, an endless string,   170
But now that time is gone and past.

And Betty's drooping at the heart,
That happy time all past and gone,
'How can it be he is so late?
The doctor he has made him wait,
Susan! they'll both be here anon.'

And Susan's growing worse and worse,
And Betty's in a sad quandary;
And then there's nobody to say
If she must go or she must stay: 180
– She's in a sad quandary.

The clock is on the stroke of one;
But neither doctor nor his guide
Appear along the moonlight road,
There's neither horse nor man abroad,
And Betty's still at Susan's side.

And Susan she begins to fear
Of sad mischances not a few,
That Johnny may perhaps be drown'd,
Or lost perhaps, and never found;   190
Which they must both for ever rue.

She prefaced half a hint of this
With, 'God forbid it should be true!'
At the first word that Susan said,
Cried Betty, rising from the bed,
'Susan, I'd gladly stay with you.

'I must be gone, I must away,
Consider, Johnny's but half-wise;
Susan, we must take care of him,
If he is hurt in life or limb' –   200
'Oh God forbid!' poor Susan cries.

'What can I do?' says Betty, going,
'What can I do to ease your pain?
Good Susan tell me, and I'll stay;
I fear you're in a dreadful way,
But I shall soon be back again.'

'Good Betty go, good Betty go,
There's nothing that can ease my pain.'
Then off she hies, but with a prayer
That God poor Susan's life would spare,   210
Till she comes back again.

So, through the moonlight lane she goes,
And far into the moonlight dale;
And how she ran, and how she walked,
And all that to herself she talked,
Would surely be a tedious tale.

In high and low, above, below,
In great and small, in round and square,
In tree and tower was Johnny seen,
In bush and brake, in black and green,   220
'Twas Johnny, Johnny, everywhere.

She's past the bridge that's in the dale,
And now the thought torments her sore,
Johnny perhaps his horse forsook,
To hunt the moon that's in the brook,
And never will be heard of more.

And now she's high upon the down,
Alone amid a prospect wide;
There's neither Johnny nor his horse,
Among the fern or in the gorse;   230
There's neither doctor nor his guide.

'Oh saints! what is become of him?
Perhaps he's climbed into an oak,
Where he will stay till he is dead;
Or sadly he has been misled,
And joined the wandering gypsy-folk.

'Or him that wicked pony's carried
To the dark cave, the goblins' hall,
Or in the castle he's pursuing,
Among the ghosts, his own undoing;   240
Or playing with the waterfall.'

At poor old Susan then she railed,
While to the town she posts away;
'If Susan had not been so ill,
Alas! I should have had him still,
My Johnny, till my dying day.'

Poor Betty! in this sad distemper,
The doctor's self would hardly spare,
Unworthy things she talked and wild,
Even he, of cattle the most mild,   250
The pony had his share.

And now she's got into the town,
And to the doctor's door she hies;
'Tis silence all on every side;
The town so long, the town so wide,
Is silent as the skies.

And now she's at the doctor's door,
She lifts the knocker, rap, rap, rap,
The doctor at the casement shows,
His glimmering eyes that peep and doze;   260
And one hand rubs his old nightcap.

'Oh Doctor! Doctor! where's my Johnny?'
'I'm here, what is't you want with me?'
'Oh Sir! you know I'm Betty Foy,
And I have lost my poor dear boy,
You know him – him you often see;

'He's not so wise as some folks be.'
'The devil take his wisdom!' said
The doctor, looking somewhat grim,
'What, woman! should I know of him?'   270
And, grumbling, he went back to bed.

'O woe is me! O woe is me!
Here will I die; here will I die;
I thought to find my Johnny here,
But he is neither far nor near,
Oh! what a wretched mother I!'

She stops, she stands, she looks about,
Which way to turn she cannot tell.
Poor Betty! it would ease her pain
If she had heart to knock again;   280
– The clock strikes three – a dismal knell!

Then up along the town she hies,
No wonder if her senses fail,
This piteous news so much it shock'd her,
She quite forgot to send the doctor,
To comfort poor old Susan Gale.

And now she's high upon the down,
And she can see a mile of road,
'Oh cruel! I'm almost three-score;
Such night as this was ne'er before,   290
There's not a single soul abroad.'

She listens, but she cannot hear
The foot of horse, the voice of man;
The streams with softest sound are flowing,
The grass you almost hear it growing,
You hear it now if e'er you can.

The owlets through the long blue night
Are shouting to each other still:
Fond lovers, yet not quite hob nob,[4]
They lengthen out the tremulous sob,   300
That echoes far from hill to hill.

Poor Betty now has lost all hope,
Her thoughts are bent on deadly sin;
A green-grown pond she just has pass'd,
And from the brink she hurries fast,
Lest she should drown herself therein.

And now she sits her down and weeps;
Such tears she never shed before;
'Oh dear, dear pony! my sweet joy!
Oh carry back my idiot boy!   310
And we will ne'er o'erload thee more.'

A thought is come into her head;
'The pony he is mild and good,
And we have always used him well;
Perhaps he's gone along the dell,
And carried Johnny to the wood.'

Then up she springs as if on wings;
She thinks no more of deadly sin;
If Betty fifty ponds should see,
The last of all her thoughts would be,   320
To drown herself therein.

Oh reader! now that I might tell
What Johnny and his horse are doing!
What they've been doing all this time,
Oh could I put it into rhyme,
A most delightful tale pursuing!

Perhaps, and no unlikely thought!
He with his pony now doth roam
The cliffs and peaks so high that are,
To lay his hands upon a star,   330
And in his pocket bring it home.

Perhaps he's turned himself about,
His face unto his horse's tail,
And still and mute, in wonder lost,
All like a silent horseman-ghost,
He travels on along the vale.

And now, perhaps, he's hunting sheep,
A fierce and dreadful hunter he!
Yon valley, that's so trim and green,
In five months' time, should he be seen,   340
A desert wilderness will be.

Perhaps, with head and heels on fire,
And like the very soul of evil,
He's galloping away, away,
And so he'll gallop on for aye,
The bane of all that dread the devil.

I to the muses have been bound,
These fourteen years, by strong indentures,[5]
Oh gentle muses! let me tell
But half of what to him befell,   350
For sure he met with strange adventures.

Oh gentle muses! is this kind?
Why will ye thus my suit repel?
Why of your further aid bereave me?
And can ye thus unfriended leave me?
Ye muses! whom I love so well.

Who's yon, that, near the waterfall,
Which thunders down with headlong force,
Beneath the moon, yet shining fair,
As careless as if nothing were,   360
Sits upright on a feeding horse?

Unto his horse, that's feeding free,
He seems, I think, the rein to give;
Of moon or stars he takes no heed;
Of such we in romances read,
– 'Tis Johnny! Johnny! as I live.

And that's the very pony too.
Where is she, where is Betty Foy?
She hardly can sustain her fears;
The roaring waterfall she hears,   370
And cannot find her idiot boy.

Your pony's worth his weight in gold,
Then calm your terrors, Betty Foy!
She's coming from among the trees,
And now, all full in view, she sees
Him whom she loves, her idiot boy.

And Betty sees the pony too:
Why stand you thus Good Betty Foy?
It is no goblin, 'tis no ghost,
'Tis he whom you so long have lost,   380
He whom you love, your idiot boy.

She looks again – her arms are up –
She screams – she cannot move for joy;
She darts as with a torrent's force,
She almost has o'erturned the horse,
And fast she holds her idiot boy.

And Johnny burrs and laughs aloud,
Whether in cunning or in joy,
I cannot tell; but while he laughs,
Betty a drunken pleasure quaffs,   390
To hear again her idiot boy.

And now she's at the pony's tail,
And now she's at the pony's head,
On that side now, and now on this,
And almost stifled with her bliss,
A few sad tears does Betty shed.

She kisses o'er and o'er again,
Him whom she loves, her idiot boy,
She's happy here, she's happy there,
She is uneasy everywhere;   400
Her limbs are all alive with joy.

She pats the pony, where or when
She knows not, happy Betty Foy!
The little pony glad may be,
But he is milder far than she,
You hardly can perceive his joy.

'Oh! Johnny, never mind the doctor;
You've done your best, and that is all.'
She took the reins, when this was said,
And gently turned the pony's head   410
From the loud waterfall.

By this the stars were almost gone,
The moon was setting on the hill,
So pale you scarcely looked at her:
The little birds began to stir,
Though yet their tongues were still.

The pony, Betty, and her boy,
Wind slowly through the woody dale:
And who is she, betimes abroad,[6]
That hobbles up the steep rough road?   420
Who is it, but old Susan Gale?

Long Susan lay deep lost in thought,
And many dreadful fears beset her,
Both for her messenger and nurse;
And as her mind grew worse and worse,
Her body it grew better.

She turned, she toss'd herself in bed,
On all sides doubts and terrors met her;
Point after point did she discuss;
And while her mind was fighting thus,   430
Her body still grew better.

'Alas! what is become of them?
These fears can never be endured,
I'll to the wood.' – The word scarce said,
Did Susan rise up from her bed,
As if by magic cured.

Away she posts up hill and down,
And to the wood at length is come,
She spies her friends, she shouts a greeting;
Oh me! it is a merry meeting,   440
As ever was in Christendom.

The owls have hardly sung their last,
While our four travellers homeward wend;
The owls have hooted all night long,
And with the owls began my song,
And with the owls must end.

For while they all were travelling home,
Cried Betty, 'Tell us Johnny, do,
Where all this long night you have been,
What you have heard, what you have seen,   450
And Johnny, mind you tell us true.'

Now Johnny all night long had heard
The owls in tuneful concert strive;
No doubt too he the moon had seen;
For in the moonlight he had been
From eight o'clock till five.

And thus to Betty's question, he
Made answer, like a traveller bold
(His very words I give to you),
'The cocks did crow to-whoo, to-whoo,   460
And the sun did shine so cold.'
– Thus answered Johnny in his glory,
And that was all his travel's story.

Lines Written near Richmond, upon
the Thames, at Evening

How rich the wave, in front, imprest
With evening-twilight's summer hues,
While, facing thus the crimson west,
The boat her silent path pursues!
And see how dark the backward stream!
A little moment past, so smiling!
And still, perhaps, with faithless gleam,
Some other loiterer beguiling.

Such views the youthful bard allure,
But, heedless of the following gloom,   10
He deems their colours shall endure
'Till peace go with him to the tomb.
– And let him nurse his fond deceit,
And what if he must die in sorrow!
Who would not cherish dreams so sweet,
Though grief and pain may come tomorrow?

Glide gently, thus for ever glide,
O Thames! that other bards may see,
As lovely visions by thy side
As now, fair river! come to me.   20
Oh glide, fair stream! for ever so;
Thy quiet soul on all bestowing,
'Till all our minds for ever flow,
As thy deep waters now are flowing.

Vain thought! yet be as now thou art,
That in thy waters may be seen
The image of a poet's heart,
How bright, how solemn, how serene!
Such heart did once the poet bless,
Who, pouring here a *later* ditty,*   30

---

* Collins's ode on the death of Thomson,[1] the last written, I believe, of the poems
which were published during his lifetime. This ode is also alluded to in the next
stanza.   (Wordsworth's footnote)

Could find no refuge from distress,
But in the milder grief of pity.

Remembrance! as we glide along,
For him suspend the dashing oar,
And pray that never child of Song
May know his freezing sorrows more.
How calm! how still! the only sound,
The dripping of the oar suspended!
– The evening darkness gathers round
By virtue's holiest powers attended.   40

Expostulation and Reply

'Why William, on that old grey stone,
Thus for the length of half a day,
Why William, sit you thus alone,
And dream your time away?

'Where are your books? that light bequeath'd
To beings else forlorn and blind!
Up! Up! and drink the spirit breath'd
From dead men to their kind.

'You look round on your mother earth,
As if she for no purpose bore you;   10
As if you were her first-born birth,
And none had lived before you!'

One morning thus, by Esthwaite lake,[1]
When life was sweet I knew not why,
To me my good friend Matthew[2] spake,
And thus I made reply.

'The eye it cannot choose but see,
We cannot bid the ear be still;
Our bodies feel, where'er they be,
Against, or with our will.   20

'Nor less I deem that there are powers,
Which of themselves our minds impress,
That we can feed this mind of ours,
In a wise passiveness.

'Think you, mid all this mighty sum
Of things for ever speaking,
That nothing of itself will come,
But we must still be seeking?

' – Then ask not wherefore, here, alone,
Conversing as I may,   30
I sit upon this old grey stone,
And dream my time away.'

The Tables Turned

An evening scene, on the same subject

Up! up! my friend, and clear your looks,
Why all this toil and trouble?
Up! up! my friend, and quit your books,
Or surely you'll grow double.

The sun above the mountain's head,
A freshening lustre mellow,
Through all the long green fields has spread,
His first sweet evening yellow.

Books! 'tis a dull and endless strife,
Come, hear the woodland linnet,   10
How sweet his music; on my life
There's more of wisdom in it.

And hark! how blithe the throstle sings!
And he is no mean preacher;
Come forth into the light of things,
Let Nature be your teacher.

She has a world of ready wealth,
Our minds and hearts to bless —
Spontaneous wisdom breathed by health,
Truth breathed by cheerfulness.   20

One impulse from a vernal wood
May teach you more of man;
Of moral evil and of good,
Than all the sages can.

Sweet is the lore which nature brings;
Our meddling intellect
Misshapes the beauteous forms of things;
– We murder to dissect.

Enough of science and of art;
Close up these barren leaves;   30
Come forth, and bring with you a heart
That watches and receives.

Old Man Travelling[1]

ANIMAL TRANQUILLITY AND DECAY – A SKETCH

       The little hedgerow birds,
That peck along the road, regard him not.
He travels on, and in his face, his step,
His gait, is one expression; every limb,
His look and bending figure, all bespeak
A man who does not move with pain, but moves
With thought – He is insensibly subdued
To settled quiet: he is one by whom
All effort seems forgotten, one to whom
Long patience has such mild composure given   10
That patience now doth seem a thing of which
He hath no need. He is by nature led
To peace so perfect that the young behold
With envy what the old man hardly feels.
– I asked him whither he was bound, and what
The object of his journey; he replied,
'Sir! I am going many miles to take
A last leave of my son, a mariner,
Who from a sea-fight has been brought to Falmouth,[2]
And there is dying in an hospital.'   20

The Complaint of a Forsaken Indian Woman

When a Northern Indian, from sickness, is unable to continue his journey with his companions, he is left behind, covered over with Deer-skins, and is supplied with water, food, and fuel if the situation of the place will afford it. He is informed of the track which his companions intend to pursue, and if he is unable to follow, or overtake them, he perishes alone in the Desert; unless he should have the good fortune to fall in with some other Tribes of Indians. It is unnecessary to add that the females are equally, or still more, exposed to the same fate. See that very interesting work, Hearne's Journey from Hudson's Bay to the Northern Ocean.[1] When the Northern Lights, as the same writer informs us, vary their position in the air, they make a rustling and a crackling noise. This circumstance is alluded to in the first stanza of the following poem.

Before I see another day,
Oh let my body die away!
In sleep I heard the northern gleams;
The stars they were among my dreams;
In sleep did I behold the skies,
I saw the crackling flashes drive;
And yet they are upon my eyes,
And yet I am alive.
Before I see another day,
Oh let my body die away!   10

My fire is dead: it knew no pain;
Yet is it dead, and I remain.
All stiff with ice the ashes lie;
And they are dead, and I will die.
When I was well, I wished to live,
For clothes, for warmth, for food, and fire;
But they to me no joy can give,
No pleasure now, and no desire.
Then here contented will I lie;
Alone I cannot fear to die.   20

Alas! you might have dragged me on
Another day, a single one!
Too soon despair o'er me prevailed;
Too soon my heartless spirit failed;
When you were gone my limbs were stronger,
And Oh how grievously I rue,
That, afterwards, a little longer,
My friends, I did not follow you!
For strong and without pain I lay,
My friends, when you were gone away.   30

My child! they gave thee to another,
A woman who was not thy mother.
When from my arms my babe they took,
On me how strangely did he look!
Through his whole body something ran,
A most strange something did I see;
– As if he strove to be a man,
That he might pull the sledge for me.
And then he stretched his arms, how wild!
Oh mercy! like a little child.   40

My little joy! my little pride!
In two days more I must have died.
Then do not weep and grieve for me;
I feel I must have died with thee.
Oh wind that o'er my head art flying,
The way my friends their course did bend,
I should not feel the pain of dying,
Could I with thee a message send.
Too soon, my friends, you went away;
For I had many things to say.   50

I'll follow you across the snow,
You travel heavily and slow:
In spite of all my weary pain,
I'll look upon your tents again.
My fire is dead, and snowy white
The water which beside it stood;

The wolf has come to me tonight,
And he has stolen away my food.
For ever left alone am I,
Then wherefore should I fear to die? 60

My journey will be shortly run,
I shall not see another sun,
I cannot lift my limbs to know
If they have any life or no.
My poor forsaken child! if I
For once could have thee close to me,
With happy heart I then would die,
And my last thoughts would happy be.
I feel my body die away,
I shall not see another day. 70

The Convict[1]

The glory of evening was spread through the west;
  – On the slope of a mountain I stood,
While the joy that precedes the calm season of rest
  Rang loud through the meadow and wood.

'And must we then part from a dwelling so fair?'
  In the pain of my spirit I said,
And with a deep sadness I turned, to repair
  To the cell where the convict is laid.

The thick-ribbed walls that o'ershadow the gate
  Resound; and the dungeons unfold: 10
I pause; and at length, through the glimmering grate,
  That outcast of pity behold.

His black matted head on his shoulder is bent,
  And deep is the sigh of his breath,
And with stedfast dejection his eyes are intent
  On the fetters that link him to death.

'Tis sorrow enough on that visage to gaze,
  That body dismiss'd from his care;
Yet my fancy has pierced to his heart, and portrays
  More terrible images there.   20

His bones are consumed, and his life-blood is dried,
  With wishes the past to undo;
And his crime, through the pains that o'erwhelm him, descried,
  Still blackens and grows on his view.

When from the dark synod, or blood-reeking field,
  To his chamber the monarch is led,
All soothers of sense their soft virtue shall yield,
  And quietness pillow his head.

But if grief, self-consumed, in oblivion would doze,
  And conscience her tortures appease,   30
'Mid tumult and uproar this man must repose;
  In the comfortless vault of disease.

When his fetters at night have so press'd on his limbs,
    That the weight can no longer be borne,
If, while a half-slumber his memory bedims,
    The wretch on his pallet should turn,

While the jail-mastiff howls at the dull clanking chain,
    From the roots of his hair there shall start
A thousand sharp punctures of cold-sweating pain,
    And terror shall leap at his heart.   40

But now he half-raises his deep-sunken eye,
    And the motion unsettles a tear;
The silence of sorrow it seems to supply,
    And asks of me why I am here.

'Poor victim! no idle intruder has stood
    With o'erweening complacence our state to compare,
But one, whose first wish is the wish to be good,
    Is come as a brother thy sorrows to share.

'At thy name though compassion her nature resign,
    Though in virtue's proud mouth thy report be a stain,   50
My care, if the arm of the mighty were mine,
    Would plant thee where yet thou might'st blossom again.'

Lines Written a Few Miles above Tintern Abbey,

on revisiting the banks of the Wye during a tour[1]
JULY 13, 1798

Five years have passed; five summers, with the length
Of five long winters! and again I hear
These waters, rolling from their mountain-springs
With a sweet inland murmur.* – Once again
Do I behold these steep and lofty cliffs,
Which on a wild secluded scene impress
Thoughts of more deep seclusion; and connect
The landscape with the quiet of the sky.
The day is come when I again repose
Here, under this dark sycamore, and view   10
These plots of cottage-ground, these orchard-tufts,
Which, at this season, with their unripe fruits,
Among the woods and copses lose themselves,
Nor, with their green and simple hue, disturb
The wild green landscape. Once again I see
These hedgerows, hardly hedgerows, little lines
Of sportive wood run wild; these pastoral farms
Green to the very door; and wreathes of smoke
Sent up, in silence, from among the trees,
With some uncertain notice, as might seem,   20
Of vagrant dwellers in the houseless woods,
Or of some hermit's cave, where by his fire
The hermit sits alone.

                    Though absent long,
These forms of beauty have not been to me
As is a landscape to a blind man's eye:
But oft, in lonely rooms, and mid the din
Of towns and cities, I have owed to them,
In hours of weariness, sensations sweet,
Felt in the blood, and felt along the heart,

---

*   The river is not affected by the tides a few miles above Tintern.
                                        (Wordsworth's footnote)

And passing even into my purer mind   30
With tranquil restoration: – feelings too
Of unremembered pleasure; such, perhaps,
As may have had no trivial influence
On that best portion of a good man's life;
His little, nameless, unremembered acts
Of kindness and of love. Nor less, I trust,
To them I may have owed another gift,
Of aspect more sublime; that blessed mood,
In which the burthen of the mystery,
In which the heavy and the weary weight   40
Of all this unintelligible world
Is lighten'd: – that serene and blessed mood,
In which the affections gently lead us on,
Until, the breath of this corporeal frame,
And even the motion of our human blood
Almost suspended, we are laid asleep
In body, and become a living soul:
While with an eye made quiet by the power
Of harmony, and the deep power of joy,
We see into the life of things.

                                    If this   50
Be but a vain belief, yet, oh! how oft,
In darkness, and amid the many shapes
Of joyless daylight; when the fretful stir
Unprofitable, and the fever of the world,
Have hung upon the beatings of my heart,
How oft, in spirit, have I turned to thee
O sylvan Wye! Thou wanderer through the woods,
How often has my spirit turned to thee!

And now, with gleams of half-extinguish'd thought,
With many recognitions dim and faint,   60
And somewhat of a sad perplexity,
The picture of the mind revives again:
While here I stand, not only with the sense
Of present pleasure, but with pleasing thoughts
That in this moment there is life and food
For future years. And so I dare to hope

Though changed, no doubt, from what I was, when first
I came among these hills; when like a roe
I bounded o'er the mountains, by the sides
Of the deep rivers, and the lonely streams,   70
Wherever nature led; more like a man
Flying from something that he dreads, than one
Who sought the thing he loved. For nature then
(The coarser pleasures of my boyish days,
And their glad animal movements all gone by)
To me was all in all. – I cannot paint
What then I was. The sounding cataract
Haunted me like a passion: the tall rock,
The mountain, and the deep and gloomy wood,
Their colours and their forms, were then to me   80
An appetite: a feeling and a love,
That had no need of a remoter charm,
By thought supplied, or any interest
Unborrowed from the eye. – That time is past,
And all its aching joys are now no more,
And all its dizzy raptures. Not for this
Faint I, nor mourn, nor murmur: other gifts
Have followed, for such loss, I would believe,
Abundant recompense. For I have learned
To look on nature, not as in the hour   90
Of thoughtless youth, but hearing oftentimes
The still, sad music of humanity,
Not harsh nor grating, though of ample power
To chasten and subdue. And I have felt
A presence that disturbs me with the joy
Of elevated thoughts; a sense sublime
Of something far more deeply interfused,
Whose dwelling is the light of setting suns,
And the round ocean, and the living air,
And the blue sky, and in the mind of man,   100
A motion and a spirit, that impels
All thinking things, all objects of all thought,
And rolls through all things. Therefore am I still
A lover of the meadows and the woods,
And mountains; and of all that we behold
From this green earth; of all the mighty world

Of eye and ear, both what they half-create,*
And what perceive; well pleased to recognise
In nature and the language of the sense,
The anchor of my purest thoughts, the nurse,   110
The guide, the guardian of my heart, and soul
Of all my moral being.

                                        Nor, perchance,
If I were not thus taught, should I the more
Suffer my genial spirits to decay:
For thou art with me, here, upon the banks
Of this fair river; thou, my dearest Friend,[3]
My dear, dear Friend, and in thy voice I catch
The language of my former heart, and read
My former pleasures in the shooting lights
Of thy wild eyes. Oh! yet a little while   120
May I behold in thee what I was once,
My dear, dear Sister! And this prayer I make,
Knowing that Nature never did betray
The heart that loved her; 'tis her privilege,
Through all the years of this our life, to lead
From joy to joy: for she can so inform
The mind that is within us, so impress
With quietness and beauty, and so feed
With lofty thoughts, that neither evil tongues,
Rash judgments, nor the sneers of selfish men,   130
Nor greetings where no kindness is, nor all
The dreary intercourse of daily life,
Shall e'er prevail against us, or disturb
Our chearful faith that all which we behold
Is full of blessings. Therefore let the moon
Shine on thee in thy solitary walk;
And let the misty mountain winds be free
To blow against thee: and in after years,
When these wild ecstasies shall be matured
Into a sober pleasure, when thy mind   140

* This line has a close resemblance to an admirable line of Young,[2] the exact
  expression of which I cannot recollect.   (Wordsworth's footnote)

Shall be a mansion for all lovely forms,
Thy memory be as a dwelling-place
For all sweet sounds and harmonies; Oh! then,
If solitude, or fear, or pain, or grief,
Should be thy portion, with what healing thoughts
Of tender joy wilt thou remember me,
And these my exhortations! Nor, perchance,
If I should be, where I no more can hear
Thy voice, nor catch from thy wild eyes these gleams
Of past existence, wilt thou then forget   150
That on the banks of this delightful stream
We stood together; and that I, so long
A worshipper of Nature, hither came,
Unwearied in that service: rather say
With warmer love, oh! with far deeper zeal
Of holier love. Nor wilt thou then forget,
That after many wanderings, many years
Of absence, these steep woods and lofty cliffs,
And this green pastoral landscape, were to me
More dear, both for themselves, and for thy sake.   160

IV   The Ruined Cottage (1798–9)

The Ruined Cottage

'Twas summer and the sun was mounted high.
Along the south the uplands feebly glared
Through a pale steam, and all the northern downs
In clearer air ascending showed far off
Their surfaces with shadows dappled o'er
Of deep embattled clouds: far as the sight
Could reach those many shadows lay in spots
Determined and unmoved, with steady beams
Of clear and pleasant sunshine interposed;
Pleasant to him who on the soft cool moss   10
Extends his careless limbs beside the root
Of some huge oak whose aged branches make
A twilight of their own, a dewy shade
Where the wren warbles while the dreaming man,
Half-conscious of that soothing melody,
With sidelong eye looks out upon the scene,
By those impending branches made more soft,
More soft and distant. Other lot was mine.
Across a bare wide Common I had toiled
With languid feet which by the slipp'ry ground   20
Were baffled still, and when I stretched myself
On the brown earth my limbs from very heat
Could find no rest nor my weak arm disperse
The insect host which gathered round my face
And joined their murmurs to the tedious noise
Of seeds of bursting gorse that crackled round.
I rose and turned towards a group of trees
Which midway in that level stood alone,
And thither come at length, beneath a shade
Of clustering elms that sprang from the same root   30
I found a ruined house, four naked walls
That stared upon each other. I looked round
And near the door I saw an aged Man,

Alone, and stretched upon the cottage bench;
An iron-pointed staff lay at his side.
With instantaneous joy I recognised
That pride of nature and of lowly life,
The venerable Armytage,[1] a friend
As dear to me as is the setting sun.
              Two days before   40
We had been fellow-travellers. I knew
That he was in this neighbourhood and now
Delighted found him here in the cool shade.
He lay, his pack of rustic merchandise
Pillowing his head – I guess he had no thought
Of his way-wandering life. His eyes were shut;
The shadows of the breezy elms above
Dappled his face. With thirsty heat oppressed
At length I hailed him, glad to see his hat
Bedewed with waterdrops, as if the brim   50
Had newly scooped a running stream. He rose
And pointing to a sunflower bade me climb
The [   ] wall[2] where that same gaudy flower
Looked out upon the road. It was a plot
Of garden-ground, now wild, its matted weeds
Marked with the steps of those whom as they passed,
The gooseberry trees that shot in long lank slips,
Or currants hanging from their leafless stems
In scanty strings, had tempted to o'erleap
The broken wall. Within that cheerless spot,   60
Where two tall hedgerows of thick willow boughs
Joined in a damp cold nook, I found a well
Half-choked with willow flowers and weeds.
I slaked my thirst and to the shady bench
Returned, and while I stood unbonneted
To catch the motion of the cooler air
The old Man said, 'I see around me here
Things which you cannot see: we die, my Friend,
Nor we alone, but that which each man loved
And prized in his peculiar nook of earth   70
Dies with him or is changed, and very soon
Even of the good is no memorial left.
The Poets in their elegies and songs

Lamenting the departed call the groves,
They call upon the hills and streams to mourn,
And senseless rocks, nor idly; for they speak
In these their invocations with a voice
Obedient to the strong creative power
Of human passion. Sympathies there are
More tranquil, yet perhaps of kindred birth,   80
That steal upon the meditative mind
And grow with thought. Beside yon spring I stood
And eyed its waters till we seemed to feel
One sadness, they and I. For them a bond
Of brotherhood is broken: time has been
When every day the touch of human hand
Disturbed their stillness, and they ministered
To human comfort. When I stooped to drink,
A spider's web hung to the water's edge,
And on the wet and slimy footstone lay   90
The useless fragment of a wooden bowl;
It moved my very heart. The day has been
When I could never pass this road but she
Who lived within these walls, when I appeared,
A daughter's welcome gave me, and I loved her
As my own child. O Sir! the good die first,
And they whose hearts are dry as summer dust
Burn to the socket. Many a passenger
Has blessed poor Margaret for her gentle looks
When she upheld the cool refreshment drawn   100
From that forsaken spring, and no one came
But he was welcome, no one went away
But that it seemed she loved him. She is dead,
The worm is on her cheek, and this poor hut,
Stripped of its outward garb of houshold flowers,
Of rose and sweet-briar, offers to the wind
A cold bare wall whose earthy top is tricked
With weeds and the rank spear-grass. She is dead,
And nettles rot and adders sun themselves
Where we have sate together while she nursed   110
Her infant at her breast. The unshod Colt,
The wand'ring heifer and the Potter's ass,
Find shelter now within the chimney-wall

Where I have seen her evening hearthstone blaze
And through the window spread upon the road
Its cheerful light. – You will forgive me, Sir,
But often on this cottage do I muse
As on a picture, till my wiser mind
Sinks, yielding to the foolishness of grief.

   She had a husband, an industrious man,   120
Sober and steady; I have heard her say
That he was up and busy at his loom
In summer ere the mower's scythe had swept
The dewy grass, and in the early spring
Ere the last star had vanished. They who passed
At evening, from behind the garden-fence
Might hear his busy spade, which he would ply
After his daily work till the daylight
Was gone and every leaf and flower were lost
In the dark hedges. So they passed their days   130
In peace and comfort, and two pretty babes
Were their best hope next to the God in Heaven.
– You may remember, now some ten years gone,
Two blighting seasons when the fields were left
With half a harvest. It pleased heaven to add
A worse affliction in the plague of war:
A happy land was stricken to the heart;
'Twas a sad time of sorrow and distress:
A wanderer among the cottages,
I with my pack of winter raiment saw   140
The hardships of that season: many rich
Sunk down as in a dream among the poor,
And of the poor did many cease to be,
And their place knew them not. Meanwhile, abridged
Of daily comforts, gladly reconciled
To numerous self-denials, Margaret
Went struggling on through those calamitous years
With cheerful hope: but ere the second autumn
A fever seized her husband. In disease
He lingered long, and when his strength returned   150
He found the little he had stored to meet
The hour of accident or crippling age
Was all consumed. As I have said, 'twas now

A time of trouble; shoals of artisans
Were from their daily labour turned away
To hang for bread on parish charity,
They and their wives and children – happier far
Could they have lived as do the little birds
That peck along the hedges or the kite
That makes her dwelling in the mountain rocks.   160
Ill fared it now with Robert, he who dwelt
In this poor cottage; at his door he stood
And whistled many a snatch of merry tunes
That had no mirth in them, or with his knife
Carved uncouth figures on the heads of sticks,
Then idly sought about through every nook
Of house or garden any casual task
Of use or ornament, and with a strange,
Amusing but uneasy novelty
He blended where he might the various tasks   170
Of summer, autumn, winter, and of spring.
But this endured not; his good-humour soon
Became a weight in which no pleasure was,
And poverty brought on a petted mood
And a sore temper: day by day he drooped,
And he would leave his home, and to the town
Without an errand would he turn his steps
Or wander here and there among the fields.
One while he would speak lightly of his babes
And with a cruel tongue: at other times   180
He played with them wild freaks of merriment:
And 'twas a piteous thing to see the looks
Of the poor innocent children. "Every smile,"
Said Margaret to me here beneath these trees,
"Made my heart bleed." ' At this the old Man paused
And looking up to those enormous elms
He said, ' 'Tis now the hour of deepest noon.
At this still season of repose and peace,
This hour when all things which are not at rest
Are cheerful, while this multitude of flies   190
Fills all the air with happy melody,
Why should a tear be in an old man's eye?
Why should we thus with an untoward mind

And in the weakness of humanity
From natural wisdom turn our hearts away,
To natural comfort shut our eyes and ears,
And feeling on disquiet thus disturb
The calm of Nature with our restless thoughts?'

SECOND PART

He spake with somewhat of a solemn tone:
But when he ended there was in his face   200
Such easy cheerfulness, a look so mild
That for a little time it stole away
All recollection, and that simple tale
Passed from my mind like a forgotten sound.
A while on trivial things we held discourse,
To me soon tasteless. In my own despite
I thought of that poor woman as of one
Whom I had known and loved. He had rehearsed
Her homely tale with such familiar power,
With such an active countenance, an eye   210
So busy, that the things of which he spake
Seemed present, and, attention now relaxed,
There was a heartfelt chillness in my veins.
I rose, and turning from that breezy shade
Went out into the open air and stood
To drink the comfort of the warmer sun.
Long time I had not stayed ere, looking round
Upon that tranquil ruin, I returned
And begged of the old man that for my sake
He would resume his story. He replied,   220
'It were a wantonness and would demand
Severe reproof, if we were men whose hearts
Could hold vain dalliance with the misery
Even of the dead, contented thence to draw
A momentary pleasure never marked
By reason, barren of all future good.
But we have known that there is often found
In mournful thoughts, and always might be found,
A power to virtue friendly; were't not so,
I am a dreamer among men, indeed   230
An idle dreamer. 'Tis a common tale,

By moving accidents uncharactered,
A tale of silent suffering, hardly clothed
In bodily form, and to the grosser sense
But ill adapted, scarcely palpable
To him who does not think. But at your bidding
I will proceed.
         While thus it fared with them
To whom this cottage till that hapless year
Had been a blessed home, it was my chance
To travel in a country far remote. 240
And glad I was when, halting by yon gate
That leads from the green lane, again I saw
These lofty elm trees. Long I did not rest:
With many pleasant thoughts I cheered my way
O'er the flat common. At the door arrived,
I knocked, and when I entered with the hope
Of usual greeting, Margaret looked at me
A little while, then turned her head away
Speechless, and sitting down upon a chair
Wept bitterly. I wist not what to do 250
Or how to speak to her. Poor wretch! at last
She rose from off her seat – and then, oh Sir!
I cannot tell how she pronounced my name:
With fervent love, and with a face of grief
Unutterably helpless, and a look
That seemed to cling upon me, she enquired
If I had seen her husband. As she spake
A strange surprise and fear came to my heart,
Nor had I power to answer ere she told
That he had disappeared – just two months gone. 260
He left his house; two wretched days had passed,
And on the third by the first break of light,
Within her casement full in view she saw
A purse of gold. "I trembled at the sight,"
Said Margaret, "for I knew it was his hand
That placed it there, and on that very day
By one, a stranger, from my husband sent,
The tidings came that he had joined a troop
Of soldiers going to a distant land.
He left me thus – Poor Man! he had not heart 270

To take a farewell of me, and he feared
That I should follow with my babes, and sink
Beneath the misery of a soldier's life."
This tale did Margaret tell with many tears:
And when she ended I had little power
To give her comfort, and was glad to take
Such words of hope from her own mouth as served
To cheer us both: but long we had not talked
Ere we built up a pile of better thoughts,
And with a brighter eye she looked around   280
As if she had been shedding tears of joy.
We parted. It was then the early spring;
I left her busy with her garden tools;
And well remember, o'er that fence she looked,
And while I paced along the footway path
Called out, and sent a blessing after me
With tender cheerfulness and with a voice
That seemed the very sound of happy thoughts.
    I roved o'er many a hill and many a dale
With this my weary load, in heat and cold,   290
Through many a wood, and many an open ground,
In sunshine or in shade, in wet or fair,
Now blithe, now drooping, as it might befall,
My best companions now the driving winds
And now the "trotting brooks"[3] and whispering trees
And now the music of my own sad steps,
With many a short-lived thought that passed between
And disappeared. I came this way again
Towards the wane of summer, when the wheat
Was yellow, and the soft and bladed grass   300
Sprang up afresh and o'er the hayfield spread
Its tender green. When I had reached the door
I found that she was absent. In the shade
Where now we sit I waited her return.
Her cottage in its outward look appeared
As cheerful as before; in any show
Of neatness little changed, but that I thought
The honeysuckle crowded round the door
And from the wall hung down in heavier wreathes,
And knots of worthless stone-crop started out   310

Along the window's edge, and grew like weeds
Against the lower panes. I turned aside
And strolled into her garden. – It was changed:
The unprofitable bindweed spread his bells
From side to side and with unwieldy wreaths
Had dragged the rose from its sustaining wall
And bent it down to earth; the border-tufts –
Daisy and thrift and lowly camomile
And thyme – had straggled out into the paths
Which they were used to deck. Ere this an hour   320
Was wasted. Back I turned my restless steps,
And as I walked before the door it chanced
A stranger passed, and guessing whom I sought
He said that she was used to ramble far.
The sun was sinking in the west, and now
I sate with sad impatience. From within
Her solitary infant cried aloud.
The spot though fair seemed very desolate:
The longer I remained more desolate.
And, looking round, I saw the corner-stones,   330
Till then unmarked, on either side the door
With dull red stains discoloured and stuck o'er
With tufts and hairs of wool, as if the sheep
That feed upon the commons thither came
Familiarly and found a couching-place
Even at her threshold. – The house-clock struck eight;
I turned and saw her distant a few steps.
Her face was pale and thin, her figure too
Was changed. As she unlocked the door she said,
"It grieves me you have waited here so long,   340
But in good truth I've wandered much of late
And sometimes, to my shame I speak, have need
Of my best prayers to bring me back again."
While on the board she spread our evening meal
She told me she had lost her elder child,
That he for months had been a serving-boy
Apprenticed by the parish. "I perceive
You look at me, and you have cause. Today
I have been travelling far, and many days
About the fields I wander, knowing this   350

Only, that what I seek I cannot find.
And so I waste my time: for I am changed;
And to myself," said she, "have done much wrong,
And to this helpless infant. I have slept
Weeping, and weeping I have waked; my tears
Have flowed as if my body were not such
As others are, and I could never die.
But I am now in mind and in my heart
More easy, and I hope," said she, "that heaven
Will give me patience to endure the things   360
Which I behold at home." It would have grieved
Your very heart to see her. Sir, I feel
The story linger in my heart. I fear
'Tis long and tedious, but my spirit clings
To that poor woman: so familiarly
Do I perceive her manner, and her look
And presence, and so deeply do I feel
Her goodness, that not seldom in my walks
A momentary trance comes over me;
And to myself I seem to muse on one   370
By sorrow laid asleep or borne away,
A human being destined to awake
To human life, or something very near
To human life, when he shall come again
For whom she suffered. Sir, it would have grieved
Your very soul to see her: evermore
Her eyelids drooped, her eyes were downward cast;
And when she at her table gave me food
She did not look at me. Her voice was low,
Her body was subdued. In every act   380
Pertaining to her house-affairs appeared
The careless stillness which a thinking mind
Gives to an idle matter – still she sighed,
But yet no motion of the breast was seen,
No heaving of the heart. While by the fire
We sate together, sighs came on my ear;
I knew not how, and hardly whence they came.
I took my staff, and when I kissed her babe
The tears stood in her eyes. I left her then
With the best hope and comfort I could give;   390

She thanked me for my will, but for my hope
It seemed she did not thank me.
                                        I returned
And took my rounds along this road again
Ere on its sunny bank the primrose flower
Had chronicled the earliest day of spring.
I found her sad and drooping; she had learned
No tidings of her husband: if he lived
She knew not that he lived; if he were dead
She knew not he was dead. She seemed the same
In person and appearance, but her house   400
Bespoke a sleepy hand of negligence;
The floor was neither dry nor neat, the hearth
Was comfortless [   ],
The windows too were dim, and her few books,
Which, one upon the other, heretofore
Had been piled up against the corner-panes
In seemly order, now with straggling leaves
Lay scattered here and there, open or shut
As they had chanced to fall. Her infant babe
Had from its mother caught the trick of grief   410
And sighed among its playthings. Once again
I turned towards the garden-gate and saw
More plainly still that poverty and grief
Were now come nearer to her: the earth was hard,
With weeds defaced and knots of withered grass;
No ridges there appeared of clear black mould,
No winter greenness: of her herbs and flowers
It seemed the better part were gnawed away
Or trampled on the earth; a chain of straw
Which had been twisted round the tender stem   420
Of a young apple tree lay at its root;
The bark was nibbled round by truant sheep.
Margaret stood near, her infant in her arms,
And seeing that my eye was on the tree
She said, 'I fear it will be dead and gone
Ere Robert come again.' Towards the house
Together we returned, and she inquired
If I had any hope. But for her Babe
And for her little friendless Boy, she said,

She had no wish to live, that she must die   430
Of sorrow. Yet I saw the idle loom
Still in its place. His Sunday garments hung
Upon the self-same nail, his very staff
Stood undisturbed behind the door. And when
I passed this way beaten by Autumn winds
She told me that her little babe was dead
And she was left alone. That very time,
I yet remember, through the miry lane
She walked with me a mile, when the bare trees
Trickled with foggy damps, and in such sort   440
That any heart had ached to hear her begged
That wheresoe'er I went I still would ask
For him whom she had lost. We parted then,
Our final parting, for from that time forth
Did many seasons pass ere I returned
Into this tract again.
                              Five tedious years
She lingered in unquiet widowhood,
A wife and widow. Needs must it have been
A sore heart-wasting. I have heard, my friend,
That in that broken arbour she would sit   450
The idle length of half a sabbath day –
There, where you see the toadstool's lazy head –
And when a dog passed by she still would quit
The shade and look abroad. On this old Bench
For hours she sate, and evermore her eye
Was busy in the distance, shaping things
Which made her heart beat quick. Seest thou that path?
(The green-sward now has broken its grey line)
There to and fro she paced through many a day
Of the warm summer, from a belt of flax   460
That girt her waist spinning the long-drawn thread
With backward steps. – Yet ever as there passed
A man whose garments showed the Soldier's red,
Or crippled Mendicant in Sailor's garb,
The little child who sate to turn the wheel
Ceased from his toil, and she with faltering voice,
Expecting still to learn her husband's fate,
Made many a fond inquiry; and when they

Whose presence gave no comfort were gone by,
Her heart was still more sad. And by yon gate   470
Which bars the traveller's road she often stood
And when a stranger horseman came, the latch
Would lift, and in his face look wistfully,
Most happy if from aught discovered there
Of tender feeling she might dare repeat
The same sad question. Meanwhile her poor hut
Sunk to decay, for he was gone whose hand
At the first nippings of October frost
Closed up each chink and with fresh bands of straw
Chequered the green-grown thatch. And so she lived   480
Through the long winter, reckless and alone,
Till this reft house by frost, and thaw, and rain
Was sapped; and when she slept the nightly damps
Did chill her breast, and in the stormy day
Her tattered clothes were ruffled by the wind
Even at the side of her own fire. Yet still
She loved this wretched spot, nor would for worlds
Have parted hence; and still that length of road
And this rude bench one torturing hope endeared,
Fast rooted at her heart, and here, my friend,   490
In sickness she remained, and here she died,
Last human tenant of these ruined walls.'
The old Man ceased: he saw that I was moved;
From that low Bench, rising instinctively,
I turned aside in weakness, nor had power
To thank him for the tale which he had told.
I stood, and leaning o'er the garden-gate
Reviewed that Woman's suff'rings, and it seemed
To comfort me while with a brother's love
I blessed her in the impotence of grief.   500
At length towards the cottage I returned
Fondly, and traced with milder interest
That secret spirit of humanity
Which, 'mid the calm oblivious tendencies
Of nature, 'mid her plants, her weeds, and flowers,
And silent overgrowings, still survived.
The old man, seeing this, resumed and said,
'My Friend, enough to sorrow have you given,

The purposes of wisdom ask no more;
Be wise and cheerful, and no longer read   510
The forms of things with an unworthy eye.
She sleeps in the calm earth, and peace is here.
I well remember that those very plumes,
Those weeds, and the high spear-grass on that wall,
By mist and silent raindrops silvered o'er,
As once I passed did to my heart convey
So still an image of tranquillity,
So calm and still, and looked so beautiful
Amid the uneasy thoughts which filled my mind,
That what we feel of sorrow and despair   520
From ruin and from change, and all the grief
The passing shows of being leave behind,
Appeared an idle dream that could not live
Where meditation was.[2] I turned away
And walked along my road in happiness.'
　　He ceased. By this the sun declining shot
A slant and mellow radiance which began
To fall upon us where beneath the trees
We sate on that low bench, and now we felt,
Admonished thus, the sweet hour coming on.   530
A linnet warbled from those lofty elms,
A thrush sang loud, and other melodies,
At distance heard, peopled the milder air.
The old man rose and hoisted up his load.
Together casting then a farewell look
Upon those silent walls, we left the shade
And ere the stars were visible attained
A rustic inn, our evening resting-place.

from *Lyrical Ballads* (1800)

Hart-Leap Well

Hart-Leap Well is a small spring of water, about five miles from Richmond in Yorkshire, and near the side of the road which leads from Richmond to Askrigg. Its name is derived from a remarkable chase, the memory of which is preserved by the monuments spoken of in the second Part of the following Poem, which monuments do now exist as I have there described them.

The Knight had ridden down from Wensley moor
With the slow motion of a summer's cloud;
He turn'd aside towards a Vassal's door,
And, 'Bring another Horse!' he cried aloud.

'Another Horse!' – That shout the Vassal heard,
And saddled his best steed, a comely Grey;
Sir Walter mounted him; he was the third
Which he had mounted on that glorious day.

Joy sparkled in the prancing Courser's eyes;
The horse and horseman are a happy pair;
But, though Sir Walter like a falcon flies,
There is a doleful silence in the air.   10

A rout this morning left Sir Walter's Hall,
That as they gallop'd made the echoes roar;
But horse and man are vanish'd, one and all;
Such race, I think, was never seen before.

Sir Walter, restless as a veering wind,
Calls to the few tired dogs that yet remain:
Brach, Swift and Music, noblest of their kind,
Follow, and up the weary mountain strain.   20

The Knight halloo'd, he chid and cheer'd them on
With suppliant gestures and upbraidings stern;
But breath and eyesight fail, and, one by one,
The dogs are stretch'd among the mountain fern.

Where is the throng, the tumult of the chase?
The bugles that so joyfully were blown?
– This race it looks not like an earthly race;
Sir Walter and the Hart are left alone.

The poor Hart toils along the mountainside;
I will not stop to tell how far he fled,   30
Nor will I mention by what death he died;
But now the Knight beholds him lying dead.

Dismounting then, he lean'd against a thorn;
He had no follower, dog, nor man, nor boy:
He neither smack'd his whip, nor blew his horn,
But gaz'd upon the spoil with silent joy.

Close to the thorn on which Sir Walter lean'd,
Stood his dumb partner in this glorious act;
Weak as a lamb the hour that it is yean'd,
And foaming like a mountain cataract.   40

Upon his side the Hart was lying stretch'd:
His nose half-touch'd a spring beneath a hill,
And with the last deep groan his breath had fetch'd
The waters of the spring were trembling still.

And now, too happy for repose or rest,
Was never man in such a joyful case,
Sir Walter walk'd all round, north, south and west,
And gaz'd, and gaz'd upon that darling place.

And turning up the hill, it was at least
Nine roods of sheer ascent, Sir Walter found   50
Three several marks which with his hoofs the beast
Had left imprinted on the verdant ground.

Sir Walter wiped his face, and cried, ' 'Till now
Such sight was never seen by living eyes:
Three leaps have borne him from this lofty brow,
Down to the very fountain where he lies.

'I'll build a Pleasure-house upon this spot,
And a small Arbour, made for rural joy;
'Twill be the traveller's shed, the pilgrim's cot,
A place of love for damsels that are coy.   60

'A cunning Artist will I have to frame
A bason for that fountain in the dell;
And they, who do make mention of the same,
From this day forth, shall call it Hart-Leap Well.

'And, gallant brute! to make thy praises known,
Another monument shall here be rais'd;
Three several pillars, each a rough hewn stone,
And planted where thy hoofs the turf have graz'd.

'And in the summer-time when days are long,
I will come hither with my paramour,   70
And with the dancers, and the minstrel's song,
We will make merry in that pleasant bower.

Till the foundations of the mountains fail
My mansion with its arbour shall endure,
– The joy of them who till the fields of Swale,
And them who dwell among the woods of Ure.'[1]

Then home he went, and left the Hart, stone-dead,
With breathless nostrils stretch'd above the spring.
And soon the Knight perform'd what he had said,
The fame whereof through many a land did ring.   80

Ere thrice the moon into her port had steer'd,
A cup of stone receiv'd the living well;
Three pillars of rude stone Sir Walter rear'd,
And built a house of pleasure in the dell.

And near the fountain, flowers of stature tall
With trailing plants and trees were intertwin'd,
Which soon composed a little sylvan hall,
A leafy shelter from the sun and wind.

And thither, when the summer days were long,
Sir Walter journey'd with his paramour;   90
And with the dancers and the minstrel's song
Made merriment within that pleasant bower.

The Knight, Sir Walter, died in course of time,
And his bones lie in his paternal vale –
But there is matter for a second rhyme,
And I to this would add another tale.

PART SECOND

The moving accident is not my trade,
To freeze the blood I have no ready arts;
'Tis my delight, alone in summer shade,
To pipe a simple song to thinking hearts.   100

As I from Hawes to Richmond did repair,
It chanc'd that I saw standing in a dell
Three aspins at three corners of a square,
And one, not four yards distant, near a well.

What this imported I could ill divine,
And, pulling now the rein my horse to stop,
I saw three pillars standing in a line,
The last stone pillar on a dark hilltop.

The trees were grey, with neither arms nor head;
Half-wasted the square mound of tawny green;   100
So that you just might say, as then I said,
'Here in old time the hand of man has been.'

I look'd upon the hills both far and near;
More doleful place did never eye survey;
It seem'd as if the springtime came not here,
And Nature here were willing to decay.

I stood in various thoughts and fancies lost,
When one who was in Shepherd's garb attir'd,
Came up the hollow. Him did I accost,
And what this place might be I then inquir'd.   120

The Shepherd stopp'd, and that same story told
Which in my former rhyme I have rehears'd.
'A jolly place,' said he, 'in times of old,
But something ails it now; the spot is curs'd.

'You see these lifeless stumps of aspin wood,
Some say that they are beeches, others elms,
These were the Bower; and here a Mansion stood,
The finest palace of a hundred realms.

'The arbour does its own condition tell,
You see the stones, the fountain, and the stream,   130
But as to the great Lodge, you might as well
Hunt half a day for a forgotten dream.

'There's neither dog nor heifer, horse nor sheep,
Will wet his lips within that cup of stone;
And, oftentimes, when all are fast asleep,
This water doth send forth a dolorous groan.

'Some say that here a murder has been done,
And blood cries out for blood: but, for my part,
I've guess'd, when I've been sitting in the sun,
That it was all for that unhappy Hart.   140

'What thoughts must through the creature's brain
                                    have pass'd!
From the stone on the summit of the steep
Are but three bounds, and look, Sir, at this last!
O Master! it has been a cruel leap.

'For thirteen hours he ran a desperate race;
And in my simple mind we cannot tell
What cause the Hart might have to love this place,
And come and make his death-bed near the well.

'Here on the grass perhaps asleep he sank,
Lull'd by this fountain in the summertide;   150
This water was perhaps the first he drank
When he had wander'd from his mother's side.

'In April here beneath the scented thorn
He heard the birds their morning carols sing,
And he, perhaps, for aught we know, was born
Not half a furlong from that self-same spring.

'But now here's neither grass nor pleasant shade;
The sun on drearier hollow never shone:
So will it be, as I have often said,
Till trees, and stones, and fountain all are gone.'   160

'Grey-headed Shepherd, thou hast spoken well;
Small difference lies between thy creed and mine;
This beast not unobserv'd by Nature fell,
His death was mourn'd by sympathy divine.

'The Being, that is in the clouds and air,
That is in the green leaves among the groves,
Maintains a deep and reverential care
For them the quiet creatures whom he loves.

'The Pleasure-house is dust: – behind, before,
This is no common waste, no common gloom;   170
But Nature, in due course of time, once more
Shall here put on her beauty and her bloom.

'She leaves these objects to a slow decay
That what we are, and have been, may be known;
But, at the coming of the milder day,
These monuments shall all be overgrown.

'One lesson, Shepherd, let us two divide,
Taught both by what she shows, and what conceals,
Never to blend our pleasure or our pride
With sorrow of the meanest thing that feels.'   180

There was a Boy[1]

There was a Boy, ye knew him well, ye Cliffs
And Islands of Winander! many a time,
At evening, when the stars had just begun
To move along the edges of the hills,
Rising or setting, would he stand alone,
Beneath the trees, or by the glimmering lake,
And there, with fingers interwoven, both hands
Press'd closely palm to palm and to his mouth
Uplifted, he, as through an instrument,
Blew mimic hootings to the silent owls   10
That they might answer him. And they would shout
Across the wat'ry vale and shout again
Responsive to his call, with quivering peals,
And long halloos, and screams, and echoes loud
Redoubled and redoubled, a wild scene
Of mirth and jocund din. And, when it chanced
That pauses of deep silence mock'd his skill,
Then, sometimes, in that silence, while he hung
Listening, a gentle shock of mild surprise
Has carried far into his heart the voice   20
Of mountain torrents, or the visible scene
Would enter unawares into his mind
With all its solemn imagery, its rocks,
Its woods, and that uncertain heaven, receiv'd
Into the bosom of the steady lake.
Fair are the woods, and beauteous is the spot,
The vale where he was born: the Churchyard hangs
Upon a slope above the village school,
And there along that bank when I have pass'd
At evening, I believe, that near his grave   30
A full half-hour together I have stood,
Mute – for he died when he was ten years old.

The Brothers*

These Tourists, Heaven preserve us! needs must live
A profitable life: some glance along,
Rapid and gay, as if the earth were air,
And they were butterflies to wheel about
Long as their summer lasted; some, as wise,
Upon the forehead of a jutting crag
Sit perch'd with book and pencil on their knee,
And look and scribble, scribble on and look,
Until a man might travel twelve stout miles,
Or reap an acre of his neighbour's corn.   10

But, for that moping son of Idleness
Why can he tarry *yonder*? – In our churchyard
Is neither epitaph nor monument,
Tombstone nor name, only the turf we tread,
And a few natural graves. To Jane, his Wife,
Thus spake the homely Priest of Ennerdale.[1]
It was a July evening, and he sate
Upon the long stone-seat beneath the eaves
Of his old cottage, as it chanced that day,
Employ'd in winter's work. Upon the stone   20
His Wife sate near him, teasing matted wool,
While, from the twin cards tooth'd with glittering wire,
He fed the spindle of his youngest child,
Who turn'd her large round wheel in the open air
With back and forward steps. Towards the field
In which the parish chapel stood alone,
Girt round with a bare ring of mossy wall,
While half an hour went by, the Priest had sent
Many a long look of wonder, and at last,
Risen from his seat, beside the snow-white ridge   30
Of carded wool which the old Man had piled,
He laid his implements with gentle care,

---

*   This Poem was intended to be the concluding poem of a series of pastorals, the
     scene of which was laid among the mountains of Cumberland and Westmoreland.
     I mention this to apologise for the abruptness with which the poem begins.
                                                          (Wordsworth's footnote)

Each in the other lock'd; and, down the path
Which from his cottage to the churchyard led,
He took his way, impatient to accost
The Stranger, whom he saw still lingering there.

   'Twas one well known to him in former days,
A Shepherd-lad: who ere his thirteenth year
Had chang'd his calling, with the mariners
A fellow-mariner, and so had fared   40
Through twenty seasons; but he had been rear'd
Among the mountains, and he in his heart
Was half a Shepherd on the stormy seas.
Oft in the piping shrouds had Leonard heard
The tones of waterfalls, and inland sounds
Of caves and trees; and when the regular wind
Between the tropics fill'd the steady sail
And blew with the same breath through days and weeks,
Lengthening invisibly its weary line
Along the cloudless main, he, in those hours   50
Of tiresome indolence, would often hang
Over the vessel's side, and gaze and gaze,
And, while the broad green wave and sparkling foam
Flash'd round him images and hues, that wrought
In union with the employment of his heart,
He, thus by feverish passion overcome,
Even with the organs of his bodily eye,
Below him, in the bosom of the deep
Saw mountains, saw the forms of sheep that graz'd
On verdant hills, with dwellings among trees,   60
And Shepherds clad in the same country grey
Which he himself had worn.*
                          And now at length,
From perils manifold, with some small wealth
Acquir'd by traffic in the Indian Isles,
To his paternal home he is return'd,

---

* This description of the Calenture is sketched from an imperfect recollection of
an admirable one in prose, by Mr Gilbert, author of the *Hurricane*.
                                            (Wordsworth's footnote)

With a determin'd purpose to resume
The life which he liv'd there, both for the sake
Of many darling pleasures, and the love
Which to an only brother he has borne   70
In all his hardships, since that happy time
When, whether it blew foul or fair, they two
Were brother Shepherds on their native hills.
– They were the last of all their race; and now,
When Leonard had approach'd his home, his heart
Fail'd in him, and, not venturing to inquire
Tidings of one whom he so dearly lov'd,
Towards the churchyard he had turn'd aside,
That, as he knew in what particular spot
His family were laid, he thence might learn   80
If still his Brother liv'd, or to the file
Another grave was added. – He had found
Another grave, near which a full half-hour
He had remain'd, but, as he gaz'd, there grew
Such a confusion in his memory,
That he began to doubt, and he had hopes
That he had seen this heap of turf before,
That it was not another grave, but one
He had forgotten. He had lost his path,
As up the vale he came that afternoon,   90
Through fields which once had been well known to him.
And Oh! what joy the recollection now
Sent to his heart! he lifted up his eyes,
And looking round he thought that he perceiv'd
Strange alteration wrought on every side
Among the woods and fields, and that the rocks,
And the eternal hills, themselves were chang'd.

   By this the Priest who down the field had come
Unseen by Leonard, at the churchyard gate
Stopp'd short, and thence, at leisure, limb by limb   100
He scann'd him with a gay complacency.
Aye, thought the Vicar, smiling to himself,
'Tis one of those who needs must leave the path
Of the world's business, to go wild alone:
His arms have a perpetual holiday,

The happy man will creep about the fields
Following his fancies by the hour, to bring
Tears down his cheek, or solitary smiles
Into his face, until the setting sun
Write Fool upon his forehead. Planted thus   110
Beneath a shed that overarch'd the gate
Of this rude churchyard, till the stars appear'd
The good man might have commun'd with himself
But that the Stranger, who had left the grave,
Approach'd; he recognis'd the Priest at once,
And after greetings interchang'd, and given
By Leonard to the Vicar as to one
Unknown to him, this dialogue ensued.

LEONARD

You live, Sir, in these dales, a quiet life:
Your years make up one peaceful family;   120
And who would grieve and fret, if, welcome come
And welcome gone, they are so like each other,
They cannot be remember'd. Scarce a funeral
Comes to this churchyard once in eighteen months;
And yet, some changes must take place among you.
And you, who dwell here, even among these rocks
Can trace the finger of mortality,
And see, that with our threescore years and ten
We are not all that perish. – I remember,
For many years ago I pass'd this road,   130
There was a footway all along the fields
By the brookside – 'tis gone – and that dark cleft!
To me it does not seem to wear the face
Which then it had.

PRIEST

                              Why, Sir, for aught I know,
That chasm is much the same –

LEONARD

                                        But, surely, yonder –

PRIEST

Aye, there indeed, your memory is a friend

That does not play you false. – On that tall pike,
(It is the loneliest place of all these hills)   140
There were two Springs which bubbled side by side,
As if they had been made that they might be
Companions for each other: ten years back,
Close to those brother fountains, the huge crag
Was rent with lightning – one is dead and gone,
The other, left behind, is flowing still. –
For accidents and changes such as these,
Why we have store of them! a water-spout
Will bring down half a mountain; what a feast
For folks that wander up and down like you,   150
To see an acre's breadth of that wide cliff
One roaring cataract – a sharp May storm
Will come with loads of January snow,
And in one night send twenty score of sheep
To feed the ravens, or a Shepherd dies
By some untoward death among the rocks:
The ice breaks up and sweeps away a bridge –
A wood is fell'd:– and then for our own homes!
A child is born or christen'd, a field plough'd,
A daughter sent to service, a web spun,   160
The old house-clock is deck'd with a new face;
And hence, so far from wanting facts or dates
To chronicle the time, we all have here
A pair of diaries, one serving, Sir,
For the whole dale, and one for each fireside,
Yours was a stranger's judgment: for historians
Commend me to these valleys.

LEONARD

                        Yet your churchyard
Seems, if such freedom may be used with you,
To say that you are heedless of the past.   170
Here's neither head- nor foot-stone, plate of brass,
An orphan could not find his mother's grave:
Cross-bones or skull, type of our earthly state
Or emblem of our hopes: the dead man's home
Is but a fellow to that pasture field.

PRIEST

Why there, Sir, is a thought that's new to me.
The Stone-cutters, 'tis true, might beg their bread
If every English churchyard were like ours:
Yet your conclusion wanders from the truth.
We have no need of names and epitaphs,
We talk about the dead by our firesides.   180
And then for our immortal part, *we* want
No symbols, Sir, to tell us that plain tale:
The thought of death sits easy on the man
Who has been born and dies among the mountains.

LEONARD

Your dalesmen, then, do in each other's thoughts
Possess a kind of second life: no doubt
You, Sir, could help me to the history
Of half these Graves?

PRIEST

          For eight-score winters past,
With what I've witness'd, and with what I've heard,
Perhaps I might, and, on a winter's evening,   190
If you were seated at my chimney's nook
By turning o'er these hillocks one by one,
We two could travel, Sir, through a strange round,
Yet all in the broad highway of the world.
Now there's a grave – your foot is half upon it,
It looks just like the rest, and yet that man
Died broken-hearted.

LEONARD

          'Tis a common case,
We'll take another: who is he that lies
Beneath yon ridge, the last of those three graves –   200
It touches on that piece of native rock
Left in the churchyard wall.

PRIEST

          That's Walter Ewbank.
He had as white a head and fresh a cheek

As ever were produc'd by youth and age
Engendering in the blood of hale fourscore.
For five long generations had the heart
Of Walter's forefathers o'erflow'd the bounds
Of their inheritance, that single cottage,
You see it yonder, and those few green fields.   210
They toil'd and wrought, and still, from sire to son,
Each struggled, and each yielded as before
A little – yet a little – and old Walter,
They left to him the family heart, and land
With other burthens than the crop it bore.
Year after year the old man still preserv'd
A chearful mind, and buffeted with bond,
Interest and mortgages; at last he sank,
And went into his grave before his time.
Poor Walter! whether it was care that spurr'd him   220
God only knows, but to the very last
He had the lightest foot in Ennerdale:
His pace was never that of an old man:
I almost see him tripping down the path
With his two Grandsons after him – but you,
Unless our Landlord be your host tonight,
Have far to travel, and in these rough paths
Even in the longest day of midsummer –

LEONARD

But these two Orphans!

PRIEST

                              Orphans! such they were –   230
Yet not while Walter liv'd – for, though their Parents
Lay buried side by side as now they lie,
The old Man was a father to the boys,
Two fathers in one father: and if tears
Shed, when he talk'd of them where they were not,
And hauntings from the infirmity of love,
Are aught of what makes up a mother's heart,
This old Man in the day of his old age
Was half a mother to them – If you weep, Sir,
To hear a stranger talking about strangers,   240

Heaven bless you when you are among your kindred!
Aye. You may turn that way – it is a grave
Which will bear looking at.

PRIEST

                              These Boys I hope
They lov'd this good old Man –

PRIEST

                                    They did – and truly,
But that was what we almost overlook'd,
They were such darlings of each other. For
Though from their cradles they had liv'd with Walter,
The only kinsman near them in the house,   250
Yet he being old, they had much love to spare,
And it all went into each other's hearts.
Leonard, the elder by just eighteen months,
Was two years taller: 'twas a joy to see,
To hear, to meet them! from their house the School
Was distant three short miles, and in the time
Of storm and thaw, when every water-course
And unbridg'd stream, such as you may have notic'd
Crossing our roads at every hundred steps,
Was swoln into a noisy rivulet,   260
Would Leonard then, when elder boys perhaps
Remain'd at home, go staggering through the fords
Bearing his Brother on his back. – I've seen him,
On windy days, in one of those stray brooks,
Aye, more than once I've seen him mid-leg deep,
Their two books lying both on a dry stone
Upon the hither side: – and once I said,
As I remember, looking round these rocks
And hills on which we all of us were born,
That God who made the great book of the world   270
Would bless such piety –

LEONARD

                              It may be then –

PRIEST

Never did worthier lads break English bread:

The finest Sunday that the Autumn saw,
With all its mealy clusters of ripe nuts,
Could never keep these boys away from church,
Or tempt them to an hour of sabbath breach.
Leonard and James! I warrant, every corner
Among these rocks and every hollow place
Where foot could come, to one or both of them   280
Was known as well as to the flowers that grow there.
Like roe-bucks they went bounding o'er the hills:
They play'd like two young ravens on the crags:
Then they could write, aye and speak too, as well
As many of their betters – and for Leonard!
The very night before he went away,
In my own house I put into his hand
A Bible, and I'd wager twenty pounds,
That, if he is alive, he has it yet.

LEONARD

It seems, these Brothers have not liv'd to be   290
A comfort to each other. –

PRIEST

                    That they might
Live to that end, is what both old and young
In this our valley all of us have wish'd,
And what, for my part, I have often pray'd:
But Leonard –

LEONARD

Then James still is left among you –

PRIEST

'Tis of the elder Brother I am speaking:
They had an Uncle, he was at that time
A thriving man, and traffick'd on the seas: 300
And, but for this same Uncle, to this hour
Leonard had never handled rope or shroud,
For the Boy lov'd the life which we lead here;
And, though a very Stripling, twelve years old,
His soul was knit to this his native soil.
But, as I said, old Walter was too weak

To strive with such a torrent; when he died,
The estate and house were sold, and all their sheep,
A pretty flock, and which, for aught I know,
Had clothed the Ewbanks for a thousand years.   310
Well – all was gone, and they were destitute.
And Leonard, chiefly for his brother's sake,
Resolv'd to try his fortune on the seas.
'Tis now twelve years since we had tidings from him.
If there was one among us who had heard
That Leonard Ewbank was come home again,
From the great Gavel,* down by Leeza's Banks,
And down the Enna, far as Egremont,
The day would be a very festival,
And those two bells of ours, which there you see   320
Hanging in the open air – but, O good Sir!
This is sad talk – they'll never sound for him
Living or dead – When last we heard of him
He was in slavery among the Moors
Upon the Barbary Coast – 'Twas not a little
That would bring down his spirit, and, no doubt,
Before it ended in his death, the Lad
Was sadly cross'd – Poor Leonard! when we parted,
He took me by the hand and said to me,
If ever the day came when he was rich,   330
He would return, and on his Father's Land
He would grow old among us.

LEONARD

If that day
Should come, 'twould needs be a glad day for him;
He would himself, no doubt, be happy then
As any that should meet him –

* The great Gavel, so called, I imagine, from its resemblance to the gable end of a house, is one of the highest of the Cumberland mountains. It stands at the head of the several vales of Ennerdale, Wastdale, and Borrowdale.
   The Leeza is a river which follows into the Lake of Ennerdale: on issuing from the lake, it changes its name, and is called the End, Eyne or Enna. It falls into the sea a little below Egremont.   (Wordsworth's footnote)

PRIEST

Happy, Sir –

LEONARD

You said his kindred all were in their graves,
And that he had one Brother –

PRIEST

                         That is but   340
A fellow tale of sorrow. From his youth
James, though not sickly, yet was delicate,
And Leonard being always by his side
Had done so many offices about him,
That, though he was not of a timid nature,
Yet still the spirit of a mountain boy
In him was somewhat check'd, and when his Brother
Was gone to sea and he was left alone
The little colour that he had was soon
Stolen from his cheek, he droop'd, and pin'd and pin'd: 350

LEONARD

But these are all the graves of full grown men!

PRIEST

Aye, Sir, that pass'd away: we took him to us.
He was the child of all the dale – he liv'd
Three months with one, and six months with another:
And wanted neither food, nor clothes, nor love,
And many, many happy days were his.
But, whether blithe or sad, 'tis my belief
His absent Brother still was at his heart.
And, when he liv'd beneath our roof, we found
(A practice till this time unknown to him)   360
That often, rising from his bed at night,
He in his sleep would walk about, and sleeping
He sought his Brother Leonard – You are mov'd!
Forgive me, Sir: before I spoke to you,
I judg'd you most unkindly.

LEONARD

                         But this youth,

How did he die at last?[2]

PRIEST

                         One sweet May morning,
It will be twelve years since, when Spring returns,
He had gone forth among the new-dropp'd lambs,   370
With two or three companions whom it chanc'd
Some further business summon'd to a house
Which stands at the Dale-head. James, tir'd perhaps,
Or from some other cause remain'd behind.
You see yon precipice – it almost looks
Like some vast building made of many crags
And in the midst is one particular rock
That rises like a column from the vale,
Whence by our Shepherds it is call'd, the Pillar.
James pointed to its summit, over which   380
They all had purpos'd to return together,
And told them that he there would wait for them:
They parted, and his comrades pass'd that way
Some two hours after, but they did not find him
At the appointed place, a circumstance
Of which they took no heed: but one of them,
Going by chance, at night, into the house
Which at this time was James's home, there learn'd
That nobody had seen him all that day:
The morning came, and still, he was unheard of: 390
The neighbours were alarm'd, and to the Brook
Some went, and some towards the Lake; ere noon
They found him at the foot of that same Rock
Dead, and with mangled limbs. The third day after
I buried him, poor Lad, and there he lies.

LEONARD

And that then *is* his grave! – Before his death
You said that he saw many happy years?

PRIEST

Aye, that he did –

LEONARD

                         And all went well with him –

PRIEST

If he had one, the Lad had twenty homes.   400

LEONARD

And you believe then, that his mind was easy –

PRIEST

Yes, long before he died, he found that time
Is a true friend to sorrow, and unless
His thoughts were turn'd on Leonard's luckless fortune,
He talk'd about him with a cheerful love.

LEONARD

He could not come to an unhallow'd end!

PRIEST

Nay, God forbid! You recollect I mention'd
A habit which disquietude and grief
Had brought upon him, and we all conjectur'd
That, as the day was warm, he had lain down   410
Upon the grass, and, waiting for his comrades
He there had fallen asleep, that in his sleep
He to the margin of the precipice
Had walked, and from the summit had fallen headlong,
And so no doubt he perish'd: at the time,
We guess, that in his hands he must have had
His Shepherd's staff; for midway in the cliff
It had been caught, and there for many years
It hung – and moulder'd there.

                      The Priest here ended –   420
The Stranger would have thank'd him, but he felt
Tears rushing in; both left the spot in silence,
And Leonard, when they reach'd the churchyard gate,
As the Priest lifted up the latch, turn'd round,
And, looking at the grave, he said, 'My Brother.'
The Vicar did not hear the words: and now,
Pointing towards the Cottage, he entreated
That Leonard would partake his homely fare:
The other thank'd him with a fervent voice,

But added, that, the evening being calm,   430
He would pursue his journey. So they parted.

It was not long ere Leonard reach'd a grove
That overhung the road: he there stopp'd short,
And, sitting down beneath the trees, review'd
All that the Priest had said: his early years
Were with him in his heart: his cherish'd hopes,
And thoughts which had been his an hour before,
All press'd on him with such a weight, that now,
This vale, where he had been so happy, seem'd
A place in which he could not bear to live: 440
So he relinquish'd all his purposes.
He travell'd on to Egremont; and thence,
That night, address'd a letter to the Priest
Reminding him of what had pass'd between them.
And adding, with a hope to be forgiven,
That it was from the weakness of his heart,
He had not dared to tell him, who he was.

This done, he went on shipboard, and is now
A Seaman, a grey-headed Mariner.

Strange Fits of Passion

Strange fits of passion I have known,
And I will dare to tell,
But in the lover's ear alone,
What once to me befell.

When she I lov'd was strong and gay
And like a rose in June,
I to her cottage bent my way,
Beneath the evening moon.

Upon the moon I fix'd my eye,
All over the wide lea;   10
My horse trudg'd on, and we drew nigh
Those paths so dear to me.

And now we reach'd the orchard plot,
And, as we climb'd the hill,
Towards the roof of Lucy's[1] cot
The moon descended still.

In one of those sweet dreams I slept,
Kind Nature's gentlest boon!
And, all the while, my eyes I kept
On the descending moon.   20

My horse mov'd on; hoof after hoof
He rais'd and never stopp'd:
When down behind the cottage roof
At once the planet dropp'd.

What fond and wayward thoughts will slide
Into a Lover's head –
'O mercy!' to myself I cried,
'If Lucy should be dead!'

Song

She dwelt among th' untrodden ways
   Beside the springs of Dove,[1]
A Maid whom there were none to praise
   And very few to love.

A Violet by a mossy stone
   Half-hidden from the Eye!
– Fair, as a star when only one
   Is shining in the sky!

She liv'd unknown, and few could know
   When Lucy[2] ceas'd to be;   10
But she is in her Grave, and Oh!
   The difference to me.

A Slumber Did My Spirit Seal

A slumber did my spirit seal,
   I had no human fears:
She[1] seem'd a thing that could not feel
   The touch of earthly years.

No motion has she now, no force,
   She neither hears nor sees,
Roll'd round in earth's diurnal course
   With rocks and stones and trees!

Lucy Gray[1]

Oft I had heard of Lucy Gray,
And when I cross'd the Wild,
I chanc'd to see at break of day
The solitary Child.

No Mate, no comrade Lucy knew;
She dwelt on a wild Moor,
The sweetest Thing that ever grew
Beside a human door!

You yet may spy the Fawn at play,
The Hare upon the Green;   10
But the sweet face of Lucy Gray
Will never more be seen.

'Tonight will be a stormy night,
You to the Town must go,
And take a lantern, Child, to light
Your Mother thro' the snow.'

'That, Father! will I gladly do;
'Tis scarcely afternoon –
The Minster-clock has just struck two,
And yonder is the Moon.'   20

At this the Father rais'd his hook
And snapp'd a faggot-band;
He plied his work, and Lucy took
The lantern in her hand.

Not blither is the mountain roe,
With many a wanton stroke
Her feet disperse the powd'ry snow
That rises up like smoke.

The storm came on before its time,
She wander'd up and down,   30
And many a hill did Lucy climb
But never reach'd the Town.

The wretched Parents all that night
Went shouting far and wide;
But there was neither sound nor sight
To serve them for a guide.

At daybreak on a hill they stood
That overlook'd the Moor;
And thence they saw the Bridge of Wood
A furlong from their door.   40

And now they homeward turn'd, and cry'd,
'In Heaven we all shall meet!'
When in the snow the Mother spied
The print of Lucy's feet.

Then downward from the steep hill's edge
They track'd the footmarks small;
And through the broken hawthorn-hedge,
And by the long stone-wall;

And then an open field they cross'd,
The marks were still the same;   50
They track'd them on, nor ever lost,
And to the Bridge they came.

They follow'd from the snowy bank
The footmarks, one by one,
Into the middle of the plank,
And further there were none.

Yet some maintain that to this day
She is a living Child,
That you may see sweet Lucy Gray
Upon the lonesome Wild.   60

O'er rough and smooth she trips along,
And never looks behind;
And sings a solitary song
That whistles in the wind.

Poor Susan

At the corner of Wood Street,[1] when daylight appears,
There's a Thrush that sings loud, it has sung for three years:
Poor Susan has pass'd by the spot and has heard
In the silence of morning the song of the bird.

'Tis a note of enchantment; what ails her? She sees
A mountain ascending, a vision of trees;
Bright volumes of vapour through Lothbury glide,
And a river flows on through the vale of Cheapside.

Green pastures she views in the midst of the dale,
Down which she so often has tripp'd with her pail,   10
And a single small cottage, a nest like a dove's,
The only one dwelling on earth that she loves.

She looks, and her heart is in Heaven, but they fade,
The mist and the river, the hill and the shade;
The stream will not flow, and the hill will not rise,
And the colours have all pass'd away from her eyes.

Poor Outcast! return – to receive thee once more
The house of thy Father will open its door,
And thou once again, in thy plain russet gown,
May'st hear the thrush sing from a tree of its own.   20

If Nature, for a Favourite Child[1]

In the School of —[2] is a tablet on which are inscribed, in gilt letters, the names of the several persons who have been school-masters there since the foundation of the school, with the time at which they entered upon and quitted their office. Opposite one of those names the author wrote the following lines:

If Nature, for a favourite Child,
In thee hath temper'd so her clay,
That every hour thy heart runs wild
Yet never once doth go astray,

Read o'er these lines; and then review
This tablet, that thus humbly rears   10
In such diversity of hue
Its history of two hundred years.

– When through this little wreck of fame,
Cypher and syllable, thine eye
Has travell'd down to Matthew's name,[3]
Pause with no common sympathy.

And if a sleeping tear should wake
Then be it neither check'd nor stay'd:
For Matthew a request I make
Which for himself he had not made.   20

Poor Matthew, all his frolics o'er,
Is silent as a standing pool,
Far from the chimney's merry roar,
And murmur of the village school.

The sighs which Matthew heav'd were sighs
Of one tir'd out with fun and madness;
The tears which came to Matthew's eyes
Were tears of light, the oil of gladness.

Yet sometimes when the secret cup
Of still and serious thought went round   30
It seem'd as if he drank it up,
He felt with spirit so profound.

– Thou soul of God's best earthly mould,
Thou happy soul, and can it be
That these two words of glittering gold
Are all that must remain of thee?

The Two April Mornings

We walk'd along, while bright and red
Uprose the morning sun,
And Matthew[1] stopp'd, he look'd, and said,
'The will of God be done!'

A village Schoolmaster was he,
With hair of glittering grey;
As blithe a man as you could see
On a spring holiday.

And on that morning, through the grass,
And by the steaming rills,   10
We travell'd merrily to pass
A day among the hills.

'Our work,' said I, 'was well begun;
Then, from thy breast what thought,
Beneath so beautiful a sun,
So sad a sigh has brought?'

A second time did Matthew stop,
And fixing still his eye
Upon the eastern mountain-top
To me he made reply.   20

'Yon cloud with that long purple cleft
Brings fresh into my mind
A day like this which I have left
Full thirty years behind.

'And on that slope of springing corn
The self-same crimson hue
Fell from the sky that April morn,
The same which now I view!

'With rod and line my silent sport
I plied by Derwent's wave,[1]   30
And, coming to the church, stopp'd short
Beside my daughter's grave.

'Nine summers had she scarcely seen
The pride of all the vale;
And then she sang! – she would have been
A very nightingale.

'Six feet in earth my Emma lay,
And yet I lov'd her more,
For so it seem'd, than till that day
I e'er had lov'd before.   40

'And, turning from her grave, I met
Beside the churchyard Yew
A blooming girl, whose hair was wet
With points of morning dew.

'A basket on her head she bare,
Her brow was smooth and white,
To see a child so very fair,
It was a pure delight!

'No fountain from its rocky cave
E'er tripp'd with foot so free,   50
She seem'd as happy as a wave
That dances on the sea.

'There came from me a sigh of pain
Which I could ill confine;
I look'd at her and look'd again;
– And did not wish her mine.'

Matthew is in his grave, yet now
Methinks I see him stand,
As at that moment, with his bough
Of wilding in his hand.   60

The Fountain

A CONVERSATION

We talk'd with open heart, and tongue
Affectionate and true,
A pair of Friends, though I was young,
And Matthew[1] seventy-two.

We lay beneath a spreading oak,
Beside a mossy seat,
And from the turf a fountain broke,
And gurgled at our feet.

Now, Matthew, let us try to match
This water's pleasant tune   10
With some old Border-song,[2] or catch
That suits a summer's noon.

Or of the Church-clock and the chimes
Sing here beneath the shade,
That half-mad thing of witty rhymes
Which you last April made!

In silence Matthew lay, and eyed
The spring beneath the tree;
And thus the dear old Man replied,
The grey-hair'd Man of glee.   20

'Down to the vale this water steers,
How merrily it goes!
'Twill murmur on a thousand years,
And flow as now it flows.

'And here, on this delightful day,
I cannot choose but think
How oft, a vigorous Man, I lay
Beside this Fountain's brink.

'My eyes are dim with childish tears,
My heart is idly stirr'd,   30
For the same sound is in my ears,
Which in those days I heard.

'Thus fares it still in our decay:
And yet the wiser mind
Mourns less for what age takes away
Than what it leaves behind.

'The blackbird in the summer trees,
The lark upon the hill,
Let loose their carols when they please,
Are quiet when they will.   40

'With Nature never do *they* wage
A foolish strife; they see
A happy youth, and their old age
Is beautiful and free:

'But we are press'd by heavy laws,
And often, glad no more,
We wear a face of joy, because
We have been glad of yore.

'If there is one who need bemoan
His kindred laid in earth,   50
The household hearts that were his own,
It is the man of mirth.

'My days, my Friend, are almost gone,
My life has been approv'd,
And many love me, but by none
Am I enough belov'd.'

'Now both himself and me he wrongs,
The man who thus complains!
I live and sing my idle songs
Upon these happy plains,   60

'And, Matthew, for thy Children dead
I'll be a son to thee!'
At this he grasp'd his hands, and said,
'Alas! that cannot be.'

We rose up from the fountain-side,
And down the smooth descent

  Of the green sheep-track did we glide,
  And through the wood we went,

  And, ere we came to Leonard's Rock,
  He sang those witty rhymes   70
  About the crazy old church-clock
  And the bewilder'd chimes.

Nutting

        It seems a day
(I speak of one from many singled out),
One of those heavenly days which cannot die,
When forth I sallied from our cottage-door,*
And with a wallet o'er my shoulder slung,
A nutting crook in hand, I turn'd my steps
Towards the distant woods, a Figure quaint,
Trick'd out in proud disguise of Beggar's weeds
Put on for the occasion, by advice
And exhortation of my frugal Dame.[1]   10
Motley accoutrement! of power to smile
At thorns, and brakes, and brambles, and, in truth,
More ragged than need was. Among the woods,
And o'er the pathless rocks, I fore'd my way
Until, at length, I came to one dear nook
Unvisited, where not a broken bough
Droop'd with its wither'd leaves, ungracious sign
Of devastation, but the hazels rose
Tall and erect, with milk-white clusters hung,
A virgin scene! – A little while I stood,   20
Breathing with such suppression of the heart
As joy delights in; and with wise restraint
Voluptuous, fearless of a rival, eyed

---

* The house at which I was boarded during the time I was at School.
                (Wordsworth's footnote)

The banquet, or beneath the trees I sate
Among the flowers, and with the flowers I play'd;
A temper known to those, who, after long
And weary expectation, have been bless'd
With sudden happiness beyond all hope.
– Perhaps it was a bower beneath whose leaves
The violets of five seasons reappear   30
And fade, unseen by any human eye,
Where fairy water-breaks do murmur on
For ever, and I saw the sparkling foam,
And with my cheek on one of those green stones
That, fleec'd with moss, beneath the shady trees,
Lay round me scatter'd like a flock of sheep,
I heard the murmur and the murmuring sound,
In that sweet mood when pleasure loves to pay
Tribute to ease, and, of its joy secure
The heart luxuriates with indifferent things,   40
Wasting its kindliness on stocks and stones,
And on the vacant air. Then up I rose,
And dragg'd to earth both branch and bough, with crash
And merciless ravage; and the shady nook
Of hazels, and the green and mossy bower
Deform'd and sullied, patiently gave up
Their quiet being: and unless I now
Confound my present feelings with the past,
Even then, when from the bower I turn'd away,
Exulting, rich beyond the wealth of kings   50
I felt a sense of pain when I beheld
The silent trees and the intruding sky.

Then, dearest Maiden! move along these shades
In gentleness of heart with gentle hand
Touch – for there is a Spirit in the woods.

Three Years She Grew

Three years she grew in sun and shower,
Then Nature said, 'A lovelier flower
On earth was never sown;
This Child I to myself will take,
She shall be mine, and I will make
A Lady of my own.

'Myself will to my darling be
Both law and impulse, and with me
The Girl in rock and plain,
In earth and heaven, in glade and bower,   10
Shall feel an overseeing power
To kindle or restrain.

'She shall be sportive as the fawn
That wild with glee across the lawn
Or up the mountain springs,
And hers shall be the breathing balm,
And hers the silence and the calm
Of mute insensate things.

'The floating clouds their state shall lend
To her, for her the willow bend,   20
Nor shall she fail to see
Even in the motions of the storm
Grace that shall mould the Maiden's form
By silent sympathy.

'The stars of midnight shall be dear
To her, and she shall lean her ear
In many a secret place
Where rivulets dance their wayward round,
And beauty born of murmuring sound
Shall pass into her face.   30

'And vital feelings of delight
Shall rear her form to stately height,
Her virgin bosom swell;

Such thoughts to Lucy I will give
While she and I together live
Here in this happy dell.'

Thus Nature spake – The work was done –
How soon my Lucy's race was run!
She died and left to me
This heath, this calm and quiet scene,   40
The memory of what has been,
And never more will be.

The Old Cumberland Beggar

A DESCRIPTION

The class of Beggars to which the old man here described belongs, will probably soon be extinct. It consisted of poor and, mostly, old and infirm persons, who confined themselves to a stated round in their neighbourhood, and had certain fixed days on which, at different houses, they regularly received charity; sometimes in money, but mostly in provisions.

I saw an aged Beggar in my walk,
And he was seated by the highway side
On a low structure of rude masonry
Built at the foot of a huge hill, that they
Who lead their horses down the steep rough road
May thence remount at ease. The aged man
Had placed his staff across the broad smooth stone
That overlays the pile, and from a bag
All white with flour, the dole of village dames,
He drew his scraps and fragments, one by one,   10
And scann'd them with a fix'd and serious look
Of idle computation. In the sun,
Upon the second step of that small pile,
Surrounded by those wild unpeopled hills,
He sate, and eat his food in solitude;
And ever, scatter'd from his palsied hand,
That still attempting to prevent the waste
Was baffled still, the crumbs in little showers
Fell on the ground, and the small mountain birds,
Not venturing yet to peck their destin'd meal,   20
Approached within the length of half his staff.

Him from my childhood have I known, and then
He was so old, he seems not older now;
He travels on, a solitary man,
So helpless in appearance, that for him
The sauntering horseman-traveller does not throw
With careless hand his alms upon the ground,

But stops, that he may safely lodge the coin
Within the old Man's hat; nor quits him so,
But still when he has given his horse the rein   30
Towards the aged Beggar turns a look,
Sidelong and half-reverted. She who tends
The toll-gate, when in summer at her door
She turns her wheel, if on the road she sees
The aged Beggar coming, quits her work,
And lifts the latch for him that he may pass.
The Post-boy when his rattling wheels o'ertake
The aged Beggar, in the woody lane,
Shouts to him from behind, and, if perchance
The old Man does not change his course, the Boy   40
Turns with less noisy wheels to the road-side,
And passes gently by, without a curse
Upon his lips, or anger at his heart.
He travels on, a solitary Man,
His age has no companion. On the ground
His eyes are turn'd, and, as he moves along,
They move along the ground; and evermore,
Instead of common and habitual sight
Of fields with rural works, of hill and dale,
And the blue sky, one little span of earth   50
Is all his prospect. Thus, from day to day,
Bowbent, his eyes for ever on the ground,
He plies his weary journey, seeing still,
And never knowing that he sees, some straw,
Some scatter'd leaf, or marks which, in one track,
The nails of cart or chariot wheel have left
Impress'd on the white road, in the same line,
At distance still the same. Poor Traveller!
His staff trails with him, scarcely do his feet
Disturb the summer dust; he is so still   60
In look and motion that the cottage curs,
Ere he have pass'd the door, will turn away
Weary of barking at him. Boys and girls,
The vacant and the busy, maids and youths,
And urchins newly breech'd, all pass him by:
Him even the slow-pac'd waggon leaves behind.

But deem not this man useless. – Statesmen![1] ye
Who are so restless in your wisdom, ye
Who have a broom still ready in your hands
To rid the world of nuisances; ye proud,   70
Heart-swoln, while in your pride ye contemplate
Your talents, power, and wisdom, deem him not
A burthen of the earth. 'Tis Nature's law
That none, the meanest of created things,
Of forms created the most vile and brute,
The dullest or most noxious, should exist
Divorced from good, a spirit and pulse of good,
A life and soul to every mode of being
Inseparably link'd. While thus he creeps
From door to door, the Villagers in him   80
Behold a record which together binds
Past deeds and offices of charity
Else unremember'd, and so keeps alive
The kindly mood in hearts which lapse of years,
And that half-wisdom half-experience gives
Make slow to feel, and by sure steps resign
To selfishness and cold oblivious cares.
Among the farms and solitary huts
Hamlets, and thinly-scattered villages,
Where'er the aged Beggar takes his rounds,   90
The mild necessity of use compels
To acts of love; and habit does the work
Of reason, yet prepares that after joy
Which reason cherishes. And thus the soul,
By that sweet taste of pleasure unpursu'd
Doth find itself insensibly dispos'd
To virtue and true goodness. Some there are,
By their good works exalted, lofty minds
And meditative, authors of delight
And happiness, which to the end of time   100
Will live, and spread, and kindle; minds like these,
In childhood, from this solitary being,
This helpless wanderer, have perchance receiv'd
(A thing more precious far than all that books
Or the solicitudes of love can do!)

That first mild touch of sympathy and thought,
In which they found their kindred with a world
Where want and sorrow were. The easy man
Who sits at his own door, and like the pear
Which overhangs his head from the green wall,   110
Feeds in the sunshine; the robust and young,
The prosperous and unthinking, they who live
Shelter'd, and flourish in a little grove
Of their own kindred, all behold in him
A silent monitor, which on their minds
Must needs impress a transitory thought
Of self-congratulation, to the heart
Of each recalling his peculiar boons,
His charters and exemptions; and perchance,
Though he to no one give the fortitude   120
And circumspection needful to preserve
His present blessings, and to husband up
The respite of the season, he, at least,
And 'tis no vulgar service, makes them felt.

Yet further. – Many, I believe, there are
Who live a life of virtuous decency,
Men who can hear the Decalogue[2] and feel
No self-reproach, who of the moral law
Establish'd in the land where they abide
Are strict observers, and not negligent,   130
Meanwhile, in any tenderness of heart
Or act of love to those with whom they dwell,
Their kindred, and the children of their blood.
Praise be to such, and to their slumbers peace!
– But of the poor man ask, the abject poor,
Go and demand of him, if there be here,
In this cold abstinence from evil deeds,
And these inevitable charities,
Wherewith to satisfy the human soul.
No – man is dear to man: the poorest poor   140
Long for some moments in a weary life
When they can know and feel that they have been
Themselves the fathers and the dealers out

Of some small blessings, have been kind to such
As needed kindness, for this single cause,
That we have all of us one human heart.
Such pleasure is to one kind Being known,
My Neighbour, when with punctual care, each week
Duly as Friday comes, though press'd herself
By her own wants, she from her chest of meal   150
Takes one unsparing handful for the scrip
Of this old Mendicant, and, from her door
Returning with exhilarated heart,
Sits by her fire and builds her hope in heav'n.

Then let him pass, a blessing on his head!
And while, in that vast solitude to which
The tide of things has led him, he appears
To breathe and live but for himself alone,
Unblam'd, uninjur'd, let him bear about
The good which the benignant law of heaven   160
Has hung around him, and, while life is his,
Still let him prompt the unletter'd Villagers
To tender offices and pensive thoughts.
Then let him pass, a blessing on his head!
And, long as he can wander, let him breathe
The freshness of the valleys, let his blood
Struggle with frosty air and winter snows,
And let the charter'd[3] wind that sweeps the heath
Beat his grey locks against his wither'd face.
Reverence the hope whose vital anxiousness   170
Gives the last human interest to his heart.
May never House, misnamed of industry,
Make him a captive; for that pent-up din,
Those life-consuming sounds that clog the air,
Be his the natural silence of old age.
Let him be free of mountain solitudes,
And have around him, whether heard or not,
The pleasant melody of woodland birds.
Few are his pleasures; if his eyes, which now
Have been so long familiar with the earth,   180
No more behold the horizontal sun

Rising or setting, let the light at least
Find a free entrance to their languid orbs.
And let him, *where* and *when* he will, sit down
Beneath the trees, or by the grassy bank
Of highway side, and with the little birds
Share his chance-gather'd meal, and, finally,
As in the eye of Nature he has liv'd,
So in the eye of Nature let him die.

A Poet's Epitaph

Art thou a Statesman, in the van
Of public business train'd and bred?
– First learn to love one living man;
Then may'st thou think upon the dead.

A Lawyer art thou? – draw not nigh;
Go, carry to some other place
The hardness of thy coward eye,
The falsehood of thy sallow face.

Art thou a man of purple cheer?[1]
A rosy man, right plump to see?   10
Approach; yet Doctor, not too near:
This grave no cushion is for thee.

Art thou a man of gallant pride,
A Soldier, and no man of chaff?
Welcome! – but lay thy sword aside,
And lean upon a Peasant's staff.

Physician art thou? One, all eyes,
Philosopher![2] a fingering slave,
One that would peep and botanise
Upon his mother's grave?   20

Wrapp'd closely in thy sensual fleece,
O turn aside, and take, I pray,
That he below may rest in peace,
Thy pin-point of a soul away!

– A Moralist perchance appears;
Led, Heaven knows how! to this poor sod:
And He has neither eyes nor ears;
Himself his world, and his own God;

One to whose smooth-rubb'd soul can cling
Nor form nor feeling great nor small,   30

A reasoning, self-sufficing thing,
An intellectual All in All!

Shut close the door! press down the latch:
Sleep in thy intellectual crust,
Nor lose ten tickings of thy watch,
Near this unprofitable dust.

But who is He with modest looks,
And clad in homely russet brown?
He murmurs near the running brooks
A music sweeter than their own.   40

He is retired as noontide dew,
Or fountain in a noonday grove;
And you must love him, ere to you
He will seem worthy of your love.

The outward shows of sky and earth,
Of hill and valley he has view'd;
And impulses of deeper birth
Have come to him in solitude.

In common things that round us lie
Some random truths he can impart,   50
The harvest of a quiet eye
That broods and sleeps on his own heart.

But he is weak, both man and boy,
Hath been an idler in the land;
Contented if he might enjoy
The things which others understand.

– Come hither in thy hour of strength,
Come, weak as is a breaking wave!
Here stretch thy body at full length;
Or build thy house upon this grave.   60

Michael

A PASTORAL[1] POEM

If from the public way you turn your steps
Up the tumultuous brook of Green-head Gill,[2]
You will suppose that with an upright path
Your feet must struggle; in such bold ascent
The pastoral Mountains front you, face to face.
But, courage! for beside that boisterous Brook
The mountains have all open'd out themselves,
And made a hidden valley of their own.
No habitation there is seen; but such
As journey thither find themselves alone   10
With a few sheep, with rocks and stones, and kites
That overhead are sailing in the sky.

It is in truth an utter solitude,
Nor should I have made mention of this Dell
But for one object which you might pass by,
Might see and notice not. Beside the brook
There is a straggling heap of unhewn stones!
And to that place a story appertains,
Which, though it be ungarnish'd with events,
Is not unfit, I deem, for the fireside,   20
Or for the summer shade. It was the first,
The earliest of those tales that spake to me
Of Shepherds, dwellers in the valleys, men
Whom I already lov'd, not verily
For their own sakes, but for the fields and hills
Where was their occupation and abode.
And hence this Tale, while I was yet a boy
Careless of books, yet having felt the power
Of Nature, by the gentle agency
Of natural objects led me on to feel   30
For passions that were not my own, and think
At random and imperfectly indeed
On man; the heart of man and human life.
Therefore, although it be a history
Homely and rude, I will relate the same

For the delight of a few natural hearts,
And with yet fonder feeling, for the sake
Of youthful Poets, who among these Hills
Will be my second self when I am gone.

Upon the Forest-side in Grasmere Vale   40
There dwelt a Shepherd, Michael was his name,
An old man, stout of heart, and strong of limb.
His bodily frame had been from youth to age
Of an unusual strength; his mind was keen,
Intense and frugal, apt for all affairs,
And in his Shepherd's calling he was prompt
And watchful more than ordinary men.
Hence he had learn'd the meaning of all winds,
Of blasts of every tone, and often-times,
When others heeded not, He heard the South[3]   50
Make subterraneous music, like the noise
Of Bagpipers on distant Highland hills;
The Shepherd, at such warning, of his flock
Bethought him, and he to himself would say
The winds are now devising work for me!
And truly at all times the storm, that drives
The Traveller to a shelter, summon'd him
Up to the mountains: he had been alone
Amid the heart of many thousand mists
That came to him and left him on the heights.   60
So liv'd he till his eightieth year was pass'd.

And grossly that man errs, who should suppose
That the green Valleys, and the Streams and Rocks
Were things indifferent to the Shepherd's thoughts.
Fields, where with cheerful spirits he had breath'd
The common air; the hills, which he so oft
Had climb'd with vigorous steps; which had impress'd
So many incidents upon his mind
Of hardship, skill or courage, joy or fear;
Which like a book preserv'd the memory   70
Of the dumb animals, whom he had sav'd,
Had fed or shelter'd, linking to such acts,
So grateful in themselves, the certainty

Of honorable gains; these fields, these hills
Which were his living Being, even more
Than his own Blood – what could they less? had laid
Strong hold on his affections, were to him
A pleasurable feeling of blind love,
The pleasure which there is in life itself.

He had not passed his days in singleness.   80
He had a Wife, a comely Matron, old
Though younger than himself full twenty years.
She was a woman of a stirring life
Whose heart was in her house: two wheels she had
Of antique form, this large for spinning wool,
That small for flax, and if one wheel had rest,
It was because the other was at work.
The Pair had but one Inmate in their house,
An only Child, who had been born to them
When Michael telling o'er his years began   90
To deem that he was old, in Shepherd's phrase,
With one foot in the grave. This only son,
With two brave sheep dogs tried in many a storm,
The one of an inestimable worth,
Made all their Household. I may truly say,
That they were as a proverb in the vale
For endless industry. When day was gone,
And from their occupations out of doors
The Son and Father were come home, even then
Their labour did not cease, unless when all   100
Turn'd to their cleanly supper-board, and there
Each with a mess of pottage and skimm'd milk,
Sate round their basket pil'd with oaten cakes,
And their plain home-made cheese. Yet when their meal
Was ended, LUKE (for so the Son was nam'd)
And his old Father, both betook themselves
To such convenient work, as might employ
Their hands by the fireside; perhaps to card
Wool for the Housewife's spindle, or repair
Some injury done to sickle, flail, or scythe,   110
Or other implement of house or field.

Down from the ceiling by the chimney's edge,
Which in our ancient uncouth country style
Did with a huge projection overbrow
Large space beneath, as duly as the light
Of day grew dim, the Housewife hung a lamp;
An aged utensil, which had perform'd
Service beyond all others of its kind.
Early at evening did it burn and late,
Surviving Comrade of uncounted Hours   120
Which going by from year to year had found
And left the Couple neither gay perhaps
Nor cheerful, yet with objects and with hopes
Living a life of eager industry.
And now, when LUKE was in his eighteenth year,
There by the light of this old lamp they sate,
Father and Son, while late into the night
The Housewife plied her own peculiar work,
Making the cottage thro' the silent hours
Murmur as with the sound of summer flies.   130
Not with a waste of words, but for the sake
Of pleasure, which I know that I shall give
To many living now, I of this Lamp
Speak thus minutely: for there are no few
Whose memories will bear witness to my tale.
The Light was famous in its neighbourhood,
And was a public Symbol of the life
The thrifty Pair had liv'd. For, as it chanc'd,
Their Cottage on a plot of rising ground
Stood single, with large prospect North and South,   140
High into Easedale, up to Dunmal-Raise,
And Westward to the village near the Lake.
And from this constant light so regular
And so far seen, the House itself by all
Who dwelt within the limits of the vale,
Both old and young, was nam'd The Evening Star.

Thus living on through such a length of years,
The Shepherd, if he lov'd himself, must needs
Have lov'd his Help-mate; but to Michael's heart
This Son of his old age was yet more dear –   150

Effect which might perhaps have been produc'd
By that instinctive tenderness, the same
Blind Spirit, which is in the blood of all,
Or that a child, more than all other gifts,
Brings hope with it, and forward-looking thoughts,
And stirrings of inquietude, when they
By tendency of nature needs must fail.
From such, and other causes, to the thoughts
Of the old Man his only Son was now
The dearest object that he knew on earth.   160
Exceeding was the love he bare to him,
His Heart and his Heart's joy! For oftentimes
Old Michael, while he was a babe in arms,
Had done him female service, not alone
For dalliance and delight, as is the use
Of Fathers, but with patient mind enforc'd
To acts of tenderness; and he had rock'd
His cradle with a woman's gentle hand.

And in a later time, ere yet the Boy
Had put on Boy's attire, did Michael love,   170
Albeit of a stern unbending mind,
To have the young one in his sight, when he
Had work by his own door, or when he sate
With sheep before him on his Shepherd's stool,
Beneath that large old Oak, which near their door
Stood, and from its enormous breadth of shade
Chosen for the Shearer's covert from the sun,
Thence in our rustic dialect was call'd
The CLIPPING TREE,* a name which yet it bears.
There, while they two were sitting in the shade,   180
With others round them, earnest all and blithe,
Would Michael exercise his heart with looks
Of fond correction and reproof bestow'd
Upon the child, if he disturb'd the sheep
By catching at their legs, or with his shouts

---

*   Clipping is the word used in the North of England for shearing.
                                                      (Wordsworth's note)

Scar'd them, while they lay still beneath the shears.
And when by Heaven's good grace the Boy grew up
A healthy Lad, and carried in his cheek
Two steady roses that were five years old,
Then Michael from a winter coppice cut   190
With his own hand a sapling, which he hoop'd
With iron, making it throughout in all
Due requisites a perfect Shepherd's Staff,
And gave it to the Boy; wherewith equipp'd
He as a Watchman oftentimes was plac'd
At gate or gap, to stem or turn the flock,
And to his office prematurely call'd
There stood the urchin, as you will divine,
Something between a hindrance and a help,
And for this cause not always, I believe,   200
Receiving from his Father hire of praise.
Though nought was left undone which staff or voice,
Or looks, or threatening gestures could perform.
But soon as Luke, full ten years old, could stand
Against the mountain blasts, and to the heights,
Not fearing toil, nor length of weary ways,
He with his Father daily went, and they
Were as companions, why should I relate
That objects which the Shepherd loved before
Were dearer now? that from the Boy there came   210
Feelings and emanations, things which were
Light to the sun and music to the wind;
And that the Old Man's heart seemed born again.
Thus in his Father's sight the Boy grew up:
And now when he had reached his eighteenth year,
He was his comfort and his daily hope.

While this good household thus were living on
From day to day, to Michael's ear there came
Distressful tidings. Long before the time
Of which I speak, the Shepherd had been bound   220
In surety for his Brother's Son, a man
Of an industrious life, and ample means,
But unforeseen misfortunes suddenly
Had press'd upon him, and old Michael now

Was summon'd to discharge the forfeiture,
A grievous penalty, but little less
Than half his substance. This unlook'd for claim,
At the first hearing, for a moment took
More hope out of his life than he supposed
That any old man ever could have lost.   230
As soon as he had gather'd so much strength
That he could look his trouble in the face,
It seem'd that his sole refuge was to sell
A portion of his patrimonial fields.
Such was his first resolve; he thought again,
And his heart fail'd him. 'Isabel,' said he,
Two evenings after he had heard the news,
'I have been toiling more than seventy years,
And in the open sunshine of God's love
Have we all liv'd, yet if these fields of ours   240
Should pass into a Stranger's hand, I think
That I could not lie quiet in my grave.
Our lot is a hard lot; the Sun itself
Has scarcely been more diligent than I,
And I have liv'd to be a fool at last
To my own family. An evil Man
That was, and made an evil choice, if he
Were false to us; and if he were not false,
There are ten thousand to whom loss like this
Had been no sorrow. I forgive him – but   250
'Twere better to be dumb than to talk thus.
When I began, my purpose was to speak
Of remedies and of a cheerful hope.
Our Luke shall leave us, Isabel; the land
Shall not go from us, and it shall be free,
He shall possess it, free as is the wind
That passes over it. We have, thou knowest,
Another Kinsman, he will be our friend
In this distress. He is a prosperous man,
Thriving in trade, and Luke to him shall go,   260
And with his Kinsman's help and his own thrift,
He quickly will repair this loss, and then
May come again to us. If here he stay,
What can be done? Where everyone is poor

What can be gain'd?' At this, the old man paus'd,
And Isabel sate silent, for her mind
Was busy, looking back into past times.
There's Richard Bateman,[4] thought she to herself;
He was a parish-boy[5] – at the church-door
They made a gathering for him, shillings, pence,   270
And halfpennies, wherewith the Neighbours bought
A Basket, which they fill'd with Pedlar's wares,
And with this Basket on his arm, the Lad
Went up to London, found a Master there,
Who out of many chose the trusty Boy
To go and overlook his merchandise
Beyond the seas, where he grew wond'rous rich,
And left estates and monies to the poor,
And at his birth-place built a Chapel, floor'd
With Marble, which he sent from foreign lands.   280
These thoughts, and many others of like sort,
Pass'd quickly thro' the mind of Isabel,
And her face brighten'd. The Old Man was glad,
And thus resum'd. 'Well! Isabel, this scheme
These two days has been meat and drink to me.
Far more than we have lost is left us yet.
– We have enough – I wish indeed that I
Were younger, but this hope is a good hope.
– Make ready Luke's best garments, of the best
Buy for him more, and let us send him forth   290
Tomorrow, or the next day, or tonight:
– If he could go, the Boy should go tonight.'

Here Michael ceas'd, and to the fields went forth
With a light heart. The Housewife for five days
Was restless morn and night, and all day long
Wrought on with her best fingers to prepare
Things needful for the journey of her Son.
But Isabel was glad when Sunday came
To stop her in her work; for, when she lay
By Michael's side, she for the two last nights   300
Heard him, how he was troubled in his sleep:
And when they rose at morning she could see
That all his hopes were gone. That day at noon

She said to Luke, while they two by themselves
Were sitting at the door, 'Thou must not go,
We have no other Child but thee to lose,
None to remember – do not go away,
For if thou leave thy Father he will die.'
The Lad made answer with a jocund voice,
And Isabel, when she had told her fears,   310
Recover'd heart. That evening her best fare
Did she bring forth, and all together sate
Like happy people round a Christmas fire.

Next morning Isabel resum'd her work,
And all the ensuing week the house appear'd
As cheerful as a grove in Spring: at length
The expected letter from their Kinsman came,
With kind assurances that he would do
His utmost for the welfare of the Boy,
To which requests were added that forthwith   320
He might be sent to him. Ten times or more
The letter was read over; Isabel
Went forth to show it to the neighbours round:
Nor was there at that time on English Land
A prouder heart than Luke's. When Isabel
Had to her house return'd, the Old Man said,
'He shall depart tomorrow.' To this word
The Housewife answered, talking much of things
Which, if at such short notice he should go,
Would surely be forgotten. But at length   330
She gave consent, and Michael was at ease.

Near the tumultous brook of Green-head Gill,
In that deep Valley, Michael had design'd
To build a Sheep-fold,[6] and, before he heard
The tidings of his melancholy loss,
For this same purpose he had gathered up
A heap of stones, which close to the brookside
Lay thrown together, ready for the work.
With Luke that evening thitherward he walk'd;
And soon as they had reach'd the place he stopp'd,   340
And thus the Old Man spake to him. 'My Son,

Tomorrow thou wilt leave me; with full heart
I look upon thee, for thou art the same
That wert a promise to me ere thy birth,
And all thy life hast been my daily joy.
I will relate to thee some little part
Of our two histories; 'twill do thee good
When thou art from me, even if I should speak
Of things thou canst not know of. – After thou
First cam'st into the world, as it befalls   350
To new-born infants, thou didst sleep away
Two days, and blessings from thy Father's tongue
Then fell upon thee. Day by day pass'd on,
And still I lov'd thee with encreasing love.
Never to living ear came sweeter sounds
Than when I heard thee by our own fireside
First uttering without words a natural tune,
When thou, a feeding babe, didst in thy joy
Sing at thy Mother's breast. Month follow'd month,
And in the open fields my life was pass'd   360
And in the mountains, else I think that thou
Hadst been brought up upon thy father's knees.
– But we were playmates, Luke; among these hills,
As well thou know'st, in us the old and young
Have play'd together, nor with me didst thou
Lack any pleasure which a boy can know.'

Luke had a manly heart; but at these words
He sobb'd aloud; the Old Man grasp'd his hand,
And said, 'Nay do not take it so – I see
That these are things of which I need not speak.   370
– Even to the utmost I have been to thee
A kind and a good Father: and herein
I but repay a gift which I myself
Receiv'd at others' hands, for, though now old
Beyond the common life of man, I still
Remember them who lov'd me in my youth.
Both of them sleep together: here they liv'd
As all their Forefathers had done, and when
At length their time was come, they were not loth
To give their bodies to the family mold.   380

I wish'd that thou should'st live the life they liv'd.
But 'tis a long time to look back, my Son,
And see so little gain from sixty years.
These fields were burthen'd when they came to me;
'Till I was forty years of age, not more
Than half of my inheritance was mine.
I toil'd and toil'd; God bless'd me in my work,
And 'till these three weeks past the land was free.
– It looks as if it never could endure
Another Master. Heaven forgive me, Luke,   390
If I judge ill for thee, but it seems good
That thou should'st go.' At this the Old Man paus'd,
Then, pointing to the Stones near which they stood,
Thus, after a short silence, he resum'd:
'This was a work for us, and now, my Son,
It is a work for me. But, lay one Stone –
Here, lay it for me, Luke, with thine own hands.
I for the purpose brought thee to this place.
Nay, Boy, be of good hope:– we both may live
To see a better day. At eighty-four   400
I still am strong and stout; – do thou thy part,
I will do mine. – I will begin again
With many tasks that were resign'd to thee;
Up to the heights, and in among the storms,
Will I without thee go again, and do
All works which I was wont to do alone,
Before I knew thy face. – Heaven bless thee, Boy!
Thy heart these two weeks has been beating fast
With many hopes – it should be so – yes – yes –
I knew that thou could'st never have a wish   410
To leave me, Luke, thou hast been bound to me
Only by links of love; when thou art gone
What will be left to us! – But, I forget
My purposes. Lay now the corner-stone,
As I requested, and hereafter, Luke,
When thou art gone away, should evil men
Be thy companions, let this Sheep-fold be
Thy anchor and thy shield; amid all fear
And all temptation, let it be to thee
An emblem of the life thy Fathers liv'd,   420

Who, being innocent, did for that cause
Bestir them in good deeds. Now, fare thee well –
When thou return'st, thou in this place wilt see
A work which is not here, a covenant
'Twill be between us – but whatever fate
Befall thee, I shall love thee to the last,
And bear thy memory with me to the grave.'

The Shepherd ended here; and Luke stoop'd down,
And as his Father had requested, laid
The first stone of the Sheep-fold; at the sight   430
The Old Man's grief broke from him, to his heart
He press'd his Son, he kissed him and wept;
And to the House together they return'd.

Next morning, as had been resolv'd, the Boy
Began his journey, and when he had reach'd
The public Way, he put on a bold face;
And all the Neighbours as he pass'd their doors
Came forth, with wishes and with farewell pray'rs,
That follow'd him 'till he was out of sight.

A good report did from their Kinsman come,   440
Of Luke and his well-doing; and the Boy
Wrote loving letters, full of wond'rous news,
Which, as the Housewife phrased it, were throughout
The prettiest letters that were ever seen.
Both parents read them with rejoicing hearts.
So, many months pass'd on: and once again
The Shepherd went about his daily work
With confident and cheerful thoughts; and now
Sometimes when he could find a leisure hour
He to that valley took his way, and there   450
Wrought at the Sheep-fold. Meantime Luke began
To slacken in his duty, and at length
He in the dissolute city gave himself
To evil courses: ignominy and shame
Fell on him, so that he was driven at last
To seek a hiding-place beyond the seas.

There is a comfort in the strength of love;

'Twill make a thing endurable, which else
Would break the heart: – Old Michael found it so.
I have convers'd with more than one who well   460
Remember the Old Man, and what he was
Years after he had heard this heavy news.
His bodily frame had been from youth to age
Of an unusual strength. Among the rocks
He went, and still look'd up upon the sun,
And listen'd to the wind; and as before
Perform'd all kinds of labour for his Sheep,
And for the land his small inheritance.
And to that hollow Dell from time to time
Did he repair, to build the Fold of which   470
His flock had need. 'Tis not forgotten yet
The pity which was then in every heart
For the Old Man – and 'tis believ'd by all
That many and many a day he thither went,
And never lifted up a single stone.

There, by the Sheep-fold, sometimes was he seen
Sitting alone, with that his faithful Dog,
Then old, beside him, lying at his feet.
The length of full seven years from time to time
He at the building of this Sheep-fold wrought,   480
And left the work unfinished when he died.

Three years, or little more, did Isabel
Survive her Husband: at her death the estate
Was sold, and went into a Stranger's hand.
The Cottage which was nam'd The Evening Star
Is gone, the ploughshare has been through the ground
On which it stood; great changes have been wrought
In all the neighbourhood, yet the Oak is left
That grew beside their Door; and the remains
Of the unfinished Sheep-fold may be seen   490
Beside the boisterous brook of Green-head Gill.

I Travelled Among Unknown Men

I travelled among unknown men,
    In lands beyond the sea;
Nor, England! did I know till then
    What love I bore to thee.

'Tis past, that melancholy dream!
    Nor will I quit thy shore
A second time; for still I seem
    To love thee more and more.

Among thy mountains did I feel
    The joy of my desire;   10
And she I cherished turned my wheel
    Beside an English fire.

Thy mornings showed, thy night concealed,
    The bowers where Lucy[1] played;
And thine too is the last green field
    That Lucy's eyes surveyed.

To a Butterfly

Stay near me – do not take thy flight!
A little longer stay in sight!
Much converse do I find in thee,
Historian of my infancy!
Float near me; do not yet depart!
Dead times revive in thee:
Thou bring'st, gay creature as thou art!
A solemn image to my heart,
My father's family!

Oh! pleasant, pleasant were the days,
The time when, in our childish plays,
My sister Emmeline[1] and I
Together chased the butterfly!
A very hunter did I rush
Upon the prey: – with leaps and springs
I followed on from brake to bush;
But she, God love her! feared to brush
The dust from off its wings.

To the Cuckoo

O blithe New-comer! I have heard,
I hear thee and rejoice.
O Cuckoo! shall I call thee Bird,
Or but a wandering Voice?

While I am lying on the grass
Thy twofold shout I hear,
From hill to hill it seems to pass,
At once far off, and near.

Though babbling only to the Vale,
Of sunshine and of flowers,   10
Thou bringest unto me a tale
Of visionary hours.

Thrice welcome, darling of the Spring!
Even yet thou art to me
No bird, but an invisible thing,
A voice, a mystery;

The same whom in my schoolboy days
I listened to; that Cry
Which made me look a thousand ways
In bush, and tree, and sky.   20

To seek thee did I often rove
Through woods and on the green;
And thou wert still a hope, a love;
Still longed for, never seen.

And I can listen to thee yet;
Can lie upon the plain
And listen, till I do beget
That golden time again.

O blessèd Bird! the earth we pace
Again appears to be   30
An unsubstantial, faery place;
That is fit home for Thee!

My Heart Leaps Up when I Behold

My heart leaps up when I behold
    A rainbow in the sky:
So was it when my life began;
So is it now I am a man;
So be it when I shall grow old,
    Or let me die!
The Child is father of the Man;
And I could wish my days to be
Bound each to each by natural piety.

Ode: Intimations of Immortality from Recollections of Early Childhood[1]

The Child is Father of the Man;
And I could wish my days to be
Bound each to each by natural piety.

1

There was a time when meadow, grove, and stream,
The earth, and every common sight,
     To me did seem
    Apparelled in celestial light,
The glory and the freshness of a dream.
It is not now as it hath been of yore; –
    Turn wheresoe'er I may,
     By night or day,
The things which I have seen I now can see no more.

2

    The Rainbow comes and goes,   10
    And lovely is the Rose;
    The Moon doth with delight
Look round her when the heavens are bare;
    Waters on a starry night
    Are beautiful and fair;
  The sunshine is a glorious birth;
  But yet I know, where'er I go,
That there hath past away a glory from the earth.

3

Now, while the birds thus sing a joyous song,
  And while the young lambs bound   20
    As to the tabor's[2] sound,
To me alone there came a thought of grief:
A timely utterance[3] gave that thought relief,
    And I again am strong:
The cataracts blow their trumpets from the steep;
No more shall grief of mine the season wrong;
I hear the Echoes through the mountains throng,

The Winds come to me from the fields of sleep,
   And all the earth is gay;
     Land and sea   30
    Give themselves up to jollity,
     And with the heart of May
   Doth every Beast keep holiday; –
    Thou Child of Joy,
Shout round me, let me hear thy shouts, thou happy
        Shepherd-boy!

4

Ye blessèd Creatures, I have heard the call
  Ye to each other make; I see
The heavens laugh with you in your jubilee;
  My heart is at your festival,
    My head hath its coronal,   40
The fullness of your bliss, I feel – I feel it all.
    Oh evil day! if I were sullen
    While Earth herself is adorning,
     This sweet May-morning,
    And the Children are culling
     On every side,
  In a thousand valleys far and wide,
   Fresh flowers; while the sun shines warm,
And the Babe leaps up on his Mother's arm: –
    I hear, I hear, with joy I hear!   50
    – But there's a Tree, of many, one,
A single Field which I have looked upon,
Both of them speak of something that is gone:
    The Pansy at my feet
    Doth the same tale repeat:
Whither is fled the visionary gleam?
Where is it now, the glory and the dream?

5

Our birth is but a sleep and a forgetting:
The Soul that rises with us, our life's Star,
    Hath had elsewhere its setting,   60
     And cometh from afar:

Not in entire forgetfulness,
And not in utter nakedness,
But trailing clouds of glory do we come
From God, who is our home:
Heaven lies about us in our infancy!
Shades of the prison-house begin to close
Upon the growing Boy,
But He
Beholds the light, and whence it flows,   70
He sees it in his joy;
The Youth, who daily farther from the east
Must travel, still is Nature's Priest,
And by the vision splendid
Is on his way attended;
At length the Man perceives it die away,
And fade into the light of common day.

6

Earth fills her lap with pleasures of her own;
Yearnings she hath in her own natural kind,
And, even with something of a Mother's mind,   80
And no unworthy aim,
The homely Nurse doth all she can
To make her Foster-child, her Inmate Man,
Forget the glories he hath known,
And that imperial palace whence he came.

7

Behold the Child among his new-born blisses,
A six years' Darling of a pigmy size!
See, where 'mid work of his own hand he lies,
Fretted by sallies of his mother's kisses,
With light upon him from his father's eyes!   90
See, at his feet, some little plan or chart,
Some fragment from his dream of human life,
Shaped by himself with newly-learnèd art;
A wedding or a festival,
A mourning or a funeral;
And this hath now his heart,
And unto this he frames his song:

       Then will he fit his tongue
To dialogues of business, love, or strife;
      But it will not be long   100
      Ere this be thrown aside,
      And with new joy and pride
The little Actor cons another part;
Filling from time to time his 'humorous stage'
With all the Persons, down to palsied Age,
That Life brings with her in her equipage;
      As if his whole vocation
      Were endless imitation.

        8

Thou, whose exterior semblance doth belie
      Thy Soul's immensity;   110
Thou best Philosopher, who yet dost keep
Thy heritage, thou Eye among the blind,
That, deaf and silent, read'st the eternal deep,
Haunted for ever by the eternal mind, –
      Mighty Prophet! Seer blest!
      On whom those truths do rest,
Which we are toiling all our lives to find,
In darkness lost, the darkness of the grave;
Thou, over whom thy Immortality
Broods like the Day, a Master o'er a Slave,   120
A Presence which is not to be put by;
Thou little Child, yet glorious in the might
Of heaven-born freedom on thy being's height,
Why with such earnest pains dost thou provoke
The years to bring the inevitable yoke,
Thus blindly with thy blessedness at strife?
Full soon thy Soul shall have her earthly freight,
And custom lie upon thee with a weight,
Heavy as frost, and deep almost as life!

        9

      O joy! that in our embers   130
      Is something that doth live,
      That nature yet remembers

What was so fugitive!
The thought of our past years in me doth breed
Perpetual benediction: not indeed
For that which is most worthy to be blest;
Delight and liberty, the simple creed
Of Childhood, whether busy or at rest,
With new-fledged hope still fluttering in his breast: –
      Not for these I raise   140
      The song of thanks and praise;
  But for those obstinate questionings
  Of sense and outward things,
  Fallings from us, vanishings;
  Blank misgivings of a Creature
Moving about in worlds not realised,
High instincts before which our mortal Nature
Did tremble like a guilty Thing surprised:
    But for those first affections,
    Those shadowy recollections,   150
  Which, be they what they may,
Are yet the fountain light of all our day,
Are yet a master light of all our seeing;
  Uphold us, cherish, and have power to make
Our noisy years seem moments in the being
Of the eternal Silence: truths that wake,
    To perish never;
Which neither listlessness, nor mad endeavour,
    Nor Man nor Boy,
Nor all that is at enmity with joy,   160
Can utterly abolish or destroy!
    Hence in a season of calm weather
    Though inland far we be,
Our Souls have sight of that immortal sea
    Which brought us hither,
  Can in a moment travel thither,
And see the Children sport upon the shore,
And hear the mighty waters rolling evermore.

10

Then sing, ye Birds, sing, sing a joyous song!
  And let the young Lambs bound   170
  As to the tabor's sound!
We in thought will join your throng,
  Ye that pipe and ye that play,
  Ye that through your hearts today
  Feel the gladness of the May!
What though the radiance which was once so bright
Be now for ever taken from my sight,
  Though nothing can bring back the hour
Of splendour in the grass, of glory in the flower;
  We will grieve not, rather find   180
  Strength in what remains behind;
  In the primal sympathy
  Which having been must ever be;
  In the soothing thoughts that spring
  Out of human suffering;
  In the faith that looks through death,
In years that bring the philosophic mind.

11

And O, ye Fountains, Meadows, Hills, and Groves,
Forebode not any severing of our loves!
Yet in my heart of hearts I feel your might;   190
I only have relinquished one delight
To live beneath your more habitual sway.
I love the Brooks which down their channels fret,
Even more than when I tripped lightly as they;
The innocent brightness of a new-born Day
   Is lovely yet;
The Clouds that gather round the setting sun
Do take a sober colouring from an eye
That hath kept watch o'er man's mortality;
Another race hath been, and other palms are won. 200
Thanks to the human heart by which we live,
Thanks to its tenderness, its joys, and fears,
To me the meanest flower that blows can give
Thoughts that do often lie too deep for tears.

Resolution and Independence

1

There was a roaring in the wind all night;
The rain came heavily and fell in floods;
But now the sun is rising calm and bright;
The birds are singing in the distant woods;
Over his own sweet voice the Stock-dove broods;[1]
The Jay makes answer as the Magpie chatters;
And all the air is filled with pleasant noise of waters.

2

All things that love the sun are out of doors;
The sky rejoices in the morning's birth;
The grass is bright with raindrops; – on the moor   10
The hare is running races in her mirth;
And with her feet she from the plashy earth
Raises a mist; that, glittering in the sun,
Runs with her all the way, wherever she doth run.

3

I was a Traveller then upon the moor;
I saw the hare that raced about with joy;
I heard the woods and distant waters roar;
Or heard them not, as happy as a boy:
The pleasant season did my heart employ:
My old remembrances went from me wholly;   20
And all the ways of men, so vain and melancholy.

4

But, as it sometimes chanceth, from the might
Of joy in minds that can no further go,
As high as we have mounted in delight
In our dejection do we sink as low;
To me that morning did it happen so;
And fears and fancies thick upon me came;
Dim sadness – and blind thoughts, I knew not, nor could name.

5

I heard the skylark warbling in the sky;
And I bethought me of the playful hare: 30
Even such a happy Child of earth am I;
Even as these blissful creatures do I fare;
Far from the world I walk, and from all care;
But there may come another day to me –
Solitude, pain of heart, distress, and poverty.

6

My whole life I have lived in pleasant thought,
As if life's business were a summer mood;
As if all needful things would come unsought
To genial faith, still rich in genial good;
But how can he expect that others should   40
Build for him, sow for him, and at his call
Love him, who for himself will take no heed at all?

7

I thought of Chatterton,[2] the marvellous Boy,
The sleepless Soul that perished in his pride;
Of Him[3] who walked in glory and in joy
Following his plough, along the mountainside:
By our own spirits are we deified:
We Poets in our youth begin in gladness;
But thereof come in the end despondency and madness.

8

Now, whether it were by peculiar grace,   50
A leading from above, a something given,
Yet it befell that, in this lonely place,
When I with these untoward thoughts had striven,
Beside a pool bare to the eye of heaven
I saw a Man before me unawares:
The oldest man he seemed that ever wore grey hairs.

9

As a huge stone is sometimes seen to lie
Couched on the bald top of an eminence;

Wonder to all who do the same espy,
By what means it could thither come, and whence;   60
So that it seems a thing endued with sense:
Like a sea-beast crawled forth, that on a shelf
Of rock or sand reposeth, there to sun itself;[4]

10

Such seemed this Man, not all alive nor dead,
Nor all asleep – in his extreme old age:
His body was bent double, feet and head
Coming together in life's pilgrimage;
As if some dire constraint of pain, or rage
Of sickness felt by him in times long past,
A more than human weight upon his frame had cast.   70

11

Himself he propped, limbs, body, and pale face,
Upon a long grey staff of shaven wood:
And, still as I drew near with gentle pace,
Upon the margin of that moorish flood
Motionless as a cloud the old Man stood,
That heareth not the loud winds when they call;
And moveth all together, if it move at all.

12

At length, himself unsettling, he the pond
Stirred with his staff, and fixedly did look
Upon the muddy water, which he conned,   80
As if he had been reading in a book:
And now a stranger's privilege I took;
And, drawing to his side, to him did say,
'This morning gives us promise of a glorious day.'

13

A gentle answer did the old Man make,
In courteous speech which forth he slowly drew:
And him with further words I thus bespake,
'What occupation do you there pursue?
This is a lonesome place for one like you.'

Ere he replied, a flash of mild surprise   90
Broke from the sable orbs of his yet-vivid eyes.

14

His words came feebly, from a feeble chest,
But each in solemn order followed each,
With something of a lofty utterance drest –
Choice word and measured phrase, above the reach
Of ordinary men; a stately speech;
Such as grave Livers do in Scotland use,
Religious men, who give to God and man their dues.

15

He told, that to these waters he had come
To gather leeches, being old and poor: 100
Employment hazardous and wearisome!
And he had many hardships to endure:
From pond to pond he roamed, from moor to moor;
Housing, with God's good help, by choice or chance;
And in this way he gained an honest maintenance.

16

The old Man still stood talking by my side;
But now his voice to me was like a stream
Scarce heard; nor word from word could I divide;
And the whole body of the Man did seem
Like one whom I had met with in a dream;   110
Or like a man from some far region sent,
To give me human strength, by apt admonishment.

17

My former thoughts returned: the fear that kills;
And hope that is unwilling to be fed;
Cold, pain, and labour, and all fleshly ills;
And mighty Poets in their misery dead.
 – Perplexed, and longing to be comforted,
My question eagerly did I renew,
'How is it that you live, and what is it you do?'

18

He with a smile did then his words repeat;   120
And said that, gathering leeches, far and wide
He travelled; stirring thus about his feet
The waters of the pools where they abide.
'Once I could meet with them on every side;
But they have dwindled long by slow decay;
Yet still I persevere, and find them where I may.'

19

While he was talking thus, the lonely place,
The old Man's shape, and speech – all troubled me:
In my mind's eye I seemed to see him pace
About the weary moors continually,   130
Wandering about alone and silently.
While I these thoughts within myself pursued,
He, having made a pause, the same discourse renewed.

20

And soon with this he other matter blended,
Cheerfully uttered, with demeanour kind,
But stately in the main; and when he ended,
I could have laughed myself to scorn to find
In that decrepit Man so firm a mind.
'God,' said I, 'be my help and stay secure;
I'll think of the Leech-gatherer on the lonely moor!'   140

1801

I grieved for Buonaparté,[1] with a vain
And an unthinking grief! The tenderest mood
Of that Man's mind – what can it be? what food
Fed his first hopes? what knowledge could *he* gain?
'Tis not in battles that from youth we train
The Governor who must be wise and good,
And temper with the sternness of the brain
Thoughts motherly, and meek as womanhood.
Wisdom doth live with children round her knees:
Books, leisure, perfect freedom, and the talk   10
Man holds with weekday man in the hourly walk
Of the mind's business: these are the degrees
By which true Sway doth mount; this is the stalk
True Power doth grow on; and her rights are these.

Great Men Have Been Among Us

Great men have been among us; hands that penned
And tongues that uttered wisdom – better none:
The later Sidney, Marvell, Harrington,
Young Vane, and others who called Milton[1] friend.
These moralists could act and comprehend:
They knew how genuine glory was put on;
Taught us how rightfully a nation shone
In splendour: what strength was, that would not bend
But in magnanimous meekness. France, 'tis strange,
Hath brought forth no such souls as we had then.   10
Perpetual emptiness! unceasing change!
No single volume paramount, no code,
No master spirit, no determined road;
But equally a want of books and men!

It Is Not To Be Thought Of That the Flood

It is not to be thought of that the Flood
Of British freedom, which, to the open sea
Of the world's praise, from dark antiquity
Hath flowed, 'with pomp of waters, unwithstood',
Roused though it be full often to a mood
Which spurns the check of salutary bands,
That this most famous Stream in bogs and sands
Should perish; and to evil and to good
Be lost for ever. In our halls is hung
Armoury of the invincible Knights of old: 10
We must be free or die, who speak the tongue
That Shakespeare spake; the faith and morals hold
Which Milton held. – In everything we are sprung
Of Earth's first blood, have titles manifold.

Personal Talk

1

I am not One who much or oft delight
To season my fireside with personal talk, –
Of friends, who live within an easy walk,
Or neighbours, daily, weekly, in my sight:
And, for my chance-acquaintance, ladies bright,
Sons, mothers, maidens withering on the stalk,
These all wear out of me, like Forms, with chalk
Painted on rich men's floors, for one feast-night.
Better than such discourse doth silence long,
Long, barren silence, square with my desire;   10
To sit without emotion, hope, or aim,
In the loved presence of my cottage-fire,
And listen to the flapping of the flame,
Or kettle whispering its faint undersong.

2

'Yet life,' you say, 'is life; we have seen and see,
And with a living pleasure we describe;
And fits of sprightly malice do but bribe
The languid mind into activity.
Sound sense, and love itself, and mirth and glee
Are fostered by the comment and the gibe.'   20
Even be it so: yet still among your tribe,
Our daily world's true Worldlings, rank not me!
Children are blest, and powerful; their world lies
More justly balanced; partly at their feet,
And part far from them: – sweetest melodies
Are those that are by distance made more sweet;
Whose mind is but the mind of his own eyes,
He is a Slave; the meanest we can meet!

3

Wings have we – and as far as we can go
We may find pleasure: wilderness and wood,   30
Blank ocean and mere sky, support that mood
Which with the lofty sanctifies the low.
Dreams, books, are each a world; and books, we know,
Are a substantial world, both pure and good:
Round these, with tendrils strong as flesh and blood,
Our pastime and our happiness will grow.
There find I personal themes, a plenteous store,
Matter wherein right voluble I am,
To which I listen with a ready ear;
Two shall be named, pre-eminently dear –   40
The gentle Lady married to the Moor;[1]
And heavenly Una[2] with her milk-white Lamb.

4

Nor can I not believe but that hereby
Great gains are mine; for thus I live remote
From evil-speaking; rancour, never sought,
Comes to me not; malignant truth, or lie.
Hence have I genial seasons, hence have I
Smooth passions, smooth discourse, and joyous thought:

And thus from day to day my little boat
Rocks in its harbour, lodging peaceably.   50
Blessings be with them – and eternal praise,
Who gave us nobler loves, and nobler cares –
The Poets, who on earth have made us heirs
Of truth and pure delight by heavenly lays!
Oh! might my name be numbered among theirs,
Then gladly would I end my mortal days.

The World is Too Much with Us

The world is too much with us; late and soon,
Getting and spending, we lay waste our powers:
Little we see in Nature that is ours;
We have given our hearts away, a sordid boon!
This Sea that bares her bosom to the moon;
The winds that will be howling at all hours,
And are up-gathered now like sleeping flowers;
For this, for everything, we are out of tune;
It moves us not. – Great God! I'd rather be
A Pagan suckled in a creed outworn;   10
So might I, standing on this pleasant lea,
Have glimpses that would make me less forlorn;
Have sight of Proteus[1] rising from the sea;
Or hear old Triton[2] blow his wreathèd horn.

Composed upon Westminster Bridge

SEPTEMBER 3, 1802

Earth has not anything to show more fair:
Dull would he be of soul who could pass by
A sight so touching in its majesty:
This City now doth, like a garment, wear
The beauty of the morning; silent, bare,
Ships, towers, domes, theatres, and temples lie
Open unto the fields, and to the sky;
All bright and glittering in the smokeless air.
Never did sun more beautifully steep
In his first splendour, valley, rock, or hill;   10
Ne'er saw I, never felt, a calm so deep!
The river glideth at his own sweet will:
Dear God! the very houses seem asleep;
And all that mighty heart is lying still!

It is a Beauteous Evening, Calm and Free

It is a beauteous evening, calm and free,
The holy time is quiet as a Nun
Breathless with adoration; the broad sun
Is sinking down in its tranquillity;
The gentleness of heaven broods o'er the Sea:
Listen! the mighty Being is awake,
And doth with his eternal motion make
A sound like thunder – everlastingly.
Dear Child! dear Girl! that walkest with me here,
If thou appear untouched by solemn thought,   10
Thy nature is not therefore less divine:
Thou liest in Abraham's bosom all the year;
And worshipp'st at the Temple's inner shrine,
God being with thee when we know it not.

To Toussaint l'Ouverture1

Toussaint,[1] the most unhappy man of men!
Whether the whistling Rustic tend his plough
Within thy hearing, or thy head be now
Pillowed in some deep dungeon's earless den; –
O miserable Chieftain! where and when
Wilt thou find patience! Yet die not; do thou
Wear rather in thy bonds a cheerful brow:
Though fallen thyself, never to rise again,
Live, and take comfort. Thou hast left behind
Powers that will work for thee; air, earth, and skies;   10
There's not a breathing of the common wind
That will forget thee; thou hast great allies;
Thy friends are exultations, agonies,
And love, and man's unconquerable mind.

London, 1802

Milton![1] thou shouldst be living at this hour:
England hath need of thee: she is a fen
Of stagnant waters: altar, sword, and pen,
Fireside, the heroic wealth of hall and bower,
Have forfeited their ancient English dower
Of inward happiness. We are selfish men;
Oh! raise us up, return to us again;
And give us manners, virtue, freedom, power.
Thy soul was like a Star, and dwelt apart:
Thou hadst a voice whose sound was like the sea: 10
Pure as the naked heavens, majestic, free,
So didst thou travel on life's common way,
In cheerful godliness; and yet thy heart
The lowliest duties on herself did lay.

The Small Celandine

There is a Flower, the lesser Celandine,
That shrinks, like many more, from cold and rain;
And, the first moment that the sun may shine,
Bright as the sun himself, 'tis out again!

When hailstones have been falling, swarm on swarm,
Or blasts the green field and the trees distrest,
Oft have I seen it muffled up from harm,
In close self-shelter, like a Thing at rest.

But lately, one rough day, this Flower I passed
And recognised it, though an altered form,   10
Now standing forth an offering to the blast,
And buffeted at will by rain and storm.

I stopped, and said with inly-muttered voice,
'It doth not love the shower, nor seek the cold:
This neither is its courage nor its choice,
But its necessity in being old.

'The sunshine may not cheer it, nor the dew;
It cannot help itself in its decay;
Stiff in its members, withered, changed of hue.'
And, in my spleen, I smiled that it was grey.   20

To be a Prodigal's Favourite – then, worse truth,
A Miser's Pensioner – behold our lot!
O Man, that from thy fair and shining youth
Age might but take the things Youth needed not!

I Wandered Lonely as a Cloud

I wandered lonely as a cloud
That floats on high o'er vales and hills,
When all at once I saw a crowd,
A host, of golden daffodils;
Beside the lake, beneath the trees,
Fluttering and dancing in the breeze.

Continuous as the stars that shine
And twinkle on the milky way,
They stretched in never-ending line
Along the margin of a bay: 10
Ten thousand saw I at a glance,
Tossing their heads in sprightly dance.

The waves beside them danced; but they
Out-did the sparkling waves in glee:
A poet could not but be gay,
In such a jocund company:
I gazed – and gazed – but little thought
What wealth the show to me had brought:

For oft, when on my couch I lie
In vacant or in pensive mood,   20
They flash upon that inward eye
Which is the bliss of solitude;
And then my heart with pleasure fills,
And dances with the daffodils.

Elegiac Stanzas
Suggested by a Picture of Peele Castle in a Storm

Painted by Sir George Beaumont[1]

I was thy neighbour once, thou rugged Pile!
Four summer weeks I dwelt in sight of thee:
I saw thee every day; and all the while
Thy Form was sleeping on a glassy sea.

So pure the sky, so quiet was the air!
So like, so very like, was day to day!
Whene'er I looked, thy Image still was there;
It trembled, but it never passed away.

How perfect was the calm! it seemed no sleep;
No mood, which season takes away, or brings: 10
I could have fancied that the mighty Deep
Was even the gentlest of all gentle Things.

Ah! THEN, if mine had been the Painter's hand,
To express what then I saw; and add the gleam,
The light that never was, on sea or land,
The consecration, and the Poet's dream;

I would have planted thee, thou hoary Pile
Amid a world how different from this!
Beside a sea that could not cease to smile;
On tranquil land, beneath a sky of bliss.   20

Thou shouldst have seemed a treasure-house divine
Of peaceful years; a chronicle of heaven; –
Of all the sunbeams that did ever shine
The very sweetest had to thee been given.

A Picture had it been of lasting ease,
Elysian quiet, without toil or strife;
No motion but the moving tide, a breeze,
Or merely silent Nature's breathing life.

Such, in the fond illusion of my heart,
Such Picture would I at that time have made: 30
And seen the soul of truth in every part,
A stedfast peace that might not be betrayed.

So once it would have been, – 'tis so no more;
I have submitted to a new control:
A power is gone, which nothing can restore;
A deep distress² hath humanised my Soul.

Not for a moment could I now behold
A smiling sea, and be what I have been:
The feeling of my loss will ne'er be old;
This, which I know, I speak with mind serene.   40

Then, Beaumont, Friend! who would have been the Friend,
If he had lived, of Him whom I deplore,
This work of thine I blame not, but commend;
This sea in anger, and that dismal shore.

O 'tis a passionate Work! – yet wise and well,
Well chosen is the spirit that is here;
That Hulk which labours in the deadly swell,
This rueful sky, this pageantry of fear!

And this huge Castle, standing here sublime,
I love to see the look with which it braves,   50
Cased in the unfeeling armour of old time,
The lightning, the fierce wind, and trampling waves.

Farewell, farewell the heart that lives alone,
Housed in a dream, at distance from the Kind!
Such happiness, wherever it be known,
Is to be pitied; for 'tis surely blind.

But welcome fortitude, and patient cheer,
And frequent sights of what is to be borne!
Such sights, or worse, as are before me here. –
Not without hope we suffer and we mourn.   60

Stepping Westward

*While my Fellow-traveller and I were walking by the side of Loch
Ketterine, one fine evening after sunset, in our road to a Hut
where, in the course of our Tour, we had been hospitably
entertained some weeks before, we met, in one of the loneliest
parts of that solitary region, two well-dressed Women, one of
whom said to us, by way of greeting, 'What, you are stepping
westward?'*

'What, you are stepping westward?' – 'Yea.'
  – 'Twould be a *wildish* destiny,
If we, who thus together roam
In a strange Land, and far from home,
Were in this place the guests of Chance:
Yet who would stop, or fear to advance,
Though home or shelter he had none,
With such a sky to lead him on?

The dewy ground was dark and cold;
Behind, all gloomy to behold;   10
And stepping westward seemed to be
A kind of *heavenly* destiny:
I liked the greeting; 'twas a sound
Of something without place or bound;
And seemed to give me spiritual right
To travel through that region bright.

The voice was soft, and she who spake
Was walking by her native lake:
The salutation had to me
The very sound of courtesy: 20
Its power was felt; and while my eye
Was fixed upon the glowing Sky,
The echo of the voice enwrought
A human sweetness with the thought
Of travelling through the world that lay
Before me in my endless way.

The Solitary Reaper

Behold her, single in the field,
Yon solitary Highland Lass!
Reaping and singing by herself;
Stop here, or gently pass!
Alone she cuts and binds the grain,
And sings a melancholy strain;
O listen! for the Vale profound
Is overflowing with the sound.

No Nightingale did ever chaunt
More welcome notes to weary bands   10
Of travellers in some shady haunt,
Among Arabian sands:
A voice so thrilling ne'er was heard
In springtime from the Cuckoo-bird,
Breaking the silence of the seas
Among the farthest Hebrides.

Will no one tell me what she sings? –
Perhaps the plaintive numbers flow
For old, unhappy, far-off things,
And battles long ago: 20
Or is it some more humble lay,
Familiar matter of today?
Some natural sorrow, loss, or pain,
That has been, and may be again?

Whate'er the theme, the Maiden sang
As if her song could have no ending;
I saw her singing at her work,
And o'er the sickle bending; –
I listened, motionless and still;
And, as I mounted up the hill,   30
The music in my heart I bore,
Long after it was heard no more.

The Simplon Pass[1]

– Brook and road
Were fellow-travellers in this gloomy Pass,
And with them did we journey several hours
At a slow step. The immeasurable height
Of woods decaying, never to be decayed,
The stationary blasts of waterfalls,
And in the narrow rent, at every turn,
Winds thwarting winds bewildered and forlorn,
The torrents shooting from the clear blue sky,
The rocks that muttered close upon our ears,   10
Black drizzling crags that spake by the wayside
As if a voice were in them, the sick sight
And giddy prospect of the raving stream,
The unfettered clouds and region of the heavens,
Tumult and peace, the darkness and the light –
Were all like workings of one mind, the features
Of the same face, blossoms upon one tree,
Characters of the great Apocalypse,[2]
The types and symbols of Eternity,
Of first, and last, and midst, and without end.   20

Yew-Trees

There is a Yew-tree, pride of Lorton Vale,
Which to this day stands single, in the midst
Of its own darkness, as it stood of yore:
Not loth to furnish weapons for the bands
Of Umfraville or Percy[1] ere they marched
To Scotland's heaths; or those that crossed the sea
And drew their sounding bows at Azincour,
Perhaps at earlier Crecy, or Poictiers.[2]
Of vast circumference and gloom profound
This solitary Tree! a living thing   10
Produced too slowly ever to decay;
Of form and aspect too magnificent
To be destroyed. But worthier still of note
Are those fraternal Four of Borrowdale,
Joined in one solemn and capacious grove;
Huge trunks! and each particular trunk a growth
Of intertwisted fibres serpentine
Up-coiling, and inveterately convolved;
Nor uninformed with Phantasy, and looks
That threaten the profane; – a pillared shade,   20
Upon whose grassless floor of red-brown hue,
By sheddings from the pining umbrage tinged
Perennially – beneath whose sable roof
Of boughs, as if for festal purpose, decked
With unrejoicing berries – ghostly Shapes
May meet at noontide; Fear and trembling Hope,
Silence and Foresight; Death the Skeleton
And Time the Shadow; – there to celebrate,
As in a natural temple scattered o'er
With altars undisturbed of mossy stone,   30
United worship; or in mute repose
To lie, and listen to the mountain flood
Murmuring from Glaramara's inmost caves.

Surprised by Joy

Surprised by joy – impatient as the Wind
I turned to share the transport – Oh! with whom
But Thee,[1] deep buried in the silent tomb,
That spot which no vicissitude can find?
Love, faithful love, recalled thee to my mind –
But how could I forget thee? Through what power,
Even for the least division of an hour,
Have I been so beguiled as to be blind
To my most grievous loss! – That thought's return
Was the worst pang that sorrow ever bore,   10
Save one, one only, when I stood forlorn,
Knowing my heart's best treasure was no more;
That neither present time, nor years unborn
Could to my sight that heavenly face restore.

Vernal Ode

Rerum Natura tota est nusquam magis quam in minimis.
                              PLINY, *Nat. Hist.*[1]

1

Beneath the concave of an April sky,
When all the fields with freshest green were dight,
Appeared, in presence of the spiritual eye
That aids or supersedes our grosser sight,
The form and rich habiliments of One
Whose countenance bore resemblance to the sun,
When it reveals, in evening majesty,
Features half lost amid their own pure light.
Poised like a weary cloud, in middle air
He hung, – then floated with angelic ease   10
(Softening that bright effulgence by degrees)
Till he had reached a summit sharp and bare,
Where oft the venturous heifer drinks the noontide breeze.
Upon the apex of that lofty cone
Alighted, there the Stranger stood alone;
Fair as a gorgeous Fabric of the east
Suddenly raised by some enchanter's power,
Where nothing was; and firm as some old Tower
Of Britain's realm, whose leafy crest
Waves high, embellished by a gleaming shower!   20

2

Beneath the shadow of his purple wings
Rested a golden harp; – he touched the strings;
And, after prelude of unearthly sound
Poured through the echoing hills around,
He sang –
                  'No wintry desolations,
Scorching blight or noxious dew,
Affect my native habitations;
Buried in glory, far beyond the scope
Of man's inquiring gaze, but to his hope
Imaged, though faintly, in the hue   30

Profound of night's ethereal blue;
And in the aspect of each radiant orb; –
Some fixed, some wandering with no timid curb;
But wandering star and fixed, to mortal eye,
Blended in absolute serenity,
And free from semblance of decline; –
Fresh as if Evening brought their natal hour,
Her darkness splendour gave, her silence power,
To testify of Love and Grace divine.

3

'What if those bright fires   40
Shine subject to decay,
Sons haply of extinguished sires,
Themselves to lose their light, or pass away
Like clouds before the wind,
Be thanks poured out to Him whose hand bestows,
Nightly, on human kind
That vision of endurance and repose.
– And though to every draught of vital breath
Renewed throughout the bounds of earth or ocean,
The melancholy gates of Death   50
Respond with sympathetic motion;
Though all that feeds on nether air,
Howe'er magnificent or fair,
Grows but to perish, and entrust
Its ruins to their kindred dust;
Yet, by the Almighty's ever-during care,
Her procreant vigils Nature keeps
Amid the unfathomable deeps;
And saves the peopled fields of earth
From dread of emptiness or dearth.   60
Thus, in their stations, lifting toward the sky
The foliaged head in cloud-like majesty,
The shadow-casting race of trees survive:
Thus, in the train of Spring, arrive
Sweet flowers; – what living eye hath viewed
Their myriads? – endlessly renewed,
Wherever strikes the sun's glad ray;
Where'er the subtle waters stray;

Wherever sportive breezes bend
Their course, or genial showers descend!   70
Mortals, rejoice! the very Angels quit
Their mansions unsusceptible of change,
Amid your pleasant bowers to sit,
And through your sweet vicissitudes to range!'

4

O, nursed at happy distance from the cares
Of a too-anxious world, mild pastoral Muse!
That, to the sparkling crown Urania² wears,
And to her sister Clio's³ laurel wreath,
Prefer'st a garland culled from purple heath,
Or blooming thicket moist with morning dews;   80
Was such bright Spectacle vouchsafed to me?
And was it granted to the simple ear
Of thy contented Votary
Such melody to hear!
Him rather suits it, side by side with thee,
Wrapped in a fit of pleasing indolence,
While thy tired lute hangs on the hawthorn tree,
To lie and listen – till o'erdrowsèd sense
Sinks, hardly conscious of the influence –
To the soft murmur of the vagrant Bee.   90
– A slender sound! yet hoary Time
Doth to the *Soul* exalt it with the chime
Of all his years; – a company
Of ages coming, ages gone;
(Nations from before them sweeping,
Regions in destruction steeping)
But every awful note in unison
With that faint utterance, which tells
Of treasure sucked from buds and bells,
For the pure keeping of those waxen cells;   100
Where She – a statist prudent to confer
Upon the common weal; a warrior bold,
Radiant all over with unburnished gold,
And armed with living spear for mortal fight;
        A cunning forager
That spreads no waste; a social builder; one

In whom all busy offices unite
With all fine functions that afford delight –
Safe through the winter storm in quiet dwells!

                          5
And is She brought within the power   110
Of vision? – o'er this tempting flower
Hovering until the petals stay
Her flight, and take its voice away! –
Observe each wing! – a tiny van!
The structure of her laden thigh,
How fragile! yet of ancestry
Mysteriously remote and high;
High as the imperial front of man;
The roseate bloom on woman's cheek;
The soaring eagle's curved beak;   120
The white plumes of the floating swan;
Old as the tiger's paw, the lion's mane
Ere shaken by that mood of stern disdain
At which the desert trembles. – Humming Bee!
Thy sting was needless then, perchance unknown,
The seeds of malice were not sown;
All creatures met in peace, from fierceness free,
And no pride blended with their dignity.
– Tears had not broken from their source;
Nor Anguish strayed from her Tartarean[4] den;   130
The golden years maintained a course
Not undiversified though smooth and even;
We were not mocked with glimpse and shadow then,
Bright Seraphs mixed familiarly with men;
And earth and stars composed a universal heaven!

Ode to Lycoris[1]

MAY 1817

1

An age hath been when Earth was proud
Of lustre too intense
To be sustained; and Mortals bowed
The front in self-defence.
Who *then*, if Dian's crescent[2] gleamed,
Or Cupid's sparkling arrow streamed
While on the wing the Urchin[3] played,
Could fearlessly approach the shade?
– Enough for one soft vernal day,
If I, a bard of ebbing time,					10
And nurtured in a fickle clime,
May haunt this hornèd bay;
Whose amorous water multiplies
The flitting halcyon's[4] vivid dyes;
And smooths her liquid breast – to show
These swan-like specks of mountain snow,
White as the pair that slid along the plains
Of heaven, when Venus[5] held the reins!

2

In youth we love the darksome lawn
Brushed by the owlet's wing;					20
Then, Twilight is preferred to Dawn,
And Autumn to the Spring.
Sad fancies do we then affect,
In luxury of disrespect
To our own prodigal excess
Of too familiar happiness.
Lycoris (if such name befit
Thee, thee my life's celestial sign!),
When Nature marks the year's decline,
Be ours to welcome it;					30
Pleased with the harvest hope that runs
Before the path of milder suns;

Pleased while the sylvan world displays
Its ripeness to the feeding gaze;
Pleased when the sullen winds resound the knell
Of the resplendent miracle.

3

But something whispers to my heart
That, as we downward tend,
Lycoris! life requires an *art*
To which our souls must bend;   40
A skill – to balance and supply;
And, ere the flowing fount be dry,
As soon it must, a sense to sip,
Or drink, with no fastidious lip.
Then welcome, above all, the Guest
Whose smiles, diffused o'er land and sea,
Seem to recall the Deity
Of youth into the breast:
May pensive Autumn ne'er present
A claim to her disparagement!   50
While blossoms and the budding spray
Inspire us in our own decay;
Still, as we nearer draw to life's dark goal,
Be hopeful Spring the favourite of the Soul!

Whence that Low Voice?

Whence that low voice? – A whisper from the heart,
That told of days long past, when here I roved
With friends and kindred tenderly beloved;
Some who had early mandates to depart,
Yet are allowed to steal my path athwart
By Duddon's side,[1] once more do we unite,
Once more beneath the kind Earth's tranquil light;
And smothered joys into new being start.
From her unworthy seat, the cloudy stall
Of Time, breaks forth triumphant Memory;   10
Her glistening tresses bound, yet light and free
As golden locks of birch, that rise and fall
On gales that breathe too gently to recall
Aught of the fading year's inclemency!

Afterthought

I thought of Thee, my partner and my guide,
As being past away. – Vain sympathies!
For, backward, Duddon![1] as I cast my eyes,
I see what was, and is, and will abide;
Still glides the Stream, and shall for ever glide;
The Form remains, the Function never dies;
While we, the brave, the mighty, and the wise,
We Men, who in our morn of youth defied
The elements, must vanish; – be it so!
Enough, if something from our hands have power   10
To live, and act, and serve the future hour;
And if, as toward the silent tomb we go,
Through love, through hope, and faith's transcendent dower,
We feel that we are greater than we know.

Extempore[1] Effusion upon the Death of James Hogg[2]

When first, descending from the moorlands,
I saw the Stream of Yarrow glide
Along a bare and open valley,
The Ettrick Shepherd was my guide.

When last along its banks I wandered,
Through groves that had begun to shed
Their golden leaves upon the pathways,
My steps the Border-minstrel[3] led.

The mighty Minstrel breathes no longer,
'Mid mouldering ruins low he lies;   10
And death upon the braes of Yarrow,
Has closed the Shepherd-poet's eyes:

Nor has the rolling year twice measured,
From sign to sign, its stedfast course,
Since every mortal power of Coleridge
Was frozen at its marvellous source;

The rapt One, of the godlike forehead,
The heaven-eyed creature sleeps in earth:
And Lamb,[4] the frolic and the gentle,
Has vanished from his lonely hearth.   20

Like clouds that rake the mountain-summits,
Or waves that own no curbing hand,
How fast has brother followed brother,
From sunshine to the sunless land!

Yet I, whose lids from infant slumber
Were earlier raised, remain to hear
A timid voice, that asks in whispers,
'Who next will drop and disappear?'

Our haughty life is crowned with darkness,
Like London with its own black wreath,   30
On which with thee, O Crabbe![5] forth-looking,
I gazed from Hampstead's breezy heath.

As if but yesterday departed,
Thou too art gone before; but why,
O'er ripe fruit, seasonably gathered,
Should frail survivors heave a sigh?

Mourn rather for that holy Spirit,
Sweet as the spring, as ocean deep;
For Her [6] who, ere her summer faded,
Has sunk into a breathless sleep.   40

No more of old romantic sorrows,
For slaughtered Youth or love-lorn Maid!
With sharper grief is Yarrow smitten,
And Ettrick mourns with her their Poet dead.

SAMUEL TAYLOR COLERIDGE

1 *Lyrical Ballads* (1798)

The Rime of the Ancient Mariner[1]

IN SEVEN PARTS

Facile credo, plures esse Naturas invisibiles quam visibiles in rerum universitate. Sed horum omnium familiam quis nobis enarrabit? et gradus et cognationes et discrimina et singulorum munera? Quid agunt? quae loca habitant? Harum rerum notitiam semper ambivit ingenium humanum, nunquam attigit. Juvat, interea, non diffiteor, quandoque in animo, tanquam in tabula, majoris et melioris mundi imaginem contemplari: ne mens assuefacta hodiernae vitae minutiis se contrahat nimis, et tota subsidat in pusillas cogitationes. Sed veritati interea invigilandum est, modusque servandus, ut certa ab incertis, diem a nocte, distinguamus.

T. BURNET, *Archaeol. Phil.*, p. 68.[2]

ARGUMENT

How a Ship, having first sailed to the Equator, was driven by Storms to the cold Country towards the South Pole; how the Ancient Mariner cruelly and in contempt of the laws of hospitality killed a seabird and how he was followed by many and strange judgements: and in what manner he came back to his own country.[3]

PART 1

It is an ancient Mariner,
And he stoppeth one of three.
'By thy long grey beard and glittering eye,
Now wherefore stopp'st thou me?

The Bridegroom's doors are opened wide,
And I am next of kin;
The guests are met, the feast is set:
May'st hear the merry din.'

An ancient Mariner meeteth three gallants bidden to a wedding-feast, and detaineth one.

He holds him with his skinny hand,
'There was a ship,' quoth he.   10
'Hold off! unhand me, grey-beard loon!'
Eftsoons⁴ his hand dropt he.

The Wedding-
Guest is
spellbound by
the eye of the old
seafaring man,
and constrained
to hear his tale.

He holds him with his glittering eye –
The Wedding-Guest stood still,
And listens like a three years' child:
The Mariner hath his will.

The Wedding-Guest sat on a stone:
He cannot choose but hear;
And thus spake on that ancient man,
The bright-eyed Mariner.   20

The Mariner tells
how the ship
sailed southward
with a good
wind and fair
weather, till it
reached the line.

'The ship was cheered, the harbour cleared,
Merrily did we drop
Below the kirk,⁵ below the hill,
Below the lighthouse top.

The Sun came up upon the left,
Out of the sea came he!
And he shone bright, and on the right
Went down into the sea.

Higher and higher every day,
Till over the mast at noon – '   30
The Wedding-Guest here beat his breast,
For he heard the loud bassoon.

The Wedding-
Guest heareth
the bridal music;
but the Mariner
continueth his
tale.

The bride hath paced into the hall,
Red as a rose is she;
Nodding their heads before her goes
The merry minstrelsy.

The Wedding-Guest he beat his breast,
Yet he cannot choose but hear;
And thus spake on that ancient man,
The bright-eyed Mariner.   40

'And now the STORM-BLAST came, and he
Was tyrannous and strong:
He struck with his o'ertaking wings,
And chased us south along.

The ship driven
by a storm
toward the
south pole.

With sloping masts and dipping prow,
As who pursued with yell and blow
Still treads the shadow of his foe,
And forward bends his head,
The ship drove fast, loud roared the blast,
50 And southward aye we fled.

And now there came both mist and snow,
And it grew wondrous cold:
And ice, mast-high, came floating by,
As green as emerald.

And through the drifts the snowy clifts
Did send a dismal sheen:
Nor shapes of men nor þeasts we ken – [6]
The ice was all between.

The land of ice,
and of fearful
sounds, where
no living thing
was to be seen.

The ice was here, the ice was there,
The ice was all around:
60 It cracked and growled, and roared and howled,
Like noises in a swound![7]

At length did cross an Albatross,
Thorough the fog it came;
As if it had been a Christian soul,
We hailed it in God's name.

Till a great seabird,
called the
Albatross, came
through the snow-
fog, and was
received with great
joy and hospitality.

It ate the food it ne'er had eat,
And round and round it flew.
The ice did split with a thunder-fit;
70 The helmsman steered us through!

And a good south wind sprung up behind;
The Albatross did follow,
And every day, for food or play,
Came to the mariners' hollo!

And lo! the
Albatross proveth a
bird of good omen,
and followeth the
ship as it returned
northward through
fog and floating ice.

In mist or cloud, on mast or shroud,
It perched for vespers nine;
Whiles all the night, through fog-smoke white,
Glimmered the white Moonshine.'

The Ancient
Mariner
inhospitably
killeth the pious
bird of good
omen.

'God save thee, Ancient Mariner!
From the fiends, that plague thee thus! –   80
Why look'st thou so?' – 'With my crossbow
I shot the ALBATROSS.

PART 2

The Sun now rose upon the right:
Out of the sea came he,
Still hid in mist, and on the left
Went down into the sea

And the good south wind still blew behind,
But no sweet bird did follow,
Nor any day for food or play
Came to the mariners' hollo!   90

His shipmates
cry out against
the Ancient
Mariner, for
killing the bird
of good luck.

And I had done a hellish thing,
And it would work 'em woe:
For all averred, I had killed the bird
That made the breeze to blow.
Ah wretch! said they, the bird to slay,
That made the breeze to blow!

But when the fog
clears off, they
justify the same,
and thus make
themselves
accomplices
in the crime.
The fair breeze
continues; the
ship enters the
Pacific Ocean, and
sails northward,
even till it reaches
the line.

Nor dim nor red, like God's own head,
The glorious Sun uprist:
Then all averred, I had killed the bird
That brought the fog and mist.   100
'Twas right, said they, such birds to slay,
That bring the fog and mist.

The fair breeze blew, the white foam flew,
The furrow followed free;
We were the first that ever burst
Into that silent sea.

Down dropt the breeze, the sails dropt down,   The ship hath
'Twas sad as sad could be;   been suddenly
And we did speak only to break   becalmed.
The silence of the sea!

All in a hot and copper sky,
The bloody Sun, at noon,
Right up above the mast did stand,
No bigger than the Moon.

Day after day, day after day,
We stuck, nor breath nor motion;
As idle as a painted ship
Upon a painted ocean.

Water, water, everywhere,   And the
And all the boards did shrink;   Albatross begins
Water, water, everywhere,   to be avenged.
Nor any drop to drink.

The very deep did rot: O Christ!
That ever this should be!
Yea, slimy things did crawl with legs
Upon the slimy sea.

About, about, in reel and rout
The death-fires danced at night;
The water, like a witch's oils,
Burnt green, and blue and white.

And some in dreams assurèd were   A Spirit had
Of the Spirit that plagued us so;   followed them;
Nine fathom deep he had followed us   one of the
From the land of mist and snow.   invisible
                                          inhabitants of
                                            this planet,
            neither departed souls nor angels; concerning whom the learned
                     Jew, Josephus, and the Platonic Constantinopolitan,
                Michael Psellus, may be consulted. They are very numerous,
                   and there is no climate or element without one or more.

110

120

130

And every tongue, through utter drought,
Was withered at the root;
We could not speak, no more than if
We had been choked with soot.

The shipmates, in
their sore
distress, would
fain throw the
whole guilt on
the Ancient
Mariner: in sign
whereof they
hang the dead
sea-bird round
his neck.

Ah! well a-day! what evil looks
Had I from old and young!   140
Instead of the cross, the Albatross
About my neck was hung.

PART 3

There passed a weary time. Each throat
Was parched, and glazed each eye.
A weary time! a weary time!
How glazed each weary eye,
When looking westward, I beheld
A something in the sky.

The Ancient
Mariner
beholdeth a sign
in the element
afar off.

At first it seemed a little speck,
And then it seemed a mist;   150
It moved and moved, and took at last
A certain shape, I wist.[8]

A speck, a mist, a shape, I wist!
And still it neared and neared:
As if it dodged a water-sprite,
It plunged and tacked and veered.

At its nearer
approach, it
seemeth to him
to be a ship; and
at a dear ransom
he freeth his
speech from the
bonds of thirst.

With throats unslaked, with black lips baked,
we could nor laugh nor wail;
Through utter drought all dumb we stood!
I bit my arm, I sucked the blood,   160
And cried, A sail! a sail!

A flash of joy;

With throats unslaked, with black lips baked,
Agape they heard me call:
Gramercy![9] they for joy did grin,
And all at once their breath drew in,
As they were drinking all.

See! see! (I cried) she tacks no more!
Hither to work us weal;
Without a breeze, without a tide,
170   She steadies with upright keel!

The western wave was all a-flame.
The day was well nigh done!
Almost upon the western wave
Rested the broad bright Sun;
When that strange shape drove suddenly
Betwixt us and the Sun.

And straight the Sun was flecked with bars,
(Heaven's Mother send us grace!)
As if through a dungeon-grate he peered
180   With broad and burning face.

Alas! (thought I, and my heart beat loud)
How fast she nears and nears!
Are those *her* sails that glance in the Sun,
Like restless gossameres?[10]

Are those *her* ribs through which the Sun
Did peer, as through a grate?
And is that Woman all her crew?
Is that a DEATH? and are there two?
Is DEATH that woman's mate?

190   *Her* lips were red, *her* looks were free,
Her locks were yellow as gold:
Her skin was as white as leprosy,
The Nightmare LIFE-IN-DEATH was she,
Who thicks man's blood with cold.

The naked hulk alongside came,
And the twain were casting dice;
"The game is done! I've won! I've won!"
Quoth she, and whistles thrice.

Marginal glosses:

And horror follows. For can it be aship that comes onward without wind or tide.

It seemeth him but a skeleton of a ship.

And its ribs are seen as bars on the face of the Sun. The Spectre-Woman and her Death-mate, and no other, on board the skeleton ship.

Like vessel, like crew!

Death and Life-in-Death have diced for the ship's crew, and she (the latter) winneth the Ancient Mariner.

No twilight in
the courts of the
Sun.

The Sun's rim dips; the stars rush out:
At one stride comes the dark;   200
With far-heard whisper, o'er the sea,
Off shot the spectre-bark.

We listened and looked sideways up!
Fear at my heart, as at a cup,
My life-blood seemed to sip!
The stars were dim, and thick the night,
The steersman's face by his lamp gleamed white;
From the sails the dew did drip –

At the rising of
the Moon,

Till clomb[11] above the eastern bar
The hornèd Moon, with one bright star   210
Within the nether tip.

one after
another,

One after one, by the star-dogged Moon,
Too quick for groan or sigh,
Each turned his face with a ghastly pang,
And cursed me with his eye.

his shipmates
drop down dead.

Four times fifty living men
(And I heard nor sigh nor groan)
With heavy thump, a lifeless lump,
They dropped down one by one.

But Life-in-Death
begins her work
on the Ancient
Mariner.

The souls did from their bodies fly –   220
They fled to bliss or woe!
And every soul, it passed me by,
Like the whizz of my crossbow!'

PART 4

The wedding-
guest feareth that
a spirit is talking
to him;

'I fear thee, ancient Mariner!
I fear thy skinny hand!
And thou art long, and lank, and brown,
As is the ribbed sea-sand.

but the Ancient
Mariner assureth
him of his bodily
life, and proceedeth
to relate his horrible
penance.

I fear thee and thy glittering eye,
And thy skinny hand, so brown.' –
'Fear not, fear not, thou Wedding-Guest!   230
This body dropt not down.

Alone, alone, all, all alone,
Alone on a wide wide sea!
And never a saint took pity on
My soul in agony.

The many men, so beautiful!   He despiseth
And they all dead did lie: the creatures of
And a thousand thousand slimy things   the calm,
Lived on; and so did I.

240   I looked upon the rotting sea,   and envieth
        And drew my eyes away;   that *they*
        I looked upon the rotting deck,   should live
        And there the dead men lay.   and so many
                                                      lie dead.

I looked to heaven, and tried to pray;
But or ever a prayer had gusht,
A wicked whisper came, and made
My heart as dry as dust.

I closed my lids, and kept them close,
And the balls like pulses beat;
250   For the sky and the sea, and the sea and the sky
Lay like a load on my weary eye,
And the dead were at my feet.

The cold sweat melted from their limbs,   But the curse
Nor rot nor reek did they: liveth for
The look with which they looked on me   him in the
Had never passed away.   eye of the
                                                dead men.

An orphan's curse would drag to hell
A spirit from on high;
But oh! more horrible than that
260   Is the curse in a dead man's eye!
Seven days, seven nights, I saw that curse,
And yet I could not die.

In his loneliness
and fixedness he
yearneth towards
the journeying
Moon, and the
stars that still
sojourn, yet still
move onward;
and everywhere
the blue sky
belongs to them,
and is their
appointed rest,

The moving Moon went up the sky,
And nowhere did abide:
Softly she was going up,
And a star or two beside –

Her beams bemocked[12] the sultry main,
Like April hoar-frost spread;
But where the ship's huge shadow lay,
The charmèd water burnt alway   270
A still and awful red.

and their native country, and their own natural homes, which
they enter unannounced, as lords that are certainly expected
and yet there is a silent joy at their arrival.

By the light of
the Moon he
beholdeth God's
creatures of the
great calm.

Beyond the shadow of the ship;
I watched the water-snakes:
They moved in tracks of shining white,
And when they reared, the elfish light
Fell off in hoary flakes.

Within the shadow of the ship
I watched their rich attire:
Blue, glossy green, and velvet black,
They coiled and swam; and every track   280
Was a flash of golden fire.

Their beauty and
their happiness.

O happy living things! no tongue
Their beauty might declare:
A spring of love gushed from my heart,

He blesseth
them in his
heart.

And I blessed them unaware:
Sure my kind saint took pity on me,
And I blessed them unaware.

The spell begins
to break.

The self-same moment I could pray;
And from my neck so free
The Albatross fell off, and sank   290
Like lead into the sea.

PART 5

Oh sleep! it is a gentle thing,
Beloved from pole to pole!
To Mary Queen[13] the praise be given!
She sent the gentle sleep from Heaven,
That slid into my soul.

The silly buckets on the deck,   By grace of the
That had so long remained,   holy Mother, the
I dreamt that they were filled with dew;   Ancient Mariner
                                             is refreshed with
300   And when I awoke, it rained.   rain.

My lips were wet, my throat was cold,
My garments all were dank;
Sure I had drunken in my dreams,
And still my body drank.

I moved, and could not feel my limbs:
I was so light – almost
I thought that I had died in sleep,
And was a blessèd ghost.

And soon I heard a roaring wind: He heareth
310   It did not come anear;   sounds and
But with its sound it shook the sails,   seeth strange
That were so thin and sere.[14]   sights and
                                             commotions in
                                             the sky and the
The upper air burst into life!   element.
And a hundred fire-flags sheen,
To and fro they were hurried about!
And to and fro, and in and out,
The wan stars danced between.

And the coming wind did roar more loud,
And the sails did sigh like sedge;
320   And the rain poured down from one black cloud;
The Moon was at its edge.

The thick black cloud was cleft, and still
The Moon was at its side:
Like waters shot from some high crag,
The lightning fell with never a jag,
A river steep and wide.

The bodies of
the ship's crew
are inspired
[inspirited]
and the ship
moves on;

The loud wind never reached the ship,
Yet now the ship moved on!
Beneath the lightning and the Moon
The dead men gave a groan.   330

They groaned, they stirred, they all uprose,
Nor spake, nor moved their eyes;
It had been strange, even in a dream,
To have seen those dead men rise.

The helmsman steered, the ship moved on;
Yet never a breeze up-blew;
The mariners all 'gan work the ropes,
Where they were wont to do;
They raised their limbs like lifeless tools –
We were a ghastly crew.   340

The body of my brother's son
Stood by me, knee to knee:
The body and I pulled at one rope,
But he said nought to me.'

But not by the
souls of the men,
nor by daemons
of earth or
middle air, but
by a blessed
troop of angelic
spirits, sent
down by the
invocation of the
guardian Saint.

'I fear thee, Ancient Mariner!'
'Be calm, thou Wedding-Guest!
'Twas not those souls that fled in pain,
Which to their corses[15] came again,
But a troop of spirits blest:

For when it dawned – they dropped their arms,   350
And clustered round the mast;
Sweet sounds rose slowly through their mouths,
And from their bodies passed.

Around, around, flew each sweet sound,
Then darted to the Sun;
Slowly the sounds came back again,
Now mixed, now one by one.

Sometimes a-dropping from the sky
I heard the skylark sing;
360 Sometimes all little birds that are,
How they seemed to fill the sea and air
With their sweet jargoning!

And now 'twas like all instruments,
Now like a lonely flute;
And now it is an angel's song,
That makes the heavens be mute.

It ceased; yet still the sails made on
A pleasant noise till noon,
A noise like of a hidden brook
370 In the leafy month of June,
That to the sleeping woods all night
Singeth a quiet tune.

Till noon we quietly sailed on,
Yet never a breeze did breathe:
Slowly and smoothly went the ship,
Moved onward from beneath.

Under the keel nine fathom deep,
From the land of mist and snow,
The spirit slid: and it was he
380 That made the ship to go.
The sails at noon left off their tune,
And the ship stood still also.

The Sun, right up above the mast,
Had fixed her to the ocean:
But in a minute she 'gan stir,
With a short uneasy motion –
Backwards and forwards half her length
With a short uneasy motion.

The lonesome Spirit from the south pole carries on the ship as far as the Line, in obedience to the angelic troop, but still requireth vengeance.

Then like a pawing horse let go,
She made a sudden bound: 390
It flung the blood into my head,
And I fell down in a swound.

How long in that same fit I lay,
I have not to declare;
But ere my living life returned,
I heard and in my soul discerned
Two voices in the air.

"Is it he?" quoth one, "Is this the man?
By him who died on cross,
With his cruel bow he laid full low   400
The harmless Albatross.

The spirit who bideth by himself
In the land of mist and snow,
He loved the bird that loved the man
Who shot him with his bow."

The other was a softer voice,
As soft as honey-dew:
Quoth he, "The man hath penance done,
And penance more will do."

The Polar Spirit's fellow-daemons, the invisible inhabitants of the element, take part in his wrong; and two of them relate, one to the other, that penance long and heavy for the ancient Mariner hath been accorded to the Polar Spirit, who returneth southward.

PART 6

FIRST VOICE
"But tell me, tell me! speak again,   410
Thy soft response renewing –
What makes that ship drive on so fast?
What is the ocean doing?"

SECOND VOICE
"Still as a slave before his lord,
The ocean hath no blast;
His great bright eye most silently
Up to the Moon is cast –

If he may know which way to go;
For she guides him smooth or grim.
See, brother, see! how graciously
She looketh down on him."

FIRST VOICE
"But why drives on that ship so fast,
Without or wave or wind?"

SECOND VOICE
"The air is cut away before,
And closes from behind.

Fly, brother, fly! more high, more high!
Or we shall be belated:
For slow and slow that ship will go,
When the Mariner's trance is abated."

I woke, and we were sailing on
As in a gentle weather:
'Twas night, calm night, the moon was high;
The dead men stood together.

All stood together on the deck,
For a charnel-dungeon[16] fitter:
All fixed on me their stony eyes,
That in the Moon did glitter.

The pang, the curse, with which they died,
Had never passed away:
I could not draw my eyes from theirs,
Nor turn them up to pray.

And now this spell was snapt: once more
I viewed the ocean green,
And looked far forth, yet little saw
Of what had else been seen –

420

430

440

Marginal glosses (right column):

The Mariner hath been cast into a trance; for the angelic power causeth the vessel to drive northward faster than human life could endure.

The supernatural motion is retarded; the Mariner awakes, and his penance begins anew.

The curse is finally expiated.

Like one, that on a lonesome road
Doth walk in fear and dread,
And having once turned round walks on,
And turns no more his head;
Because he knows, a frightful fiend   450
Doth close behind him tread.

But soon there breathed a wind on me,
Nor sound nor motion made:
Its path was not upon the sea,
In ripple or in shade.

It raised my hair, it fanned my cheek
Like a meadow-gale of spring –
It mingled strangely with my fears,
Yet it felt like a welcoming.

Swiftly, swiftly flew the ship,   460
Yet she sailed softly too:
Sweetly, sweetly blew the breeze –
On me alone it blew.

And the Ancient Mariner beholdeth his native country.

Oh! dream of joy! is this indeed
The lighthouse top I see?
Is this the hill? is this the kirk?
Is this mine own countree?

We drifted o'er the harbour-bar,
And I with sobs did pray –
O let me be awake, my God!   470
Or let me sleep alway.

The harbour-bay was clear as glass,
So smoothly it was strewn!
And on the bay the moonlight lay,
And the shadow of the Moon.

The rock shone bright, the kirk no less,
That stands above the rock:
The moonlight steeped in silentness
The steady weathercock.

480 And the bay was white with silent light,   The angelic
   Till rising from the same,   spirits leave the
   Full many shapes, that shadows were,   dead bodies,
   In crimson colours came.

   A little distance from the prow   And appear in
   Those crimson shadows were: their own forms
   I turned my eyes upon the deck –   of light.
   Oh, Christ! what saw I there!

   Each corse lay flat, lifeless and flat,
   And, by the holy rood!
490 A man all light, a seraph-man,[17]
   On every corse there stood.

   This seraph-band, each waved his hand:
   It was a heavenly sight!
   They stood as signals to the land,
   Each one a lovely light;

   This seraph-band, each waved his hand,
   No voice did they impart –
   No voice; but oh! the silence sank
   Like music on my heart.

500 But soon I heard the dash of oars,
   I heard the Pilot's cheer;
   My head was turned perforce away
   And I saw a boat appear.

   The Pilot and the Pilot's boy,
   I heard them coming fast:
   Dear Lord in Heaven! it was a joy
   The dead men could not blast.

   I saw a third – I heard his voice:
   It is the Hermit good!
510 He singeth loud his godly hymns
   That he makes in the wood.
   He'll shrieve my soul, he'll wash away
   The Albatross's blood.

PART 7

The Hermit of
the Wood

This Hermit good lives in that wood
Which slopes down to the sea.
How loudly his sweet voice he rears!
He loves to talk with marineres
That come from a far countree.

He kneels at morn, and noon, and eve –
He hath a cushion plump: 520
It is the moss that wholly hides
The rotted old oak-stump.

The skiff-boat neared: I heard them talk,
"Why, this is strange, I trow!
Where are those lights so many and fair,
That signal made but now?"

approacheth the
ship with
wonder.

"Strange, by my faith!" the Hermit said –
"And they answered not our cheer!
The planks looked warped! and see those sails,
How thin they are and sere!   530
I never saw aught like to them,
Unless perchance it were

Brown skeletons of leaves that lag
My forest-brook along;
When the ivy-tod[18] is heavy with snow,
And the owlet whoops to the wolf below,
That eats the she-wolf's young."

"Dear Lord! it hath a fiendish look – "
(The Pilot made reply)
"I am a-feared" – "Push on, push on!"   540
Said the Hermit cheerily.

The boat came closer to the ship,
But I nor spake nor stirred;
The boat came close beneath the ship,
And straight a sound was heard.

Under the water it rumbled on,
Still louder and more dread:
It reached the ship, it split the bay;
The ship went down like lead.

The ship suddenly sinketh.

550   Stunned by that loud and dreadful sound,
Which sky and ocean smote,
Like one that hath been seven days drowned
My body lay afloat;
But swift as dreams, myself I found
Within the Pilot's boat.

The Ancient Mariner is saved in the Pilot's boat.

Upon the whirl, where sank the ship,
The boat spun round and round;
And all was still, save that the hill
Was telling of the sound.

560   I moved my lips – the Pilot shrieked
And fell down in a fit;
The holy Hermit raised his eyes,
And prayed where he did sit.

I took the oars: the Pilot's boy,
Who now doth crazy go,
Laughed loud and long, and all the while
His eyes went to and fro.
"Ha! ha!" quoth he, "full plain I see,
The Devil knows how to row."

570   And now, all in my own countree,
I stood on the firm land!
The Hermit stepped forth from the boat,
And scarcely he could stand.

"O shrieve[19] me, shrieve me, holy man!"
The Hermit crossed his brow.
"Say quick," quoth he, "I bid thee say –
What manner of man art thou?"

The Ancient Mariner earnestly entreateth the Hermit to shrieve him; and the penance of life falls on him.

Forthwith this frame of mine was wrenched
With a woful agony,
Which forced me to begin my tale;   580
And then it left me free.

And ever and
anon through
out his future life
an agony
constraineth him
to travel from
land to land;

Since then, at an uncertain hour,
That agony returns:
And till my ghastly tale is told,
This heart within me burns.

I pass, like night, from land to land;
I have strange power of speech;
That moment that his face I see,
I know the man that must hear me:
To him my tale I teach.   590

What loud uproar bursts from that door!
The wedding-guests are there:
But in the garden-bower the bride
And bride-maids singing are:
And hark the little vesper bell,[20]
Which biddeth me to prayer!

O Wedding-Guest! this soul hath been
Alone on a wide wide sea:
So lonely 'twas, that God himself
Scarce seemèd there to be.   600

O sweeter than the marriage-feast,
'Tis sweeter far to me,
To walk together to the kirk
With a goodly company! –

To walk together to the kirk,
And all together pray,
While each to his great Father bends,
Old men, and babes, and loving friends,
And youths and maidens gay!

610   Farewell, farewell! but this I tell
       To thee, thou Wedding-Guest!
       He prayeth well, who loveth well
       Both man and bird and beast.

       He prayeth best, who loveth best
       All things both great and small;
       For the dear God who loveth us,
       He made and loveth all.'

       The Mariner, whose eye is bright,
       Whose beard with age is hoar,
620   Is gone: and now the Wedding-Guest
       Turned from the bridegroom's door.

       He went like one that hath been stunned,
       And is of sense forlorn:[21]
       A sadder and a wiser man,
       He rose the morrow morn.

And to teach, by his own example, love and reverence to all things that God made and loveth.

The Foster-Mother's Tale,

A DRAMATIC FRAGMENT[1]

FOSTER-MOTHER
I never saw the man whom you describe.

MARIA
'Tis strange! he spake of you familiarly
As mine and Albert's common Foster-mother.

FOSTER-MOTHER
Now blessings on the man, whoe'er he be,
That joined your names with mine! O my sweet lady,
As often as I think of those dear times
When you two little ones would stand at eve
On each side of my chair, and make me learn
All you had learnt in the day; and how to talk
In gentle phrase, then bid me sing to you –   10
'Tis more like heaven to come than what *has* been.

MARIA
O my dear Mother! this strange man has left me
Troubled with wilder fancies than the moon
Breeds in the love-sick maid who gazes at it,
Till lost in inward vision, with wet eye
She gazes idly! – But that entrance, Mother!

FOSTER-MOTHER
Can no one hear? It is a perilous tale!

MARIA
No one.

FOSTER-MOTHER
My husband's father told it me,
Poor old Leoni! – Angels rest his soul!   20
He was a woodman, and could fell and saw
With lusty arm. You know that huge round beam
Which props the hanging wall of the old chapel?
Beneath that tree, while yet it was a tree
He found a baby wrapt in mosses, lined

With thistle-beards, and such small locks of wool
As hang on brambles. Well, he brought him home,
And reared him at the then Lord Velez' cost;
And so the babe grew up a pretty boy,
A pretty boy, but most unteachable –   30
And never learnt a prayer, nor told a bead,
But knew the names of birds, and mocked their notes,
And whistled, as he were a bird himself:
And all the autumn 'twas his only play
To get the seeds of wild flowers, and to plant them,
With earth and water, on the stumps of trees.
A Friar, who gathered simples in the wood,
A grey-haired man – he loved this little boy,
The boy loved him – and, when the Friar taught him,
He soon could write with the pen: and from that time,   40
Lived chiefly at the Convent or the Castle.
So he became a very learned youth.
But Oh! poor wretch! – he read, and read, and read,
'Till his brain turned – and ere his twentieth year,
He had unlawful thoughts of many things:
And though he prayed, he never loved to pray
With holy men, nor in a holy place –
But yet his speech, it was so soft and sweet,
The late Lord Velez ne'er was wearied with him.
And once, as by the north side of the Chapel   50
They stood together, chained in deep discourse,
The earth heaved under them with such a groan,
That the wall tottered, and had well-nigh fallen
Right on their heads. My Lord was sorely frightened;
A fever seized him, and he made confession
Of all the heretical and lawless talk
Which brought this judgment: so the youth was seized
And cast into that hole. My husband's father
Sobbed like a child – it almost broke his heart:
And once as he was working in the cellar,   60
He heard a voice distinctly; 'twas the youth's,
Who sung a doleful song about green fields,
How sweet it were on lake or wild savannah,
To hunt for food, and be a naked man,
And wander up and down at liberty.

He always doted on the youth, and now
His love grew desperate; and defying death,
He made that cunning entrance I described:
And the young man escaped.

MARIA
'Tis a sweet tale: 70
Such as would lull a listening child to sleep,
His rosy face besoiled with unwiped tears. –
And what became of him?

FOSTER-MOTHER
He went on shipboard
With those bold voyagers, who made discovery
Of golden lands. Leoni's younger brother
Went likewise, and when he returned to Spain,
He told Leoni that the poor mad youth,
Soon after they arrived in that new world,
In spite of his dissuasion, seized a boat,   80
And all alone, set sail by silent moonlight
Up a great river, great as any sea,
And ne'er was heard of more: but 'tis supposed,
He lived and died among the savage men.

The Nightingale

A CONVERSATION POEM,[1] APRIL 1798

No cloud, no relique of the sunken day
Distinguishes the West, no long thin slip
Of sullen light, no obscure trembling hues.
Come, we will rest on this old mossy bridge!
You see the glimmer of the stream beneath,
But hear no murmuring: it flows silently,
O'er its soft bed of verdure. All is still,
A balmy night! And though the stars be dim,
Yet let us think upon the vernal showers
That gladden the green earth, and we shall find   10
A pleasure in the dimness of the stars.
And hark! the Nightingale begins its song,
'Most musical, most melancholy' bird![2]
A melancholy bird? Oh! idle thought!
In Nature there is nothing melancholy.
But some night-wandering man whose heart was pierced
With the remembrance of a grievous wrong,
Or slow distemper, or neglected love
(And so, poor wretch! filled all things with himself,
And made all gentle sounds tell back the tale   20
Of his own sorrow), he, and such as he,
First named these notes a melancholy strain.
And many a poet echoes the conceit;[3]
Poet who hath been building up the rhyme
When he had better far have stretched his limbs
Beside a brook in mossy forest-dell,
By sun or moonlight, to the influxes
Of shapes and sounds and shifting elements
Surrendering his whole spirit, of his song
And of his fame forgetful! so his fame   30
Should share in Nature's immortality,
A venerable thing! and so his song
Should make all Nature lovelier, and itself
Be loved like Nature! But 'twill not be so;
And youths and maidens most poetical,
Who lose the deepening twilights of the spring

In ballrooms and hot theatres, they still
Full of meek sympathy must heave their sighs
O'er Philomela's[4] pity-pleading strains.

My Friend, and thou, our Sister![5] we have learnt   40
A different lore: we may not thus profane
Nature's sweet voices, always full of love
And joyance! 'Tis the merry Nightingale
That crowds, and hurries, and precipitates
With fast thick warble his delicious notes,
As he were fearful that an April night
Would be too short for him to utter forth
His love-chant, and disburthen his full soul
Of all its music!
          And I know a grove
Of large extent, hard by a castle huge,   50
Which the great lord inhabits not; and so
This grove is wild with tangling underwood,
And the trim walks are broken up, and grass,
Thin grass and king-cups grow within the paths.
But never elsewhere in one place I knew
So many nightingales; and far and near,
In wood and thicket, over the wide grove,
They answer and provoke each other's song,
With skirmish and capricious passagings,
And murmurs musical and swift jug jug,   60
And one low piping sound more sweet than all –
Stirring the air with such a harmony,
That should you close your eyes, you might almost
Forget it was not day! On moonlight bushes,
Whose dewy leaflets are but half-disclosed,
You may perchance behold them on the twigs,
Their bright, bright eyes, their eyes both bright and full,
Glistening, while many a glow-worm in the shade,
Lights up her love-torch.
          A most gentle Maid,
Who dwelleth in her hospitable home   70
Hard by the castle, and at latest eve
(Even like a Lady vowed and dedicate
To something more than Nature in the grove)

Glides through the pathways; she knows all their notes,
That gentle Maid! and oft, a moment's space,
What time the moon was lost behind a cloud,
Hath heard a pause of silence; till the moon
Emerging, hath awakened earth and sky
With one sensation, and those wakeful birds
Have all burst forth in choral minstrelsy,   80
As if some sudden gale had swept at once
A hundred airy harps! And she hath watched
Many a nightingale perch giddily
On blossomy twig still swinging from the breeze,
And to that motion tune his wanton song
Like tipsy Joy that reels with tossing head.

Farewell, O Warbler! till tomorrow eve,
And you, my friends! farewell, a short farewell!
We have been loitering long and pleasantly,
And now for our dear homes. – That strain again!   90
Full fain it would delay me! My dear babe,
Who, capable of no articulate sound,
Mars all things with his imitative lisp,
How he would place his hand beside his ear,
His little hand, the small forefinger up,
And bid us listen! And I deem it wise
To make him Nature's playmate. He knows well
The evening-star; and once, when he awoke
In most distressful mood (some inward pain
Had made up that strange thing, an infant's dream –)   100
I hurried with him to our orchard-plot,
And he beheld the moon, and, hushed at once,
Suspends his sobs, and laughs most silently,
While his fair eyes, that swam with undropped tears,
Did glitter in the yellow moonbeam! Well! –
It is a father's tale: But if that Heaven
Should give me life, his childhood shall grow up
Familiar with these songs, that with the night
He may associate joy. – Once more, farewell,
Sweet Nightingale! once more, my friends! farewell.   110

The Dungeon[1]

And this place our forefathers made for man!
This is the process of our love and wisdom,
To each poor brother who offends against us –
Most innocent, perhaps – and what if guilty?
Is this the only cure? Merciful God?
Each pore and natural outlet shrivell'd up
By ignorance and parching poverty,
His energies roll back upon his heart,
And stagnate and corrupt; till changed to poison,
They break out on him, like a loathsome plague-spot;   10
Then we call in our pamper'd mountebanks–
And this is their best cure! uncomforted
And friendless solitude, groaning and tears,
And savage faces, at the clanking hour,
Seen through the steams and vapour of his dungeon,
By the lamp's dismal twilight! So he lies
Circled with evil, till his very soul
Unmoulds its essence, hopelessly deformed
By sights of ever more deformity!

With other ministrations thou, O nature!   20
Healest thy wandering and distempered child:
Thou pourest on him thy soft influences,
Thy sunny hues, fair forms, and breathing sweets,
Thy melodies of woods, and winds, and waters,
Till he relent, and can no more endure
To be a jarring and a dissonant thing,
Amid this general dance and minstrelsy;
But, bursting into tears, wins back his way,
His angry spirit healed and harmonised
By the benignant touch of love and beauty.   30

II Other Poems

The Eolian Harp[1]

COMPOSED AT CLEVEDON, SOMERSETSHIRE

My pensive Sara! thy soft cheek reclined
Thus on mine arm, most soothing sweet it is
To sit beside our Cot,[2] our Cot o'ergrown
With white-flower'd Jasmin, and the broad-leav'd Myrtle
(Meet[3] emblems they of Innocence and Love!),
And watch the clouds, that late were rich with light,
Slow saddening round, and mark the star of eve
Serenely brilliant (such should Wisdom be)
Shine opposite! How exquisite the scents
Snatch'd from yon beanfield! and the world *so* hush'd!   10
The stilly murmur of the distant Sea
Tells us of silence.
                              And that simplest Lute,
Placed lengthways in the clasping casement, hark!
How by the desultory breeze caress'd,
Like some coy maid half yielding to her lover,
It pours such sweet upbraiding, as must needs
Tempt to repeat the wrong! And now, its strings
Boldlier swept, the long sequacious[4] notes
Over delicious surges sink and rise,
Such a soft floating witchery of sound   20
As twilight Elfins make, when they at eve
Voyage on gentle gales from Fairy-Land,
Where Melodies round honey-dropping flowers,
Footless and wild, like birds of Paradise,
Nor pause, nor perch, hovering on untam'd wing!
O! the one Life within us and abroad,
Which meets all motion and becomes its soul,
A light in sound, a sound-like power in light,
Rhythm in all thought, and joyance everywhere –
Methinks, it should have been impossible   30
Not to love all things in a world so fill'd;

Where the breeze warbles, and the mute still air
Is Music slumbering on her instrument.

  And thus, my Love! as on the midway slope
Of yonder hill I stretch my limbs at noon,
Whilst through my half-clos'd eyelids I behold
The sunbeams dance, like diamonds, on the main,
And tranquil muse upon tranquillity;
Full many a thought uncall'd and undetain'd,
And many idle flitting phantasies,   40
Traverse my indolent and passive brain,
As wild and various as the random gales
That swell and flutter on this subject Lute!
  And what if all of animated nature
Be but organic Harps diversely fram'd,
That tremble into thought, as o'er them sweeps
Plastic[5] and vast, one intellectual breeze,
At once the Soul of each, and God of all?
  But thy more serious eye a mild reproof
Darts, O beloved Woman! nor such thoughts   50
Dim and unhallow'd dost thou not reject,
And biddest me walk humbly with my God.
Meek Daughter in the family of Christ!
Well hast thou said and holily disprais'd
These shapings of the unregenerate mind;
Bubbles that glitter as they rise and break
On vain Philosophy's aye-babbling spring.
For never guiltless may I speak of him,
The Incomprehensible! save when with awe
I praise him, and with Faith that inly *feels*;   60
Who with his saving mercies healed me,
A sinful and most miserable man,
Wilder'd[6] and dark, and gave me to possess
Peace, and this Cot, and thee, heart-honour'd Maid!

Reflections on Having Left a Place of Retirement

Sermoni propriora. – HORACE

Low was our pretty Cot:[1] our tallest Rose
Peep'd at the chamber-window. We could hear
At silent noon, and eve, and early morn,
The Sea's faint murmur. In the open air
Our Myrtles blossom'd; and across the porch
Thick Jasmins twined: the little landscape round
Was green and woody, and refresh'd the eye.
It was a spot which you might aptly call
The Valley of Seclusion! Once I saw
(Hallowing his Sabbath-day by quietness)   10
A wealthy son of Commerce saunter by,
Bristowa's[2] citizen: methought, it calm'd
His thirst of idle gold, and made him muse
With wiser feelings: for he paus'd, and look'd
With a pleas'd sadness, and gaz'd all around,
Then eyed our Cottage, and gaz'd round again,
And sigh'd, and said, it was a Blessèd Place.
And we *were* bless'd. Oft with patient ear
Long-listening to the viewless skylark's note
(Viewless, or haply for a moment seen   20
Gleaming on sunny wing) in whisper'd tones
I've said to my Belovèd, 'Such, sweet Girl!
The inobtrusive song of Happiness,
Unearthly minstrelsy! then only heard
When the Soul seeks to hear; when all is hush'd,
And the Heart listens!'
                       But the time, when first
From that low Dell, steep up the stony Mount
I climb'd with perilous toil and reach'd the top,
Oh! what a goodly scene! *Here* the bleak mount,
The bare bleak mountain speckled thin with sheep;   30
Grey clouds, that shadowing spot the sunny fields;
And river, now with bushy rocks o'er-brow'd,
Now winding bright and full, with naked banks;
And seats, and lawns, the Abbey and the wood,
And cots, and hamlets, and faint city-spire;

The Channel *there*, the Islands and white sails,
Dim coasts, and cloud-like hills, and shoreless Ocean –
It seem'd like Omnipresence! God, methought,
Had built him there a Temple: the whole World
Seem'd *imag'd* in its vast circumference: 40
No *wish* profan'd my overwhelmèd heart.
Blest hour! It was a luxury – to be!

   Ah! quiet Dell! dear Cot, and Mount sublime!
I was constrain'd to quit you. Was it right,
While my unnumber'd brethren toil'd and bled,
That I should dream away the entrusted hours
On rose-leaf beds, pampering the coward heart
With feelings all too delicate for use?
Sweet is the tear that from some Howard's[3] eye
Drops on the cheek of one he lifts from earth: 50
And he that works me good with unmov'd face,
Does it but half: he chills me while he aids,
My benefactor, not my brother man!
Yet even this, this cold beneficence
Praise, praise it, O my Soul! oft as thou scann'st
The sluggard Pity's vision-weaving tribe!
Who sigh for Wretchedness, yet shun the Wretched,
Nursing in some delicious solitude
Their slothful loves and dainty sympathies!
I therefore go, and join head, heart, and hand,   60
Active and firm, to fight the bloodless fight
Of Science, Freedom, and the Truth in Christ.

   Yet oft when after honourable toil
Rests the tir'd mind, and waking loves to dream,
My spirit shall revisit thee, dear Cot!
Thy Jasmin and thy window-peeping Rose,
And Myrtles fearless of the mild sea-air.
And I shall sigh fond wishes – sweet Abode!
Ah! – had none greater! And that all had such!
It might be so – but the time is not yet.   70
Speed it, O Father! Let thy Kingdom come!

This Lime-Tree Bower My Prison

*In the June of 1797 some long-expected friends paid a
visit to the author's cottage; and on the morning of their
arrival, he met with an accident,[1] which disabled him
from walking during the whole time of their stay. One
evening, when they had left him for a few hours, he
composed the following lines in the garden-bower.*

Well, they are gone, and here must I remain,
This lime-tree bower my prison! I have lost
Beauties and feelings, such as would have been
Most sweet to my remembrance even when age
Had dimm'd mine eyes to blindness! They, meanwhile,
Friends, whom I never more may meet again,
On spring heath, along the hilltop edge,
Wander in gladness, and wind down, perchance,
To that still roaring dell, of which I told;
The roaring dell, o'erwooded, narrow, deep,   10
And only speckled by the midday sun;
Where its slim trunk the ash from rock to rock
Flings arching like a bridge; – that branchless ash,
Unsunn'd and damp, whose few poor yellow leaves
Ne'er tremble in the gale, yet tremble still,
Fann'd by the waterfall! and there my friends
Behold the dark green file of long lank weeds,
That all at once (a most fantastic sight!)
Still nod and drip beneath the dripping edge
Of the blue clay-stone.
                                Now, my friends emerge   20
Beneath the wide wide Heaven – and view again
The many-steepled tract magnificent
Of hilly fields and meadows, and the sea,
With some fair bark, perhaps, whose sails light up
The slip of smooth clear blue betwixt two Isles
Of purple shadow! Yes! they wander on
In gladness all; but thou, methinks, most glad,
My gentle-hearted Charles![2] for thou hast pined

And hunger'd after Nature, many a year,
In the great City pent, winning thy way   30
With sad yet patient soul, through evil and pain
And strange calamity![3] Ah! slowly sink
Behind the western ridge, thou glorious Sun!
Shine in the slant beams of the sinking orb,
Ye purple heath-flowers! richlier burn, ye clouds!
Live in the yellow light, ye distant groves!
And kindle, thou blue Ocean! So my friend
Struck with deep joy may stand, as I have stood,
Silent with swimming sense; yea, gazing round
On the wide landscape, gaze till all doth seem   40
Less gross than bodily; and of such hues
As veil the Almighty Spirit, when yet he makes
Spirits perceive his presence.
                              A delight
Comes sudden on my heart, and I am glad
As I myself were there! Nor in this bower,
This little lime-tree bower, have I not mark'd
Much that has sooth'd me. Pale beneath the blaze
Hung the transparent foliage; and I watch'd
Some broad and sunny leaf, and lov'd to see
The shadow of the leaf and stem above   50
Dappling its sunshine! And that walnut tree
Was richly ting'd, and a deep radiance lay
Full on the ancient ivy, which usurps
Those fronting elms, and now, with blackest mass
Makes their dark branches gleam a lighter hue
Through the late twilight: and though now the bat
Wheels silent by, and not a swallow twitters,
Yet still the solitary humble-bee
Sings in the bean-flower! Henceforth I shall know
That Nature ne'er deserts the wise and pure;   60
No plot so narrow, be but Nature there,
No waste so vacant, but may well employ
Each faculty of sense, and keep the heart
Awake to Love and Beauty! and sometimes
'Tis well to be bereft of promis'd good,
That we may lift the soul, and contemplate
With lively joy the joys we cannot share.

My gentle-hearted Charles! when the last rook
Beat its straight path along the dusky air
Homewards, I blest it! deeming its black wing   70
(Now a dim speck, now vanishing in light)
Had cross'd the mighty Orb's dilated glory,
While thou stood'st gazing; or, when all was still,
Flew creeking o'er thy head, and had a charm
For thee, my gentle-hearted Charles, to whom
No sound is dissonant which tells of Life.

Frost at Midnight

The Frost performs its secret ministry,
Unhelped by any wind. The owlet's cry
Came loud – and hark, again! loud as before.
The inmates of my cottage, all at rest,
Have left me to that solitude, which suits
Abstruser musings; save that at my side
My cradled infant[1] slumbers peacefully.
'Tis calm indeed! so calm, that it disturbs
And vexes meditation with its strange
And extreme silentness. Sea, hill, and wood,   10
This populous village! Sea, and hill, and wood,
With all the numberless goings-on of life,
Inaudible as dreams! the thin blue flame
Lies on my low-burnt fire, and quivers not;
Only that film, which fluttered on the grate,
Still flutters there, the sole unquiet thing.
Methinks, its motion in this hush of nature
Gives it dim sympathies with me who live,
Making it a companionable form,
Whose puny flaps and freaks the idling Spirit   20
By its own moods interprets, everywhere
Echo or mirror seeking of itself,
And makes a toy of Thought.
                              But O! how oft,
How oft, at school, with most believing mind,
Presageful, have I gazed upon the bars,
To watch that fluttering *stranger*![2] and as oft
With unclosed lids, already had I dreamt
Of my sweet birthplace, and the old church-tower,
Whose bells, the poor man's only music, rang
From morn to evening, all the hot Fair-day,   30
So sweetly, that they stirred and haunted me
With a wild pleasure, falling on mine ear
Most like articulate sounds of things to come!
So gazed I, till the soothing things, I dreamt,
Lulled me to sleep, and sleep prolonged my dreams!
And so I brooded all the following morn,

Awed by the stern preceptor's[3] face, mine eye
Fixed with mock study on my swimming book
Save if the door half opened, and I snatched
A hasty glance, and still my heart leaped up,   40
For still I hoped to see the *stranger's* face,
Townsman, or aunt, or sister more beloved,
My playmate when we both were clothed alike!

    Dear Babe, that sleepest cradled by my side,
Whose gentle breathings, heard in this deep calm,
Fill up the interspersed vacancies
And momentary pauses of the thought!
My babe so beautiful! it thrills my heart
With tender gladness, thus to look at thee,
And think that thou shalt learn far other lore,   50
And in far other scenes! For I was reared
In the great city, pent 'mid cloisters dim,
And saw nought lovely but the sky and stars.
But *thou*, my babe! shalt wander like a breeze
By lakes and sandy shores, beneath the crags
Of ancient mountain, and beneath the clouds,
Which image in their bulk both lakes and shores
And mountain crags: so shalt thou see and hear
The lovely shapes and sounds intelligible
Of that eternal language, which thy God   60
Utters, who from eternity doth teach
Himself in all, and all things in himself.
Great universal Teacher! he shall mould
Thy spirit, and by giving make it ask.

    Therefore all seasons shall be sweet to thee,
Whether the summer clothe the general earth
With greenness, or the redbreast sit and sing
Betwixt the tufts of snow on the bare branch
Of mossy apple tree, while the nigh thatch
Smokes in the sun-thaw; whether the eave-drops fall   70
Heard only in the trances of the blast,
Or if the secret ministry of frost
Shall hang them up in silent icicles,
Quietly shining to the quiet Moon.

France: An Ode

1

Ye Clouds! that far above me float and pause,
   Whose pathless march no mortal may control!
   Ye Ocean-Waves! that, wheresoe'er ye roll,
Yield homage only to eternal laws!
Ye Woods! that listen to the night-birds singing,
   Midway the smooth and perilous slope reclined,
Save when your own imperious branches swinging,
   Have made a solemn music of the wind!
Where, like a man beloved of God,
Through glooms, which never woodman trod,   10
      How oft, pursuing fancies holy,
My moonlight way o'er flowering weeds I wound,
      Inspired, beyond the guess of folly,
By each rude shape and wild unconquerable sound!
O ye loud Waves! and O ye Forests high!
   And O ye Clouds that far above me soared!
Thou rising Sun! thou blue rejoicing Sky!
   Yea, everything that is and will be free!
   Bear witness for me, wheresoe'er ye be,
With what deep worship I have still adored   20
      The spirit of divinest Liberty.

2

When France in wrath her giant-limbs upreared,[1]
   And with that oath, which smote air, earth, and sea,
   Stamped her strong foot and said she would be free,
Bear witness for me, how I hoped and feared!
With what a joy my lofty gratulation
   Unawed I sang, amid a slavish band:
And when to whelm the disenchanted nation,
   Like fiends embattled by a wizard's wand,
      The Monarchs marched in evil day,   30
      And Britain[2] joined the dire array;
   Though dear her shores and circling ocean,
Though many friendships, many youthful loves
   Had swoln the patriot emotion

And flung a magic light o'er all her hills and groves;
Yet still my voice, unaltered, sang defeat
   To all that braved the tyrant-quelling lance,
And shame too long delayed and vain retreat!
For ne'er, O Liberty! with partial aim
I dimmed thy light or damped thy holy flame;   40
   But blessed the paeans of delivered France,
And hung my head and wept at Britain's name.

3

'And what,' I said, 'though Blasphemy's loud scream[3]
   With that sweet music of deliverance strove!
   Though all the fierce and drunken passions wove
A dance more wild than e'er was maniac's dream!
   Ye storms, that round the dawning East assembled,
The Sun was rising, though ye hid his light!'
   And when, to soothe my soul, that hoped and trembled,
The dissonance ceased, and all seemed calm and bright;   50
   When France her front deep-scarr'd and gory
   Concealed with clustering wreaths of glory;
     When, insupportably advancing,
   Her arm made mockery of the warrior's ramp;
     While timid looks of fury glancing,
   Domestic treason, crushed beneath her fatal stamp,
Writhed like a wounded dragon in his gore;
   Then I reproached my fears that would not flee;
'And soon,' I said, 'shall Wisdom teach her lore
In the low huts of them that toil and groan!   60
And, conquering by her happiness alone,
   Shall France compel the nations to be free,
Till Love and Joy look round, and call the Earth their own.'

4

Forgive me, Freedom! O forgive those dreams!
   I hear thy voice, I hear thy loud lament,
   From bleak Helvetia's[4] icy caverns sent –
I hear thy groans upon her blood-stained streams!
   Heroes, that for your peaceful country perished,
And ye that, fleeing, spot your mountain-snows
   With bleeding wounds; forgive me, that I cherished   70

One thought that ever blessed your cruel foes!
   To scatter rage, and traitorous guilt,
   Where Peace her jealous home had built;
     A patriot-race to disinherit
Of all that made their stormy wilds so dear;
     And with inexpiable spirit
To taint the bloodless freedom of the mountaineer –
O France, that mockest Heaven, adulterous, blind,
   And patriot only in pernicious toils!
Are these thy boasts, Champion of human kind?   80
   To mix with Kings in the low lust of sway,
Yell in the hunt, and share the murderous prey;
To insult the shrine of Liberty with spoils
   From freemen torn; to tempt and to betray?

5

   The Sensual and the Dark rebel in vain,
   Slaves by their own compulsion! In mad game
   They burst their manacles and wear the name
     Of Freedom, graven on a heavier chain!
   O Liberty! with profitless endeavour
Have I pursued thee, many a weary hour;   90
   But thou nor swell'st the victor's strain, nor ever
Didst breathe thy soul in forms of human power.
   Alike from all, howe'er they praise thee
   (Nor prayer, nor boastful name delays thee),
     Alike from Priestcraft's harpy minions,
   And factious Blasphemy's obscener slaves,
     Thou speedest on thy subtle pinions,
The guide of homeless winds, and playmate of the waves!
And there I felt thee! – on that sea-cliff's verge,
   Whose pines, scarce travelled by the breeze above,   100
Had made one murmur with the distant surge!
Yes, while I stood and gazed, my temples bare,
And shot my being through earth, sea, and air,
   Possessing all things with intensest love,
     O Liberty! my spirit felt thee there.

Fears in Solitude

Written in April 1798, during the alarm of an invasion[1]

A green and silent spot, amid the hills,
A small and silent dell! O'er stiller place
No singing skylark ever poised himself.
The hills are heathy, save that swelling slope,
Which hath a gay and gorgeous covering on,
All golden with the never-bloomless furze,
Which now blooms most profusely: but the dell,
Bathed by the mist, is fresh and delicate
As vernal cornfield, or the unripe flax,
When, through its half-transparent stalks, at eve,   10
The level sunshine glimmers with green light.
Oh! 'tis a quiet spirit-healing nook!
Which all, methinks, would love; but chiefly he,
The humble man, who, in his youthful years,
Knew just so much of folly as had made
His early manhood more securely wise!
Here he might lie on fern or withered heath,
While from the singing lark (that sings unseen
The minstrelsy that solitude loves best),
And from the sun, and from the breezy air,   20
Sweet influences trembled o'er his frame;
And he, with many feelings, many thoughts,
Made up a meditative joy, and found
Religious meanings in the forms of Nature!
And so, his senses gradually wrapt
In a half sleep, he dreams of better worlds,
And dreaming hears thee still, O singing lark,
That singest like an angel in the clouds!

    My God! it is a melancholy thing
For such a man, who would full fain preserve   30
His soul in calmness, yet perforce must feel
For all his human brethren – O my God!
It weighs upon the heart, that he must think
What uproar and what strife may now be stirring

This way or that way o'er these silent hills –
Invasion, and the thunder and the shout,
And all the crash of onset; fear and rage,
And undetermined conflict – even now,
Even now, perchance, and in his native isle:
Carnage and groans beneath this blessed sun!   40
We have offended, Oh! my countrymen!
We have offended very grievously,
And been most tyrannous. From east to west
A groan of accusation pierces Heaven!
The wretched plead against us; multitudes
Countless and vehement, the sons of God,
Our brethren! Like a cloud that travels on,
Steamed up from Cairo's swamps of pestilence,
Even so, my countrymen! have we gone forth
And borne to distant tribes slavery and pangs,   50
And, deadlier far, our vices, whose deep taint
With slow perdition murders the whole man,
His body and his soul! Meanwhile, at home,
All individual dignity and power
Engulfed in Courts, Committees, Institutions,
Associations and Societies,
A vain, speech-mouthing, speech-reporting Guild,
One Benefit-Club for mutual flattery,
We have drunk up, demure as at a grace,
Pollutions from the brimming cup of wealth;   60
Contemptuous of all honourable rule,
Yet bartering freedom and the poor man's life
For gold, as at a market! The sweet words
Of Christian promise, words that even yet
Might stem destruction, were they wisely preached,
Are muttered o'er by men, whose tones proclaim
How flat and wearisome they feel their trade:
Rank scoffers some, but most too indolent
To deem them falsehoods or to know their truth.
Oh! blasphemous! the Book of Life is made   70
A superstitious instrument, on which
We gabble o'er the paths we mean to break;
For all must swear² – all and in every place,
College and wharf, council and justice-court;

All, all must swear, the briber and the bribed,
Merchant and lawyer, senator and priest,
The rich, the poor, the old man and the young;
All, all make up one scheme of perjury,
That faith doth reel; the very name of God
Sounds like a juggler's charm; and, bold with joy,   80
Forth from his dark and lonely hiding-place
(Portentous sight!), the owlet Atheism,
Sailing on obscene wings athwart the noon,
Drops his blue-fringed lids, and holds them close,
And hooting at the glorious sun in Heaven,
Cries out, 'Where is it?'
                            Thankless too for peace
(Peace long preserved by fleets and perilous seas),
Secure from actual warfare, we have loved
To swell the war-whoop, passionate for war!
Alas! for ages ignorant of all   90
Its ghastlier workings (famine or blue plague,
Battle, or siege, or flight through wintry snows),
We, this whole people, have been clamorous
For war and bloodshed; animating sports,
The which we pay for as a thing to talk of,
Spectators and not combatants! No guess
Anticipative of a wrong unfelt,
No speculation on contingency,
However dim and vague, too vague and dim
To yield a justifying cause; and forth   100
(Stuffed out with big preamble, holy names,
And adjurations of the God in Heaven)
We send our mandates for the certain death
Of thousands and ten thousands! Boys and girls,
And women, that would groan to see a child
Pull off an insect's leg, all read of war,
The best amusement for our morning meal!
The poor wretch, who has learnt his only prayers
From curses, who knows scarcely words enough
To ask a blessing from his Heavenly Father,   110
Becomes a fluent phraseman, absolute
And technical in victories and defeats,
And all our dainty terms for fratricide;

Terms which we trundle smoothly o'er our tongues
Like mere abstractions, empty sounds to which
We join no feeling and attach no form!
As if the soldier died without a wound;
As if the fibres of this godlike frame
Were gored without a pang; as if the wretch,
Who fell in battle, doing bloody deeds,   120
Passed off to Heaven, translated and not killed;
As though he had no wife to pine for him;
No God to judge him! Therefore, evil days
Are coming on us, O my countrymen!
And what if all-avenging Providence,
Strong and retributive, should make us know
The meaning of our words, force us to feel
The desolation and the agony
Of our fierce doings?
                         Spare us yet awhile,
Father and God! O! spare us yet awhile!   130
Oh! let not English women drag their flight
Fainting beneath the burthen of their babes,
Of the sweet infants, that but yesterday
Laughed at the breast! Sons, brothers, husbands, all
Who ever gazed with fondness on the forms
Which grew up with you round the same fireside,
And all who ever heard the sabbath-bells
Without the infidel's scorn, make yourselves pure!
Stand forth! be men! repel an impious foe,
Impious and false, a light yet cruel race,   140
Who laugh away all virtue, mingling mirth
With deeds of murder; and still promising
Freedom, themselves too sensual to be free,
Poison life's amities, and cheat the heart
Of faith and quiet hope, and all that soothes,
And all that lifts the spirit! Stand we forth;
Render them back upon the insulted ocean,
And let them toss as idly on its waves
As the vile seaweed, which some mountain-blast
Swept from our shores! And oh! may we return   150
Not with a drunken triumph, but with fear,
Repenting of the wrongs with which we stung

So fierce a foe to frenzy!
                          I have told,
O Britons! O my brethren! I have told
Most bitter truth, but without bitterness.
Nor deem my zeal or factious or mistimed;
For never can true courage dwell with them,
Who, playing tricks with conscience, dare not look
At their own vices. We have been too long
Dupes of a deep delusion! Some, belike,   160
Groaning with restless enmity, expect
All change from change of constituted power;
As if a Government had been a robe,
On which our vice and wretchedness were tagged
Like fancy-points and fringes, with the robe
Pulled off at pleasure. Fondly these attach
A radical causation to a few
Poor drudges of chastising Providence,
Who borrow all their hues and qualities
From our own folly and rank wickedness,   170
Which gave them birth and nursed them. Others, meanwhile,
Dote with a mad idolatry; and all
Who will not fall before their images,
And yield them worship, they are enemies
Even of their country!
                        Such have I been deemed. –
But, O dear Britain! O my Mother Isle!
Needs must thou prove a name most dear and holy
To me, a son, a brother, and a friend,
A husband, and a father! who revere
All bonds of natural love, and find them all   180
Within the limits of thy rocky shores.
O native Britain! O my Mother Isle!
How shouldst thou prove aught else but dear and holy
To me, who from thy lakes and mountain-hills,
Thy clouds, thy quiet dales, thy rocks and seas,
Have drunk in all my intellectual life,
All sweet sensations, all ennobling thoughts,
All adoration of the God in nature,
All lovely and all honourable things,
Whatever makes this mortal spirit feel   190

The joy and greatness of its future being?
There lives nor form nor feeling in my soul
Unborrowed from my country! O divine
And beauteous island! thou hast been my sole
And most magnificent temple, in the which
I walk with awe, and sing my stately songs,
Loving the God that made me! –
                                        May my fears,
My filial fears, be vain! and may the vaunts
And menace of the vengeful enemy
Pass like the gust, that roared and died away   200
In the distant tree: which heard, and only heard
In this low dell, bowed not the delicate grass.

But now the gentle dew-fall sends abroad
The fruit-like perfume of the golden furze:
The light has left the summit of the hill,
Though still a sunny gleam lies beautiful,
Aslant the ivied beacon. Now farewell,
Farewell, awhile, O soft and silent spot!
On the green sheep-track, up the heathy hill,
Homeward I wind my way; and lo! recalled   210
From bodings that have well-nigh wearied me,
I find myself upon the brow, and pause
Startled! And after lonely sojourning
In such a quiet and surrounded nook,
This burst of prospect, here the shadowy main,
Dim-tinted, there the mighty majesty
Of that huge amphitheatre of rich
And elmy fields, seems like society –
Conversing with the mind, and giving it
A livelier impulse and a dance of thought!   220
And now, beloved Stowey! I behold
Thy church-tower, and, methinks, the four huge elms
Clustering, which mark the mansion of my friend;[3]
And close behind them, hidden from my view,
Is my own lowly cottage, where my babe
And my babe's mother dwell in peace! With light
And quickened footsteps thitherward I tend,
Remembering thee, O green and silent dell!

And grateful, that by nature's quietness
And solitary musings, all my heart   230
Is softened, and made worthy to indulge
Love, and the thoughts that yearn for human kind.

Kubla Khan

OR, A VISION IN A DREAM. A FRAGMENT.

In the summer of the year 1797, the Author, then in ill health, had retired to a lonely farmhouse between Porlock and Linton, on the Exmoor confines of Somerset and Devonshire. In consequence of a slight indisposition, an anodyne had been prescribed, from the effects of which he fell asleep in his chair at the moment that he was reading the following sentence, or words of the same substance, in 'Purchas's Pilgrimage':[1] 'Here the Khan Kubla commanded a palace to be built, and a stately garden thereunto. And thus ten miles of fertile ground were inclosed with a wall.' The Author continued for about three hours in a profound sleep, at least of the external senses, during which time he has the most vivid confidence, that he could not have composed less than from two to three hundred lines; if that indeed can be called composition in which all the images rose up before him as things, with a parallel production of the correspondent expressions, without any sensation or consciousness of effort. On awaking he appeared to himself to have a distinct recollection of the whole, and taking his pen, ink, and paper, instantly and eagerly wrote down the lines that are here preserved. At this moment he was unfortunately called out by a person on business from Porlock, and detained by him above an hour, and on his return to his room, found, to his no small surprise and mortification, that though he still retained some vague and dim recollection of the general purport of the vision, yet, with the exception of some eight or ten scattered lines and images, all the rest had passed away like the images on the surface of a stream into which a stone has been cast, but, alas! without the after restoration of the latter!

> Then all the charm
> Is broken – all that phantom-world so fair
> Vanishes, and a thousand circlets spread,
> And each misshape[s] the other. Stay awhile,
> Poor youth! who scarcely dar'st lift up thine eyes –
> The stream will soon renew its smoothness, soon
> The visions will return! And lo, he stays,
> And soon the fragments dim of lovely forms
> Come trembling back, unite, and now once more
> The pool becomes a mirror.[2]

Yet from the still surviving recollections in his mind, the Author has frequently purposed to finish for himself what had been originally, as it were, given to him.

Αὔριον ἄδιον ἄσω,[3] but the tomorrow is yet to come.

As a contrast to this vision, I have annexed a fragment of a very different character, describing with equal fidelity the dream of pain and disease.

Kubla Khan[4]

In Xanadu did Kubla Khan
A stately pleasure-dome decree:
Where Alph,[5] the sacred river, ran
Through caverns measureless to man
   Down to a sunless sea.
So twice five miles of fertile ground
With walls and towers were girdled round:
And there were gardens bright with sinuous rills,
Where blossomed many an incense-bearing tree;
And here were forests ancient as the hills,   10
Enfolding sunny spots of greenery.

But oh! that deep romantic chasm which slanted
Down the green hill athwart a cedarn cover!
A savage place! as holy and enchanted
As e'er beneath a waning moon was haunted
By woman wailing for her demon-lover!

And from this chasm, with ceaseless turmoil seething,
As if this earth in fast thick pants were breathing,
A mighty fountain momently was forced:
Amid whose swift half-intermitted burst   20
Huge fragments vaulted like rebounding hail,
Or chaffy grain beneath the thresher's flail:
And 'mid these dancing rocks at once and ever
It flung up momently the sacred river.
Five miles meandering with a mazy motion
Through wood and dale the sacred river ran,
Then reached the caverns measureless to man,
And sank in tumult to a lifeless ocean:
And 'mid this tumult Kubla heard from far
Ancestral voices prophesying war!   30
   The shadow of the dome of pleasure
   Floated midway on the waves;
   Where was heard the mingled measure
   From the fountain and the caves.
It was a miracle of rare device,
A sunny pleasure-dome with caves of ice!

   A damsel with a dulcimer
   In a vision once I saw:
   It was an Abyssinian maid,
   And on her dulcimer she played,   40
   Singing of Mount Abora.[6]
   Could I revive within me
   Her symphony and song,
   To such a deep delight 'twould win me,
That with music loud and long,
I would build that dome in air,
That sunny dome! those caves of ice!
And all who heard should see them there,
And all should cry, Beware! Beware!
His flashing eyes, his floating hair!   50
Weave a circle round him thrice,
And close your eyes with holy dread,
For he on honey-dew hath fed,
And drunk the milk of Paradise.

Christabel

PREFACE[1]

The first part of the following poem was written in the year 1797, at Stowey, in the county of Somerset. The second part, after my return from Germany, in the year 1800, at Keswick, Cumberland. It is probable that if the poem had been finished at either of the former periods, or if even the first and second part had been published in the year 1800, the impression of its originality would have been much greater than I dare at present expect. But for this I have only my own indolence to blame. The dates are mentioned for the exclusive purpose of precluding charges of plagiarism or servile imitation from myself. For there is amongst us a set of critics who seem to hold that every possible thought and image is traditional; who have no notion that there are such things as fountains in the world, small as well as great; and who would therefore charitably derive every rill they behold flowing from a perforation made in some other man's tank. I am confident, however, that as far as the present poem is concerned, the celebrated poets whose writings I might be suspected of having imitated, either in particular passages, or in the tone and the spirit of the whole, would be among the first to vindicate me from the charge, and who, on any striking coincidence, would permit me to address them in this doggerel version of two monkish Latin hexameters.

> *'Tis mine and it is likewise yours;*
> *But an if this will not do;*
> *Let it be mine, good friend! for I*
> *Am the poorer of the two.*

I have only to add that the metre of Christabel is not, properly speaking, irregular, though it may seem so from its being founded on a new principle: namely, that of counting in each line the accents, not the syllables. Though the latter may vary from seven to twelve, yet in each line the accents will be found to be only four. Nevertheless, this occasional variation in number of syllables is not introduced wantonly, or for the mere ends of convenience, but in correspondence with some transition in the nature of the imagery or passion.

PART 1

'Tis the middle of night by the castle clock,
And the owls have awakened the crowing cock;
Tu – whit! – Tu – whoo!
And hark, again! the crowing cock,
How drowsily it crew.
Sir Leoline, the Baron rich,
Hath a toothless mastiff bitch;
From her kennel beneath the rock
She maketh answer to the clock,
Four for the quarters, and twelve for the hour;   10
Ever and aye, by shine and shower,
Sixteen short howls, not over loud;
Some say, she sees my lady's shroud.

Is the night chilly and dark?
The night is chilly, but not dark.
The thin grey cloud is spread on high,
It covers but not hides the sky.
The moon is behind, and at the full;
And yet she looks both small and dull.
The night is chill, the cloud is grey: 20
'Tis a month before the month of May,
And the Spring comes slowly up this way.

The lovely lady, Christabel,
Whom her father loves so well,
What makes her in the wood so late,
A furlong from the castle gate?
She had dreams all yesternight
Of her own betrothèd knight;
And she in the midnight wood will pray
For the weal² of her lover that's far away.   30

She stole along, she nothing spoke,
The sighs she heaved were soft and low,
And naught was green upon the oak
But moss and rarest misletoe:
She kneels beneath the huge oak tree,
And in silence prayeth she.

The lady sprang up suddenly,
The lovely lady, Christabel!
It moaned as near, as near can be,
But what it is she cannot tell. –   40
On the other side it seems to be,
Of the huge, broad-breasted, old oak tree.

The night is chill; the forest bare;
Is it the wind that moaneth bleak?
There is not wind enough in the air
To move away the ringlet curl
From the lovely lady's cheek –
There is not wind enough to twirl
The one red leaf, the last of its clan,
That dances as often as dance it can,   50
Hanging so light, and hanging so high,
On the topmost twig that looks up at the sky.

Hush, beating heart of Christabel!
Jesu, Maria, shield her well!
She folded her arms beneath her cloak,
And stole to the other side of the oak.
          What sees she there?

There she sees a damsel bright,
Drest in a silken robe of white,
That shadowy in the moonlight shone: 60
The neck that made that white robe wan,
Her stately neck, and arms were bare;
Her blue-veined feet unsandal'd were,
And wildly glittered here and there
The gems entangled in her hair.
I guess, 'twas frightful there to see
A lady so richly clad as she –
Beautiful exceedingly!

Mary mother,[3] save me now!
(Said Christabel), And who art thou?   70

The lady strange made answer meet,

And her voice was faint and sweet:
Have pity on my sore distress,
I scarce can speak for weariness:
Stretch forth thy hand, and have no fear!
Said Christabel, How camest thou here?
And the lady, whose voice was faint and sweet,
Did thus pursue her answer meet:

My sire is of a noble line,
And my name is Geraldine: 80
Five warriors seized me yestermorn,
Me, even me, a maid forlorn:
They choked my cries with force and fright,
And tied me on a palfrey⁴ white.
The palfrey was as fleet as wind,
And they rode furiously behind.
They spurred amain,⁵ their steeds were white:
And once we crossed the shade of night.
As sure as Heaven shall rescue me,
I have no thought what men they be;   90
Nor do I know how long it is
(For I have lain entranced I wis)⁶
Since one, the tallest of the five,
Took me from the palfrey's back,
A weary woman, scarce alive.
Some muttered words his comrades spoke:
He placed me underneath this oak;
He swore they would return with haste;
Whither they went I cannot tell –
I thought I heard, some minutes past,   100
Sounds as of a castle bell.
Stretch forth thy hand (thus ended she),
And help a wretched maid to flee.

Then Christabel stretched forth her hand,
And comforted fair Geraldine:
O well, bright dame! may you command
The service of Sir Leoline;
And gladly our stout chivalry
Will he send forth and friends withal

To guide and guard you safe and free   110
Home to your noble father's hall.

She rose: and forth with steps they passed
That strove to be, and were not, fast.
Her gracious stars the lady blest,
And thus spake on sweet Christabel:
All our household are at rest,
The hall as silent as the cell;
Sir Leoline is weak in health,
And may not well awakened be,
But we will move as if in stealth,   120
And I beseech your courtesy,
This night, to share your couch with me.

They crossed the moat, and Christabel
Took the key that fitted well;
A little door she opened straight,
All in the middle of the gate;
The gate that was ironed within and without,
Where an army in battle array had marched out.
The lady sank, belike through pain,
And Christabel with might and main   130
Lifted her up, a weary weight,
Over the threshold of the gate:
Then the lady rose again,
And moved, as she were not in pain.

So free from danger, free from fear,
They crossed the court: right glad they were.
And Christabel devoutly cried
To the lady by her side,
Praise we the Virgin all divine
Who hath rescued thee from thy distress!   140
Alas, alas! said Geraldine,
I cannot speak for weariness.
So free from danger, free from fear,
They crossed the court: right glad they were.

Outside her kennel, the mastiff old

Lay fast asleep, in moonshine cold.
The mastiff old did not awake,
Yet she an angry moan did make!
And what can ail the mastiff bitch?
Never till now she uttered yell   150
Beneath the eye of Christabel.
Perhaps it is the owlet's scritch:
For what can ail the mastiff bitch?

They passed the hall, that echoes still,
Pass as lightly as you will!
The brands were flat, the brands were dying,
Amid their own white ashes lying;
But when the lady passed, there came
A tongue of light, a fit of flame;
And Christabel saw the lady's eye,   160
And nothing else saw she thereby,
Save the boss of the shield of Sir Leoline tall,
Which hung in a murky old niche in the wall.
O softly tread, said Christabel,
My father seldom sleepeth well.

Sweet Christabel her feet doth bare,
And jealous of the listening air
They steal their way from stair to stair,
Now in glimmer, and now in gloom,
And now they pass the Baron's room,   170
As still as death, with stifled breath!
And now have reached her chamber door;
And now doth Geraldine press down
The rushes of the chamber floor.

The moon shines dim in the open air,
And not a moonbeam enters here.
But they without its light can see
The chamber carved so curiously,
Carved with figures strange and sweet,
All made out of the carver's brain,   180
For a lady's chamber meet:

The lamp with twofold silver chain
Is fastened to an angel's feet.

The silver lamp burns dead and dim;
But Christabel the lamp will trim.
She trimmed the lamp, and made it bright,
And left it swinging to and fro,
While Geraldine, in wretched plight,
Sank down upon the floor below.

O weary lady, Geraldine,   190
I pray you, drink this cordial wine!
It is a wine of virtuous powers;
My mother made it of wild flowers.

And will your mother pity me,
Who am a maiden most forlorn?
Christabel answered – Woe is me!
She died the hour that I was born.
I have heard the grey-haired friar tell
How on her death-bed she did say,
That she should hear the castle-bell   200
Strike twelve upon my wedding-day.
O mother dear! that thou wert here!
I would, said Geraldine, she were!

But soon with altered voice, said she –
'Off, wandering mother! Peak and pine!
I have power to bid thee flee.'
Alas! what ails poor Geraldine?
Why stares she with unsettled eye?
Can she the bodiless dead espy?
And why with hollow voice cries she,   210
'Off, woman, off! this hour is mine –
Though thou her guardian spirit be,
Off, woman, off! 'tis given to me.'

Then Christabel knelt by the lady's side,
And raised to heaven her eyes so blue –
Alas! said she, this ghastly ride –

Dear lady! it hath wildered you!
The lady wiped her moist cold brow,
And faintly said, ' 'Tis over now!'

Again the wild-flower wine she drank: 220
Her fair large eyes 'gan glitter bright,
And from the floor whereon she sank,
The lofty lady stood upright:
She was most beautiful to see,
Like a lady of a far countrée.

And thus the lofty lady spake –
'All they who live in the upper sky,
Do love you, holy Christabel!
And you love them, and for their sake
And for the good which me befell,   230
Even I in my degree will try,
Fair maiden, to requite you well.
But now unrobe yourself; for I
Must pray, ere yet in bed I lie.'

Quoth Christabel, So let it be!
And as the lady bade, did she.
Her gentle limbs did she undress,
And lay down in her loveliness.

But through her brain of weal and woe
So many thoughts moved to and fro,   240
That vain it were her lids to close;
So halfway from the bed she rose,
And on her elbow did recline
To look at the lady Geraldine.

Beneath the lamp the lady bowed,
And slowly rolled her eyes around;
Then drawing in her breath aloud,
Like one that shuddered, she unbound
The cincture[7] from beneath her breast:
Her silken robe, and inner vest,   250
Dropt to her feet, and full in view,

Behold! her bosom and half her side –
A sight to dream of, not to tell!
O shield her! shield sweet Christabel!

Yet Geraldine nor speaks nor stirs;
Ah! what a stricken look was hers!
Deep from within she seems halfway
To lift some weight with sick assay,
And eyes the maid and seeks delay;
Then suddenly, as one defied,   260
Collects herself in scorn and pride,
And lay down by the Maiden's side! –
And in her arms the maid she took,
                    Ah well-a-day!
And with low voice and doleful look
These words did say:
'In the touch of this bosom there worketh a spell,
Which is lord of thy utterance, Christabel!
Thou knowest tonight, and wilt know tomorrow,
This mark of my shame, this seal of my sorrow;   270
          But vainly thou warrest,
               For this is alone in
               Thy power to declare,
                    That in the dim forest
                    Thou heard'st a low moaning,
And found'st a bright lady, surpassingly fair;
And didst bring her home with thee in love and in charity,
To shield her and shelter her from the damp air.'

THE CONCLUSION TO PART 1

It was a lovely sight to see
The lady Christabel, when she   280
Was praying at the old oak tree.
          Amid the jagged shadows
          Of mossy leafless boughs,
          Kneeling in the moonlight,
          To make her gentle vows;
Her slender palms together prest,
Heaving sometimes on her breast;

Her face resigned to bliss or bale[8]
Her face, oh call it fair not pale,
And both blue eyes more bright than clear,   290
Each about to have a tear.

With open eyes (ah woe is me!)
Asleep, and dreaming fearfully,
Fearfully dreaming, yet, I wis,[9]
Dreaming that alone, which is –
O sorrow and shame! Can this be she,
The lady, who knelt at the old oak tree?
And lo! the worker of these harms,
That holds the maiden in her arms,
Seems to slumber still and mild,   300
As a mother with her child.

A star hath set, a star hath risen,
O Geraldine! since arms of thine
Have been the lovely lady's prison.
O Geraldine! one hour was thine –
Thou'st had thy will! By tairn and rill,
The night-birds all that hour were still.
But now they are jubilant anew,
From cliff and tower, tu – whoo! tu – whoo!
Tu – whoo! tu – whoo! from wood and fell!   310

And see! the lady Christabel
Gathers herself from out her trance;
Her limbs relax, her countenance
Grows sad and soft; the smooth thin lids
Close o'er her eyes; and tears she sheds –
Large tears that leave the lashes bright!
And oft the while she seems to smile
As infants at a sudden light!

Yes, she doth smile, and she doth weep,
Like a youthful hermitess,   320
Beauteous in a wilderness,
Who, praying always, prays in sleep.
And, if she move unquietly,

Perchance, 'tis but the blood so free
Comes back and tingles in her feet.
No doubt, she hath a vision sweet.
What if her guardian spirit 'twere,
What if she knew her mother near?
But this she knows, in joys and woes,
That saints will aid if men will call: 330
For the blue sky bends over all!

PART 2

Each matin bell, the Baron saith,
Knells us back to a world of death.
These words Sir Leoline first said,
When he rose and found his lady dead:
These words Sir Leoline will say
Many a morn to his dying day!

And hence the custom and law began
That still at dawn the sacristan,
Who duly pulls the heavy bell,   340
Five and forty beads must tell
Between each stroke – a warning knell,
Which not a soul can choose but hear
From Bratha Head to Wyndermere.

Saith Bracy the bard, So let it knell!
And let the drowsy sacristan
Still count as slowly as he can!
There is no lack of such, I ween,
As well fill up the space between.
In Langdale Pike and Witch's Lair,   350
And Dungeon-ghyll so foully rent,
With ropes of rock and bells of air
Three sinful sextons' ghosts are pent,
Who all give back, one after t'other,
The death-note to their living brother;
And oft too, by the knell offended,
Just as their one! two! three! is ended,

The devil mocks the doleful tale
With a merry peal from Borodale.

The air is still! through mist and cloud   360
That merry peal comes ringing loud;
And Geraldine shakes off her dread,
And rises lightly from the bed;
Puts on her silken vestments white,
And tricks her hair in lovely plight,[10]
And nothing doubting of her spell
Awakens the lady Christabel.
'Sleep you, sweet lady Christabel?
I trust that you have rested well.'

And Christabel awoke and spied   370
The same who lay down by her side –
O rather say, the same whom she
Raised up beneath the old oak tree!
Nay, fairer yet! and yet more fair!
For she belike hath drunken deep
Of all the blessedness of sleep!
And while she spake, her looks, her air
Such gentle thankfulness declare,
That (so it seemed) her girded vests
Grew tight beneath her heaving breasts.   380
'Sure I have sinn'd!' said Christabel,
'Now heaven be praised if all be well!'
And in low faltering tones, yet sweet,
Did she the lofty lady greet
With such perplexity of mind
As dreams too lively leave behind.

So quickly she rose, and quickly arrayed
Her maiden limbs, and having prayed
That He, who on the cross did groan,
Might wash away her sins unknown,   390
She forthwith led fair Geraldine
To meet her sire, Sir Leoline.

The lovely maid and the lady tall

Are pacing both into the hall,
And pacing on through page and groom,
Enter the Baron's presence-room.[11]

The Baron rose, and while he prest
His gentle daughter to his breast,
With cheerful wonder in his eyes
The lady Geraldine espies,   400
And gave such welcome to the same,
As might beseem so bright a dame!

But when he heard the lady's tale,
And when she told her father's name,
Why waxed Sir Leoline so pale,
Murmuring o'er the name again,
Lord Roland de Vaux of Tryermaine?
Alas! they had been friends in youth;
But whispering tongues can poison truth;
And constancy lives in realms above;   410
And life is thorny; and youth is vain;
And to be wroth with one we love
Doth work like madness in the brain.
And thus it chanced, as I divine,
With Roland and Sir Leoline.
Each spake words of high disdain
And insult to his heart's best brother:
They parted – ne'er to meet again!
But never either found another
To free the hollow heart from paining –   420
They stood aloof, the scars remaining,
Like cliffs which had been rent asunder;
A dreary sea now flows between; –
But neither heat, nor frost, nor thunder,
Shall wholly do away, I ween,
The marks of that which once hath been.

Sir Leoline, a moment's space,
Stood gazing on the damsel's face:
And the youthful Lord of Tryermaine
Came back upon his heart again.   430

O then the Baron forgot his age,
His noble heart swelled high with rage;
He swore by the wounds in Jesu's side
He would proclaim it far and wide,
With trump and solemn heraldry,
That they, who thus had wronged the dame,
Were base as spotted infamy!
'And if they dare deny the same,
My herald shall appoint a week,
And let the recreant traitors seek   440
My tourney court – that there and then
I may dislodge their reptile souls
From the bodies and forms of men!'
He spake: his eye in lightning rolls!
For the lady was ruthlessly seized; and he kenned[12]
In the beautiful lady the child of his friend!
And now the tears were on his face,
And fondly in his arms he took
Fair Geraldine, who met the embrace,
Prolonging it with joyous look.   450
Which when she viewed, a vision fell
Upon the soul of Christabel,
The vision of fear, the touch and pain!
She shrunk and shuddered, and saw again –
(Ah, woe is me! Was it for thee,
Thou gentle maid! such sights to see?)

Again she saw that bosom old,
Again she felt that bosom cold,
And drew in her breath with a hissing sound:
Whereat the Knight turned wildly round,   460
And nothing saw, but his own sweet maid
With eyes upraised, as one that prayed.

The touch, the sight, had passed away,
And in its stead that vision blest,
Which comforted her after-rest
While in the lady's arms she lay,
Had put a rapture in her breast,
And on her lips and o'er her eyes

Spread smiles like light!
                              With new surprise,
'What ails then my belovèd child?'   470
The Baron said – His daughter mild
Made answer, 'All will yet be well!'
I ween,[13] she had no power to tell
Aught else: so mighty was the spell.

Yet he, who saw this Geraldine,
Had deemed her sure a thing divine:
Such sorrow with such grace she blended,
As if she feared she had offended
Sweet Christabel, that gentle maid!
And with such lowly tones she prayed   480
She might be sent without delay
Home to her father's mansion.
                                       'Nay!
Nay, by my soul!' said Leoline.
'Ho! Bracy the bard, the charge be thine!
Go thou, with music sweet and loud,
And take two steeds with trappings proud,
And take the youth whom thou lov'st best
To bear thy harp, and learn thy song,
And clothe you both in solemn vest,
And over the mountains haste along,   490
Lest wandering folk, that are abroad,
Detain you on the valley road.

'And when he has crossed the Irthing flood,
My merry bard! he hastes, he hastes
Up Knorren Moor, through Halegarth Wood,
And reaches soon that castle good
Which stands and threatens Scotland's wastes.

'Bard Bracy! bard Bracy! your horses are fleet,
Ye must ride up the hall, your music so sweet,
More loud than your horses' echoing feet!   500
And loud and loud to Lord Roland call,
Thy daughter is safe in Langdale hall!
Thy beautiful daughter is safe and free –

Sir Leoline greets thee thus through me!
He bids thee come without delay
With all thy numerous array
And take thy lovely daughter home:
And he will meet thee on the way
With all his numerous array
White with their panting palfreys' foam: 510
And, by mine honour! I will say,
That I repent me of the day
When I spake words of fierce disdain
To Roland de Vaux of Tryermaine! –
– For since that evil hour hath flown,
Many a summer's sun hath shone;
Yet ne'er found I a friend again
Like Roland de Vaux of Tryermaine.'

The lady fell, and clasped his knees,
Her face upraised, her eyes o'erflowing;   520
And Bracy replied, with faltering voice,
His gracious Hail on all bestowing! –
'Thy words, thou sire of Christabel,
Are sweeter than my harp can tell;
Yet might I gain a boon[14] of thee,
This day my journey should not be,
So strange a dream hath come to me,
That I had vowed with music loud
To clear yon wood from thing unblest,
Warned by a vision in my rest!   530
For in my sleep I saw that dove,
That gentle bird, whom thou dost love,
And call'st by thy own daughter's name –
Sir Leoline! I saw the same
Fluttering, and uttering fearful moan,
Among the green herbs in the forest alone.
Which when I saw and when I heard,
I wonder'd what might ail the bird;
For nothing near it could I see,
Save the grass and green herbs underneath the old tree.   540

'And in my dream methought I went

To search out what might there be found;
And what the sweet bird's trouble meant,
That thus lay fluttering on the ground.
I went and peered, and could descry[15]
No cause for her distressful cry;
But yet for her dear lady's sake
I stooped, methought, the dove to take,
When lo! I saw a bright green snake
Coiled around its wings and neck.   550
Green as the herbs on which it couched,
Close by the dove's its head it crouched;
And with the dove it heaves and stirs,
Swelling its neck as she swelled hers!
I woke; it was the midnight hour,
The clock was echoing in the tower;
But though my slumber was gone by,
This dream it would not pass away –
It seems to live upon my eye!
And thence I vowed this self-same day   560
With music strong and saintly song
To wander through the forest bare,
Lest aught unholy loiter there.'
Thus Bracy said: the Baron, the while,
Half-listening heard him with a smile;
Then turned to Lady Geraldine,
His eyes made up of wonder and love;
And said in courtly accents fine,
'Sweet maid, Lord Roland's beauteous dove,
With arms more strong than harp or song,   570
Thy sire and I will crush the snake!'
He kissed her forehead as he spake,
And Geraldine in maiden wise
Casting down her large bright eyes,
With blushing cheek and courtesy fine
She turned her from Sir Leoline;
Softly gathering up her train,
That o'er her right arm fell again;
And folded her arms across her chest,
And couched her head upon her breast,   580

And looked askance[16] at Christabel –
Jesu, Maria, shield her well!

A snake's small eye blinks dull and shy;
And the lady's eyes they shrunk in her head,
Each shrunk up to a serpent's eye,
And with somewhat of malice, and more of dread,
At Christabel she looked askance –
One moment – and the sight was fled!
But Christabel in dizzy trance
Stumbling on the unsteady ground   590
Shuddered aloud, with a hissing sound;
And Geraldine again turned round,
And like a thing, that sought relief,
Full of wonder and full of grief,
She rolled her large bright eyes divine
Wildly on Sir Leoline.

The maid, alas! her thoughts are gone,
She nothing sees – no sight but one!
The maid, devoid of guile and sin,
I know not how, in fearful wise,   600
So deeply had she drunken in
That look, those shrunken serpent eyes,
That all her features were resigned
To this sole image in her mind:
And passively did imitate
That look of dull and treacherous hate!
And thus she stood, in dizzy trance,
Still picturing that look askance
With forced unconscious sympathy
Full before her father's view –   610
As far as such a look could be
In eyes so innocent and blue!

And when the trance was o'er, the maid
Paused awhile, and inly prayed:
Then falling at the Baron's feet,
'By my mother's soul do I entreat
That thou this woman send away!'

She said: and more she could not say:
For what she knew she could not tell,
O'er-mastered by the mighty spell.   620

Why is thy cheek so wan and wild,
Sir Leoline? Thy only child
Lies at thy feet, thy joy, thy pride,
So fair, so innocent, so mild;
The same, for whom thy lady died!
O by the pangs of her dear mother
Think thou no evil of thy child!
For her, and thee, and for no other,
She prayed the moment ere she died:
Prayed that the babe for whom she died,   630
Might prove her dear lord's joy and pride!
    That prayer her deadly pangs beguiled,
            Sir Leoline!
    And wouldst thou wrong thy only child,
            Her child and thine?

Within the Baron's heart and brain
If thoughts, like these, had any share,
They only swelled his rage and pain,
And did but work confusion there.
His heart was cleft with pain and rage,   640
His cheeks they quivered, his eyes were wild,
Dishonoured thus in his old age;
Dishonoured by his only child,
And all his hospitality
To the wronged daughter of his friend
By more than woman's jealousy
Brought thus to a disgraceful end –
He rolled his eye with stern regard
Upon the gentle minstrel bard,
And said in tones abrupt, austere –   650
'Why, Bracy! dost thou loiter here?
I bade thee hence!' The bard obeyed;
And turning from his own sweet maid,
The agèd knight, Sir Leoline,
Led forth the lady Geraldine!

THE CONCLUSION TO PART II[17]

A little child, a limber elf,
Singing, dancing to itself,
A fairy thing with red round cheeks,
That always finds, and never seeks,
Makes such a vision to the sight   660
As fills a father's eyes with light;
And pleasures flow in so thick and fast
Upon his heart, that he at last
Must needs express his love's excess
With words of unmeant bitterness.
Perhaps 'tis pretty to force together
Thoughts so all unlike each other;
To mutter and mock a broken charm,
To dally with wrong that does no harm.
Perhaps 'tis tender too and pretty   670
At each wild word to feel within

A sweet recoil of love and pity.
And what if, in a world of sin
(O sorrow and shame should this be true!),
Such giddiness of heart and brain
Comes seldom save from rage and pain,
So talks as it's most used to do.

Dejection: An Ode

Late, late yestreen I saw the new Moon,
With the old Moon in her arms;
And I fear, I fear, my Master dear!
We shall have a deadly storm.
                    Ballad of Sir Patrick Spence[1]

1

Well! If the Bard was weather-wise, who made
  The grand old ballad of Sir Patrick Spence,
This night, so tranquil now, will not go hence
Unroused by winds, that ply a busier trade
Than those which mould yon cloud in lazy flakes,
Or the dull sobbing draft, that moans and rakes
Upon the strings of this Aeolian lute,[2]
    Which better far were mute.
  For lo! the New-moon winter-bright!
  And overspread with phantom light   10
  (With swimming phantom light o'erspread
  But rimmed and circled by a silver thread),
Is the old Moon in her lap, foretelling
  The coming-on of rain and squally blast.
And oh! that even now the gust were swelling,
  And the slant night-shower driving loud and fast!
Those sounds which oft have raised me, whilst they awed,
    And sent my soul abroad,
Might now perhaps their wonted impulse give,
Might startle this dull pain, and make it move and live!   20

2

A grief without a pang, void, dark, and drear,
  A stifled, drowsy, unimpassioned grief,
  Which finds no natural outlet, no relief,
    In word, or sigh, or tear –
O Lady![3] in this wan and heartless mood,
To other thoughts by yonder throstle woo'd,
  All this long eve, so balmy and serene,
Have I been gazing on the western sky,

    And its peculiar tint of yellow green:
And still I gaze – and with how blank an eye!   30
And those thin clouds above, in flakes and bars,
That give away their motion to the stars;
Those stars, that glide behind them or between,
Now sparkling, now bedimmed, but always seen:
Yon crescent Moon, as fixed as if it grew
In its own cloudless, starless lake of blue;
I see them all so excellently fair,
I see, not feel, how beautiful they are!

3

    My genial spirits fail;
    And what can these avail   40
To lift the smothering weight from off my breast?
    It were a vain endeavour,
    Though I should gaze for ever
On that green light that lingers in the west:
I may not hope from outward forms to win
The passion and the life, whose fountains are within.

4

O Lady! we receive but what we give,
And in our life alone does Nature live:
Ours is her wedding garment, ours her shroud!
    And would we aught behold, of higher worth,   50
Than that inanimate cold world allowed
To the poor loveless ever-anxious crowd,
    Ah! from the soul itself must issue forth
A light, a glory, a fair luminous cloud
    Enveloping the Earth –
And from the soul itself must there be sent
    A sweet and potent voice, of its own birth,
Of all sweet sounds the life and element!

5

O pure of heart! thou need'st not ask of me
What this strong music in the soul may be!   60
What, and wherein it doth exist,
This light, this glory, this fair luminous mist,

This beautiful and beauty-making power.
   Joy, virtuous Lady! Joy that ne'er was given,
Save to the pure, and in their purest hour,
Life, and Life's effluence, cloud at once and shower,
Joy, Lady! is the spirit and the power,
Which wedding Nature to us gives in dower
   A new Earth and new Heaven,
Undreamt of by the sensual and the proud –   70
Joy is the sweet voice, Joy the luminous cloud –
    We in ourselves rejoice!
And thence flows all that charms or ear or sight,
   All melodies the echoes of that voice,
All colours a suffusion from that light.

6

There was a time when, though my path was rough,
   This joy within me dallied with distress,
And all misfortunes were but as the stuff
   Whence Fancy made me dreams of happiness:
For hope grew round me, like the twining vine,   80
And fruits, and foliage, not my own, seemed mine.
But now afflictions bow me down to earth:
Nor care I that they rob me of my mirth;
   But oh! each visitation
Suspends what nature gave me at my birth,
   My shaping spirit of Imagination.
For not to think of what I needs must feel,
   But to be still and patient, all I can;
And haply by abstruse research to steal
   From my own nature all the natural man –   90
   This was my sole resource, my only plan:
Till that which suits a part infects the whole,
And now is almost grown the habit of my soul.

7

Hence, viper thoughts, that coil around my mind,
    Reality's dark dream!
turn from you, and listen to the wind,
   Which long has raved unnoticed. What a scream
Of agony by torture lengthened out

That lute sent forth! Thou Wind, that rav'st without,
   Bare crag, or mountain-tairn, or blasted tree, 100
Or pine-grove whither woodman never clomb,
Or lonely house, long held the witches' home,
   Methinks were fitter instruments for thee,
Mad Lutanist! who in this month of showers,
Of dark-brown gardens, and of peeping flowers,
Mak'st Devils' yule, with worse than wintry song,
The blossoms, buds, and timorous leaves among.
   Thou Actor, perfect in all tragic sounds!
Thou mighty Poet, e'en to frenzy bold!
     What tell'st thou now about? 110
     'Tis of the rushing of an host in rout,
  With groans, of trampled men, with smarting wounds –
At once they groan with pain, and shudder with the cold!
But hush! there is a pause of deepest silence!
   And all that noise, as of a rushing crowd,
With groans, and tremulous shudderings – all is over –
   It tells another tale, with sounds less deep and loud!
     A tale of less affright,
     And tempered with delight,
As Otway's self[4] had framed the tender lay, – 120
     'Tis of a little child
     Upon a lonesome wild,
Not far from home, but she hath lost her way:
And now moans low in bitter grief and fear,
And now screams loud, and hopes to make her mother hear.

8

'Tis midnight, but small thoughts have I of sleep:
Full seldom may my friend such vigils keep!
Visit her, gentle Sleep! with wings of healing,
   And may this storm be but a mountain-birth,
May all the stars hang bright above her dwelling, 130
   Silent as though they watched the sleeping Earth!
     With light heart may she rise,
     Gay fancy, cheerful eyes,
   Joy lift her spirit, joy attune her voice;
To her may all things live, from pole to pole,
Their life the eddying of her living soul!

O simple spirit, guided from above,
Dear Lady! friend devoutest of my choice,
Thus mayest thou ever, evermore rejoice.

Hymn before Sunrise, in the Vale of Chamouni [1]

Besides the Rivers Arve and Arveiron, which have their sources in the foot of Mont Blanc, five conspicuous torrents rush down its sides; and within a few paces of the Glaciers, the Gentiana Major *grows in immense numbers, with its 'flowers of loveliest blue'.*

Hast thou a charm to stay the morning-star
In his steep course? So long he seems to pause
On thy bald awful head. O sovran BLANC,
The Arve and Arveiron [2] at thy base
Rave ceaselessly; but thou, most awful Form!
Risest from forth thy silent sea of pines,
How silently! Around thee and above
Deep is the air and dark, substantial, black,
An ebon mass: methinks thou piercest it,
As with a wedge! But when I look again,   10
It is thine own calm home, thy crystal shrine,
Thy habitation from eternity!
O dread and silent Mount! I gazed upon thee,
Till thou, still present to the bodily sense,
Didst vanish from my thought: entranced in prayer
I worshipped the Invisible alone.

Yet, like some sweet beguiling melody,
So sweet, we know not we are listening to it,
Thou, the meanwhile, wast blending with my Thought,
Yea, with my Life and Life's own secret joy: 20
Till the dilating Soul, enrapt, transfused,
Into the mighty vision passing – there
As in her natural form, swelled vast to Heaven!

Awake, my soul! not only passive praise
Thou owest! not alone these swelling tears,
Mute thanks and secret ecstasy! Awake,
Voice of sweet song! Awake, my Heart, awake!
Green vales and icy cliffs, all join my Hymn.

Thou first and chief, sole sovereign of the Vale!
O struggling with the darkness all the night,   30
And visited all night by troops of stars,
Or when they climb the sky or when they sink:
Companion of the morning-star at dawn,
Thyself Earth's rosy star, and of the dawn
Co-herald: wake, O wake, and utter praise!
Who sank thy sunless pillars deep in Earth?
Who filled thy countenance with rosy light?
Who made thee parent of perpetual streams?

And you, ye five wild torrents fiercely glad!
Who called you forth from night and utter death,   40
From dark and icy caverns called you forth,
Down those precipitous, black, jaggèd rocks,
For ever shattered and the same for ever?
Who gave you your invulnerable life,
Your strength, your speed, your fury, and your joy,
Unceasing thunder and eternal foam?
And who commanded (and the silence came),
Here let the billows stiffen, and have rest?

Ye Ice-falls! ye that from the mountain's brow
Adown enormous ravines slope amain –   50
Torrents, methinks, that heard a mighty voice,
And stopped at once amid their maddest plunge!
Motionless torrents! silent cataracts!
Who made you glorious as the Gates of Heaven
Beneath the keen full moon? Who bade the sun
Clothe you with rainbows? Who, with living flowers
Of loveliest blue, spread garlands at your feet? –
GOD! let the torrents, like a shout of nations,
Answer! and let the ice-plains echo, GOD!
GOD! sing ye meadow-streams with gladsome voice!   60

Ye pine-groves, with your soft and soul-like sounds!
And they too have a voice, yon piles of snow,
And in their perilous fall shall thunder, GOD!

Ye living flowers that skirt the eternal frost!
Ye wild goats sporting round the eagle's nest!
Ye eagles, playmates of the mountain-storm!
Ye lightnings, the dread arrows of the clouds!
Ye signs and wonders of the element!
Utter forth GOD, and fill the hills with praise!

Thou too, hoar Mount! with thy sky-pointing peaks,   70
Oft from whose feet the avalanche, unheard,
Shoots downward, glittering through the pure serene
Into the depth of clouds, that veil thy breast –
Thou too again, stupendous Mountain! thou
That as I raise my head, awhile bowed low
In adoration, upward from thy base
Slow travelling with dim eyes suffused with tears,
Solemnly seemest, like a vapoury cloud,
To rise before me – Rise, O ever rise,

Rise like a cloud of incense, from the Earth!   80
Thou kingly Spirit throned among the hills,
Thou dread ambassador from Earth to Heaven,
Great Hierarch![3] tell thou the silent sky,
And tell the stars, and tell yon rising sun,
Earth, with her thousand voices, praises GOD!

Answer to a Child's Question

Do you ask what the birds say? The Sparrow, the Dove,
The Linnet and Thrush say, 'I love and I love!'
In the winter they're silent – the wind is so strong;
What it says, I don't know, but it sings a loud song.
But green leaves, and blossoms, and sunny warm weather,
And singing, and loving – all come back together.
But the Lark is so brimful of gladness and love,
The green fields below him, the blue sky above,
That he sings, and he sings; and for ever sings he –
'I love my Love, and my Love loves me!'   10

The Pains of Sleep

Ere on my bed my limbs I lay,
It hath not been my use to pray
With moving lips or bended knees;
But silently, by slow degrees,
My spirit I to Love compose,
In humble trust mine eyelids close,
With reverential resignation,
No wish conceived, no thought exprest,
Only a sense of supplication;
A sense o'er all my soul imprest   10
That I am weak, yet not unblest,
Since in me, round me, everywhere
Eternal Strength and Wisdom are.

But yesternight I prayed aloud
In anguish and in agony,
Up-starting from the fiendish crowd
Of shapes and thoughts that tortured me:
A lurid light, a trampling throng,
Sense of intolerable wrong,
And whom I scorned, those only strong!   20

Thirst of revenge, the powerless will
Still baffled, and yet burning still!
Desire with loathing strangely mixed
On wild or hateful objects fixed.
Fantastic passions! maddening brawl!
And shame and terror over all!
Deeds to be hid which were not hid,
Which all confused I could not know
Whether I suffered, or I did:
For all seemed guilt, remorse or woe,   30
My own or others still the same
Life-stifling fear, soul-stifling shame.

So two nights passed: the night's dismay
Saddened and stunned the coming day.
Sleep, the wide blessing, seemed to me
Distemper's worst calamity.
The third night, when my own loud scream
Had waked me from the fiendish dream,
O'ercome with sufferings strange and wild,
I wept as I had been a child;   40
And having thus by tears subdued
My anguish to a milder mood,
Such punishments, I said, were due
To natures deepliest stained with sin, –
For aye entempesting anew
The unfathomable hell within,
The horror of their deeds to view,
To know and loathe, yet wish and do!

Such griefs with such men well agree,
But wherefore, wherefore fall on me?   50
To be beloved is all I need,
And whom I love, I love indeed.

To William Wordsworth

*Composed on the night after his recitation of a poem
on the growth of an individual mind*[1]

Friend of the wise! and Teacher of the Good!
Into my heart have I received that Lay
More than historic, that prophetic Lay
Wherein (high theme by thee first sung aright)
Of the foundations and the building up
Of a Human Spirit thou hast dared to tell
What may be told, to the understanding mind
Revealable; and what within the mind
By vital breathings secret as the soul
Of vernal growth, oft quickens in the heart   10
Thoughts all too deep for words! –
                              Theme hard as high!
Of smiles spontaneous, and mysterious fears
(The first-born they of Reason and twin-birth),
Of tides obedient to external force,
And currents self-determined, as might seem,
Or by some inner Power; of moments awful,
Now in thy inner life, and now abroad,
When power streamed from thee, and thy soul received
The light reflected, as a light bestowed –
Of fancies fair, and milder hours of youth,   20
Hyblean[2] murmurs of poetic thought
Industrious in its joy, in vales and glens
Native or outland, lakes and famous hills!
Or on the lonely high-road, when the stars
Were rising; or by secret mountain-streams,
The guides and the companions of thy way!

Of more than Fancy, of the Social Sense
Distending wide, and man beloved as man,
Where France in all her towns lay vibrating
Like some becalmèd bark beneath the burst   30
Of Heaven's immediate thunder, when no cloud
Is visible, or shadow on the main.
For thou wert there,[3] thine own brows garlanded,

Amid the tremor of a realm aglow,
Amid a mighty nation jubilant.
When from the general heart of human kind
Hope sprang forth like a full-born Deity!
 – Of that dear Hope afflicted and struck down,
So summoned homeward, thenceforth calm and sure
From the dread watchtower of man's absolute self,   40
With light unwaning on her eyes, to look
Far on – herself a glory to behold,
The Angel of the vision! Then (last strain)
Of Duty, chosen Laws controlling choice,
Action and joy! – An Orphic song[4] indeed,
A song divine of high and passionate thoughts
To their own music chaunted!
                              O great Bard![5]
Ere yet that last strain dying awed the air,
With stedfast eye I viewed thee in the choir
Of ever-enduring men. The truly great   50
Have all one age, and from one visible space
Shed influence! They, both in power and act,
Are permanent, and Time is not with them,
Save as it worketh for them, they in it.
Nor less a sacred Roll, than those of old,
And to be placed, as they, with gradual fame
Among the archives of mankind, thy work
Makes audible a linkèd lay of Truth,
Of Truth profound a sweet continuous lay,
Not learnt, but native, her own natural notes!   60
Ah! as I listened with a heart forlorn,
The pulses of my being beat anew:
And even as Life returns upon the drowned,
Life's joy rekindling roused a throng of pains –
Keen pangs of Love, awakening as a babe
Turbulent, with an outcry in the heart;
And fears self-willed, that shunned the eye of Hope;
And Hope that scarce would know itself from Fear;
Sense of past Youth, and Manhood come in vain,
And Genius given, and Knowledge won in vain;   70
And all which I had culled in wood-walks wild,
And all which patient toil had reared, and all,

Commune with thee had opened out – but flowers
Strewed on my corse, and borne upon my bier
In the same coffin, for the self-same grave!

    That way no more! and ill beseems it me,
Who came a welcomer in herald's guise,
Singing of Glory, and Futurity,
To wander back on such unhealthful road,
Plucking the poisons of self-harm! And ill   80
Such intertwine beseems triumphal wreaths
Strew'd before thy advancing!
                              Nor do thou,
Sage Bard! impair the memory of that hour
Of thy communion with my nobler mind
By pity or grief, already felt too long!
Nor let my words import more blame than needs.
The tumult rose and ceased: for Peace is nigh
Where Wisdom's voice has found a listening heart.
Amid the howl of more than wintry storms,
The Halcyon hears the voice of vernal hours[6]   90
Already on the wing.
                        Eve following eve,
Dear tranquil time, when the sweet sense of Home
Is sweetest! moments for their own sake hailed
And more desired, more precious, for thy song,
In silence listening, like a devout child,
My soul lay passive, by thy various strain
Driven as in surges now beneath the stars,
With momentary stars of my own birth,
Fair constellated foam,[7] still darting off
Into the darkness; now a tranquil sea,   100
Outspread and bright, yet swelling to the moon.

And when – O Friend! my comforter and guide!
Strong in thyself, and powerful to give strength! –
Thy long sustained Song finally closed,
And thy deep voice had ceased – yet them thyself
Wert still before my eyes, and round us both
That happy vision of belovèd faces –
Scarce conscious, and yet conscious of its close

I sate, my being blended in one thought
(Thought was it? or aspiration? or resolve?)   110
Absorbed, yet hanging still upon the sound –
And when I rose, I found myself in prayer.

Work Without Hope

Lines composed 21 February 1825

All Nature seems at work. Slugs leave their lair –
The bees are stirring – birds are on the wing –
And Winter slumbering in the open air,
Wears on his smiling face a dream of Spring!
And I the while, the sole unbusy thing,
Nor honey make, nor pair, nor build, nor sing.

   Yet well I ken the banks where amaranths[1] blow,
Have traced the fount whence streams of nectar flow.
Bloom, O ye amaranths! bloom for whom ye may,
For me ye bloom not! Glide, rich streams, away!   10
With lips unbrightened, wreathless brow, I stroll:
And would you learn the spells that drowse my soul?
Work without Hope draws nectar in a sieve,
And Hope without an object cannot live.

Notes

A note on the texts used in this edition

The text of *Lyrical Ballads* (1798) – except that of 'The Rime of the Ancient Mariner' – and of the poems and Preface from the edition of 1800 are those of the first editions. The text of Wordsworth's other poems is that of Wordsworth's last edition of his poems, 1849–50, except that of 'The Ruined Cottage', which is from the MSS of 1798–9. The text of 'The Rime of the Ancient Mariner', and of Coleridge's poems other than the rest in *Lyrical Ballads*, is that of *The Poems of Samuel Taylor Coleridge*, edited by E. H. Coleridge, 1912, which follows the last edition (1834) published in Coleridge's lifetime. Spelling and punctuation have been sparingly modernised where the practice of the copy-texts might be distracting or unclear.

Abbreviations used in the Notes

The dates in brackets after the titles of the poems are those of composition. W = Wordsworth; C = Coleridge; IF = Notes dictated by Wordsworth to Isabella Fenwick in 1843; *OED* = Oxford English Dictionary; *c.* = circa. MS(S) = Manuscript(s)

WILLIAM WORDSWORTH

I **Advertisement to *Lyrical Ballads*** (1798)   pp. 3–4

1 *gaudiness . . . writers* writers like Thomas Gray (one of whose sonnets W discusses in his Preface of 1800, see p. 11 and Note 7, p. 290, below). Coleridge had also parodied this phraseology in *The Monthly Magazine*, November 1797, e.g.,

> Mine eye perus'd
> With tearful vacancy the *dampy* grass
> Which wept and glittered in the paly ray . . .

2 *those . . . passions* W probably had in mind a writer like Robert Burns (1759–96), of whose poetry W wrote: 'Everywhere you have the presence of human life' (*Early Letters,* p. 322).

3 *Sir Joshua Reynolds . . . composition* Sir Joshua Reynolds (1723–92), artist and art critic, discussed this in his *Discourses*, Vol. XII (ed. R. Wark, San Marino [Huntingdon Library Press, 1959, p. 219]).

4 *Goody Blake . . . Warwickshire* W took the story from Erasmus Darwin's *Zoonomia* (1794–6), a study of the laws of organic life.

5 *elder poets* W is probably thinking of the old ballad writers, as collected for example in Percy's *Reliques of Ancient English Poetry* (1765).

6 *friend* traditionally supposed to have been Hazlitt

II Preface to *Lyrical Ballads* (1800/1802)   pp. 5–25

1 *Preface . . . Poems* Wordsworth first published his Preface in the second edition of *Lyrical Ballads* (1800). In the third edition (1802), to the same Preface (with a few changes) he added a substantial passage (pp. 12–18; see Notes 13 and 19 below), which includes the celebrated discussion of the nature of the poet and poetry (beginning, 'What is a poet? To whom does he address himself?'). The text here is that of the 1802 edition.

2 *Friend* Coleridge

3 *Love* This poem was not included in the first edition of *Lyrical Ballads*, and is not included in the present edition.

4 *several of my Friends* This seems to refer mainly, again, to Coleridge, but may also refer to other friends like Charles Lamb.

5 *the age of Catullus . . . that of Statius or Claudian* Catullus (*c*.84–*c*.54BC), Terence (*c*.190–159BC) and Lucretius (99–55BC) were citizens of Rome when it was a Republic. Statius (AD45–96) and Claudian (writing *c*.AD95–404) were poets of Rome in two of its imperial phases. Michael Mason points out that Statius' poetry 'was noted for its stylistic inflatedness'. The language of the earlier period was plainer and more colloquial.

6 *the age of Shakespeare . . . and that of Donne . . . or Pope* The dramatic poetry of William Shakespeare (1564–1616), Francis Beaumont (1584–1616) and John Fletcher (1579–1625) is contrasted here with the complex 'metaphysical' styles of John Donne (1572–1631) and Abraham Cowley (1618–67), and the polished and 'polite' styles of John Dryden (1631–1700) and Alexander Pope (1688–1744).

7 *many modern writers* W probably has in mind writers like Thomas Gray (1716–71), whose 'Sonnet on the Death of Richard West' he criticises later in the Preface (p. 11), and William Collins (1721–59); both these poets were often notable for what W saw as an artificial poetic diction.

8 *great national events* probably the events of Britain's war with France. See also Coleridge's 'France: An Ode' (p. 244 and Note 2, p. 305) and 'Fears in Solitude' (p. 247 and Note 1, p. 305).

9 *sickly and stupid German tragedies* W probably has in mind those of August von Kotzbue (1761–1819). Many of Kotzbue's plays (like his comedy *Lovers' Vows*, translated by Mrs Inchbald, which features in Jane Austen's *Mansfield Park*, 1814) were popular in England in translation.

10 *composition of Gray* See Note 7, above.

11 *'such as Angels weep'* John Milton (1608–74), *Paradise Lost*, I, l. 620

12 *celestial Ichor* mythical fluid which was the equivalent of blood in the veins of the Greek gods

13 *the language . . . recommending* The passage (pp. 12–18) added in 1802 begins here.

14 *a man . . . men* See Introduction, footnote 37, p. xxx.

15 *Frontiniac* a sweet white wine

16 *Aristotle . . . writing* This slightly changes the dictum of the Greek philosopher Aristotle (384–322BC) in his *Poetics*, where he says that poetry is more philosophic than history.

17 *Man* Cf. Note 14, above.

18 *'that he looks before and after'* adapted from *Hamlet*, 4, 4, 37

19 *as . . . Reader* The passage (pp. 12–18) added in 1802 ends here.

20 *poems . . . extant* W is probably referring to traditional ballads like those in Thomas Percy's *Reliques of Ancient English Poetry* (1765).

21 *Clarissa Harlowe . . . the Gamester* The former is the novel by Samuel Richardson (1689–1761) published in 1747–8; the latter a tragedy by Edward Moore (1712–57), published in 1753.

22 *Dr Johnson's stanza* These lines by Samuel Johnson (1709–84) appeared (with slightly different wording) in *The London Magazine,* April 1785, p. 284.

23 *'Babes in the Wood'* an anonymous traditional poem. The stanza here appears in a pamphlet of 1800; a slightly different version appears in 'The Children in the Wood', in Percy's *Reliques* (see Note 20, above).

24 *Sir Joshua Reynolds* painter and critic (1723–92); see, for instance, *Works* (1798), xvii–xviii, or III, p. 136.

III   *Lyrical Ballads* (1798)

Lines Left upon a Seat in a Yew-Tree (1797)   p. 27

1 *Lake of Esthwaite* near Hawkshead (where W went to school), in Westmoreland

The Female Vagrant (1793–4 or earlier)   p. 29
1 *Derwent's side*   the shores of Derwentwater, a lake in Westmoreland
2 *rue*   regret the loss of, long for
3 *the western world*   America. The war described in lines 124–6 and 149–
   53 is the American War of Independence (1775–83).
4 *devoted*   doomed (*OED*, sense 3)

Goody Blake, and Harry Gill (1798)   p. 37
1 *drover*   driver of droves (of cattle) to market; cattle-dealer
2 *canty*   lively, brisk, cheerful
3 *rout*   disturbance, uproar

Lines Written at a Small Distance from My House (1798)   p. 41
1 *House ... little boy ... person ...*   The house was at Alfoxden in
   Somerset; the little boy was the son of W's friend, Basil Montagu; the
   person W's sister, Dorothy.

Simon Lee (1798)   p. 43
1 *Simon Lee* 'This old man had been huntsman to the Squires of
   Alfoxden' (IF)
2 *Cardigan*   a county in Wales
3 *Ivor Hall*   This name may be taken from the ruins of a hall in
   Monmouthshire.
4 *He dearly loves their voices* 'The expression when the hounds were out,
   "I dearly love their voice," was word for word from his own lips.' (IF)

Anecdote for Fathers (1798)   p. 46
1 *boy*   The boy was Basil Montagu's son and the conversation took place
   in Alfoxden.
2 *Kilve*   a village on the Bristol Channel, near Alfoxden
3 *Liswyn farm* 'a beautiful spot on the River Wye' (IF). Kilve and Liswyn
   Farm may also stand for Alfoxden and Racedown, where W lived at
   different times.

We Are Seven (1798)   p. 48
1   *dear ... Jim*   In editions from 1815, W changed the first line to the
   more meditative (and surely more effective) half-line ' – A simple child',
   the version which is usually printed in editions of W's poems. The
   version here, with the phrase 'dear brother Jim', presumably aims at a
   more chattily conversational opening. W in his IF note says that the first

stanza, with the line 'A little child, dear brother Jem' (containing a joking allusion to a friend, James Tobin), was suggested by Coleridge.

Lines Written in Early Spring (1798)   p. 51

The Thorn (1798)   p. 52
1 *The Thorn* W said that this poem 'arose out of my observing, on the ridge of Quantock Hill, on a stormy day, a thorn which I had often passed in calm and bright weather without noticing it. I said to myself, "Cannot I by some invention do as much to make this thorn permanently an impressive object as the storm has made it to my eyes at this moment?" I began the poem accordingly, and composed it with great rapidity' (IF). In the Advertisement to the first edition of *Lyrical Ballads*, W said he felt he should have made it clear, in an introductory poem, that this poem is spoken by a dramatic narrator who is other than the poet. In an end-of-volume note to the 1800 edition he gave as an example a retired sea-captain who is loquacious and superstitious. This was presumably meant to explain the speaker's obsession with the topic and his repetitiousness; but the character of the speaker is not otherwise apparent in the poem as it stands, and it is doubtful if the idea improves the poem. In editions from 1815, Wordsworth set the first speaker's narrative (as well as the interjections of the imagined listener) within quotation marks (repeated at the beginning of each stanza).

The Last of the Flock (1798)   p. 60
1 *They ... man* The Speenhamland system of parish relief had been introduced in 1795: its drawback was that relief was only given to those who had no property, so that needy land-owning farmers or sheep-owners could not benefit by it.

The Mad Mother (1798)   p. 63

The Idiot Boy (1798)   p. 66
1 *The Idiot Boy* W commented to IF: 'I never wrote anything with so much glee.' He wrote a critical account of the poem in a letter to John Wilson, 7 June 1802.
2 *hurly-burly* commotion, uproar
3 *porringer* bowl
4 *hob nob* in close companionship (*OED*, sense 3b)
5 *indentures* contracts binding apprentices to masters
6 *betimes abroad* out early in the morning

Lines Written near Richmond (1798)   p. 80
1 *Collins's Ode . . . Thomson*   William Collins (1721–59); James Thomson,
   poet (1700–48)

Expostulation and Reply (1798)   p. 82
1 *Esthwaite lake*   See 'Lines Left upon a Seat in a Yew Tree', Note 1, p. 291.
2 *Matthew*   a fictional name. See 'If Nature . . . ', Note 3, p. 296. Compare
   other 'Matthew' poems: 'If Nature, for a Favourite Child', 'The Two
   April Mornings' and 'The Fountain, A Conversation'.

The Tables Turned (1798)   p. 83

Old Man Travelling (between 1795 and 1798)   p. 84
1 *Old Man Travelling*   W recalled to IF that these lines were an 'overflowing'
   from 'The Old Cumberland Beggar' (see p. 145).
2 *Falmouth*   a port in Cornwall

The Complaint of a Forsaken Indian Woman (1798)   p. 85
1 *Hearne's Journey*   Samuel Hearne's *A Journey from Prince of Wales's Fort
   in Hudson's Bay to the Northern Ocean . . . 1769–1772* (London 1795)

The Convict (?1793)   p. 88
1 *The Convict*   The poem was influenced by the penal theories of William
   Godwin (1756–1836). It was not reprinted after 1798.

Lines Written a Few Miles above Tintern Abbey (1798)   p. 90
1 *tour*   Wordsworth recalled to IF that the poem was composed during 'a
   ramble of 4 or 5 days' with his sister Dorothy up the Wye valley from
   Bristol.
2 *line of Young*   Edward Young (1683–1765); the line echoes Young's *Night
   Thoughts,* VI, l. 427, 'And half create the wondrous worlds they see.'
3 *my dearest Friend*   the 'Sister' of line 122, Dorothy Wordsworth

IV   *The Ruined Cottage* (1798–9, revised 1802–3); first published with
further revisions in the first book of *The Excursion* (1814), Book I, lines
453–970.   p. 95
1 *Armytage*   a fictional character, similar to the 'Matthew' of the Matthew
   poems (see Note 3 to 'If Nature, for a Favourite Child', p. 296, below).
   In the text of this story in Book I of *The Excursion* he becomes 'the
   Wanderer'.
2 [   ] *wall*   The gap in the text here and at line 403 are those of the MSS
   of 1798–9.

3 *"trotting brooks"* quotation from Burns's 'To W. S****' [Simpson], *Ochiltree,* Stanza xv, l. 3

V   from *Lyrical Ballads* (1800)

Hart-Leap Well (1800)   p. 109
1 *Swale . . . Ure*   The rivers Swale and Ure flow through North Yorkshire

There was a Boy (1798)   p. 115
1 *a Boy*   A first-person version of this poem, in one of W's manuscripts, suggests that the boy was at least partly W himself. The lines also appear, with some changes and excluding lines 26–32, in W's autobiographical poem *The Prelude* (1805), V, ll. 389–413.

The Brothers (1799)   p. 116
1 *Ennerdale*   in Cumberland.
2 *How . . . last?*   The story that follows is based on two real-life accidents which took place near Ennerdale.

Strange Fits of Passion . . . (1799)   p. 130
1 *Lucy's*   Lucy seems to be primarily a fictional figure, though critics have related her, variously, to Dorothy Wordsworth, Mary Hutchinson (W's wife), Annette Vallon (with whom W had a love affair in France in 1791–2) and others. 'Lucy' is also the subject of the next poem ('Song') and 'Three Years She Grew . . . ' (p. 143), and 'A Slumber Did My Spirit Seal' (p. 131) is usually taken to be one of the same group. See also Note 1 to the latter poem, below.

Song (She dwelt among th'untrodden ways) (1799)   p. 131
1 *springs of Dove*   W knew a River Dove in Derbyshire, in Yorkshire and in Westmoreland. But the phrase sounds both actual and romantic.
2 *Lucy*   See 'Strange Fits of Passion', Note 1, above.

A Slumber Did My Spirit Seal (1799)   p. 131
1 *She*   Coleridge commented on what he called this 'sublime epitaph': 'Whether it had any reality I cannot say. – Most probably, in some gloomier moment he [W] had fancied the moment in which his Sister might die.' But we do not need to try to identify the figure to understand and respond to this great poem. (See Introduction, p. xviii.)

Lucy Gray (1799)   p. 132
1 *Lucy Gray*   Some commentators associate this Lucy with that of the

preceding 'Lucy' poems ('Strange Fits of Passion', 'Song' and 'A Slumber Did My Spirit Seal'), but the mode of the poem is more that of an 'objective' narrative ballad than a subjective lyric and most critics see it as distinct from the others.

Poor Susan (1797)   p. 134

1 *Wood Street* a street in London (cf. *Lothbury* and *Cheapside* in lines 7 and 8)

If Nature, for a Favourite Child (1799)   p. 135

1 *If Nature . . .* In editions of this poem from 1836 it is given the title of 'Matthew'.

2 *In the School of* — In his comments to IF, W identified this as Hawkshead School, where he himself was a pupil.

3 *Matthew's name* W later commented: 'This and other poems connected with Matthew would not gain by a literal detail of facts. Like the Wanderer in the Excursion, this Schoolmaster was made up of several of both of his class & men of other occupations. I do not ask pardon for what there is of untruth in such verses, considered strictly as matters of fact. It is enough if, being true and consistent in spirit, they move and teach in a manner not unworthy of a poet's calling' (IF).

The Two April Mornings (1799)   p. 137

1 *Matthew* See 'If Nature, for a Favourite Child', Note 3, above.

2 *Derwent's wave* Derwentwater, near Keswick in Cumberland

The Fountain (1799)   p. 139

1 *Matthew* See 'If Nature, for a Favourite Child', Note 3, above.

2 *Border-song* a song of the Scottish or Welsh border

Nutting (1798)   p. 141

1 *Dame* Ann Tyson, with whom Wordsworth stayed while attending Hawkshead School

Three Years She Grew (1799)   p. 143

1 *Lucy* See 'Strange fits of passion . . . ', note 1, p. 408.

The Old Cumberland Beggar (1797)   p. 145

1 *Statesmen!* W commented to IF: 'The political economists were about that time beginning their war upon mendicity in all its forms & by implication, if not directly, on Alms-giving also. This heartless process has been carried as far as it can go by the AMENDED poor-law bill [of 1834] . . . '

2 *Decalogue* the Ten Commandments (Exodus 20:3–17)

3 *charter'd* unrestrained

A Poet's Epitaph (1799)   p. 151

1 *man . . . cheer* clergyman or doctor of divinity

2 *Philosopher* a natural scientist

Michael (1800)   p. 153

1 *pastoral* concerned with shepherds and life in the country (Latin *pastor* = shepherd)

2 *Green-head Gill* in the north-east of Grasmere Vale, in Westmoreland. A gill or 'ghyll' is 'a steep, narrow valley, with a stream running through it' (W in a note to 'The Idle Shepherd-Boys').

3 *South* the south wind

4 *Richard Bateman* 'The story alluded to here is well known in the country' (W).

5 *parish-boy* a poor boy supported by the parish

6 *Sheep-fold* 'an unroofed building of stone walls, with different divisions. It is generally placed by the side of a Brook, for the convenience of washing the sheep' (W).

VI   from *Poems in Two Volumes* (1807)

I Travelled Among Unknown Men (1801)   p. 167

1 *Lucy* See 'Strange Fits of Passion . . . ', Note 1, p. 295.

To a Butterfly (1802)   p. 167

1 *Emmeline* usually identified as Dorothy Wordsworth

To the Cuckoo (1802)   p. 168

My Heart Leaps Up when I Behold (1802)   p. 169

Ode: Intimations of Immortality from Recollections of Early Childhood (1802–4)   p. 170

1 *Intimations . . . Childhood* W commented: 'To the attentive and competent reader the whole sufficiently explains itself; but there may be no harm in adverting here to the particular feelings or *experiences* of my own mind on which the structure of the poem partly rests. Nothing was more difficult for me in childhood than to admit the notion of death as a state applicable to my own being. I have said elsewhere [in 'We Are Seven']:

> – A simple child,
> That lightly draws its breath,
> And feels its life in every limb,
> What should it know of death? –

But it was not so much from [feelings] of animal vivacity that *my* difficulty came as from a sense of the indomitableness of the spirit within me. I used to brood over the stories of Enoch and Elijah, and almost to persuade myself that, whatever might become of others, I should be translated, in something of the same way, to heaven. With a feeling congenial to this, I was often unable to think of external things as having external existence, and I communed with all that I saw as something not apart from, but inherent in, my own immaterial nature. Many times when going to school have I grasped at a wall or tree to recall myself from this abyss of idealism to the reality. At that time I was afraid of such processes. In later periods of life, I have deplored, as we have all reason to do, a subjugation of an opposite character, and have rejoiced over the remembrances, as is expressed in the lines:

> Obstinate questionings
> Of sense and outward things,
> Fallings from us, vanishings; etc.

To that dream-like vividness and splendour which invests objects of sight in childhood, everyone, I believe, if he would look back, could bear testimony . . . but having in the Poem regarded it as presumptive evidence of a prior state of existence, I think it right to protest against a conclusion, which has given pain to some good and pious persons, that I meant to inculcate such a belief. It is far too shadowy a notion to be recommended to faith, as more than an element in our instincts of immortality' (IF).

2 *tabor* small drum; often an attribute, with musical pipes, of shepherds in classical pastoral poetry

3 *a timely utterance* usually considered to be a reference to the lines from 'My Heart Leaps Up' (see p. 169) quoted as an epigraph at the head of this poem.

Resolution and Independence (1802)   p. 176

1 *the Stock-dove broods* In his Preface to *Poems* (1815), W commented: 'The Stock-dove is said to *coo,* a sound well imitating the note of the bird; but, by intervention of the metaphor *broods,* the affections are called in by the imagination to assist in marking the manner in which the bird

reiterates and prolongs her soft note, as if herself delighting to listen to it, and participating of a still and quiet satisfaction, like that which may be supposed inseparable from a continuous process of incubation.'

2 *Chatterton* Thomas Chatterton (1752–70), poet, who committed suicide at the age of eighteen

3 *Him* Robert Burns, poet (1759–96), son of a farmer in Ayrshire

4 *As a huge stone . . . to sun itself* In his Preface to *Poems* (1815), W commented on this stanza: 'In these images, the conferring, the abstracting, and the modifying powers of the Imagination, immediately and mediately acting, are all called into conjunction. The stone is endowed with something of the power of life to approximate it to the sea-beast; and the sea-beast stripped of some of its vital qualities to assimilate it to the stone; which intermediate image is thus treated for the purpose of bringing the original image, that of the stone, to a nearer resemblance to the figure and condition of the aged Man; who is divested of so much of the indications of life and motion as to bring him to the point where the two objects unite and coalesce in just comparison.'

1801 (I grieved for Buonaparté . . .) (1802)   p. 181

1 *Buonaparté* Napoleon Bonaparte (1769–1821), First Consul of France (1799–1804) and Emperor (1804–14 and 1814–15). Wordsworth came to hate Napoleon as the betrayer of the ideals and principles of the French Revolution.

Great Men Have Been Among Us (1802)   p. 181

1 *The later Sidney . . . Milton* Algernon Sidney, political writer (1622–83); Andrew Marvell, poet and pamphleteer (1621–78); James Harrington, republican and political writer (1611–77), Sir Henry Vane the Younger (1613–62); John Milton, republican and poet (1608–74). All these men were active under Cromwell's Commonwealth (1649–60).

It Is Not To Be Thought Of That the Flood (1802)   p. 182

Personal Talk (between 1802 and 1804)   p. 182

1 *Lady . . . Moor* Desdemona, married to Othello, in Shakespeare's play

2 *Una* Lady in *The Faerie Queene* by Edmund Spenser (c.1552–99)

The World is Too Much with Us (between 1802 and 1804)   p. 184

1 *Proteus* the herdsman of Neptune, god of the sea, in Roman mythology

2 *Triton* son of Poseidon and Amphitrite, god and goddess of the sea, in Greek mythology

Composed upon Westminster Bridge (1802)   p. 185

It is a Beauteous Evening, Calm and Free (1802)   p. 185

Toussaint L'Ouverture (1802)   p. 186
1 *Toussaint L'Ouverture* (1743–1803) Negro revolutionary who in 1802
   resisted Napoleon's reimposition of tyranny in the French colony of San
   Domingo (Haiti) when the decree of 1791, which freed the Negroes, was
   revoked, and who was imprisoned and died in captivity

London, 1802 (Milton! thou shouldst be living at this hour) (1802)   p. 186
1 *Milton* John Milton (1608–74), author of *Paradise Lost* (1667) and
   Areopagitica (on the liberty of the press, 1644), whom W admired as a
   great poet and writer on political freedom

The Small Celandine (1803–4)   p. 187

I Wandered Lonely as a Cloud (between 1804 and 1807)   p. 188

Elegiac Stanzas Suggested by a Picture of Peele Castle (1806)   p. 189
1   *Peele Castle . . . Sir George Beaumont* Peele Castle is near Barrow-in-
Furness in North Lancashire. Sir George Beaumont (1753–1827) was a
friend and financial supporter of both Wordsworth and Coleridge. He gave
one of his two paintings of Peele Castle to Mrs Wordsworth.
2   *deep distress* the death of W's brother, John Wordsworth, lost at sea
on 6 February 1805.

Stepping Westward (1805)   p. 191

The Solitary Reaper (1805)   p. 192

VII   from *Poems* (1815, 1820, 1835, 1845)

The Simplon Pass (?1799, ?1804)   p. 193
1 *The Simplon Pass* W walked through the Simplon Pass, in Switzerland,
   during a walking tour in September 1790. The poem is incorporated in
   The Prelude (1805), V, ll. 553–72 (1850: VI, ll. 621–40).
2 *Apocalypse* revelation, in particular that of the end of the world in the
   Revelation of John the Divine in the New Testament

Yew-Trees (1804 and 1814; published 1815)   p. 194
1 *Umfraville . . . Percy* probably Robert de Umfraville (1277–1325) and
   Sir Henry Percy (1364–1403), who fought against the Scots

2 *Azincour ... Crecy ... Poictiers*   three battles in the Hundred Years War
   between England and France (1337–1453)

Surprised by Joy (1813–14)   p. 195

1 *Thee*   W commented that the poem 'was in fact suggested by my
   daughter Catherine, long after her death' (IF). She died on 4 June 1812
   at the age of three.

Vernal Ode (1817)   p. 196

1 *'Rerum ... minimis'*   (Latin) 'Nature in her entirety is to be found
   nowhere more than in the smallest things' (Pliny, *Natural History*, XI, i).

2 *Urania*   the muse of astronomy

3 *Clio*   the muse of history

4 *Tartarean den*   the infernal underworld of classical mythology, where
   the wicked are punished

Ode to Lycoris (1817)   p. 200

1 *Lycoris*   This name is used by the Latin poets Virgil (in *Eclogues*, X) and
   Ovid (in *Ars Amatoria*, III), but W makes no further allusion to these
   instances in this poem.

2 *Dian's crescent*   the moon

3 *Cupid ... Urchin*   the Roman god of love, usually depicted as a winged
   boy

4 *halcyon's*   (Greek) kingfisher's

5 *Venus*   the Roman goddess of love

Whence that Low Voice? (between 1806 and 1820)   p. 202

1 *Duddon's side*   the River Duddon in Cumberland and Lancashire. This
   sonnet is number 21 of *The River Duddon*, a series of thirty-four sonnets
   on subjects connected with the river.

Afterthought (between 1806 and 1820)   p. 202

1 *Duddon*   This sonnet is the last in the *River Duddon* sequence (see
   previous note).

Extempore Effusion on the Death of James Hogg (1835)   p. 203

1 *Extempore*   spontaneous

2 *James Hogg*   Scottish poet and novelist (1770–1835). He was born in the
   Ettrick Forest and became known as the 'Ettrick Shepherd' (see line 4).

3 *the Border-minstrel*   Sir Walter Scott (1771–1832), Scottish poet and
   novelist

4 *Lamb* Charles Lamb (1775–1834), essayist and poet, and friend of
   Wordsworth and Coleridge (see also Coleridge's 'This Lime Tree Bower
   My Prison', p. 239)

5 *Crabbe* George Crabbe (1754–1832), poet

6 *Her* Felicia Hemans (1793–1835), poet

SAMUEL TAYLOR COLERIDGE

I *Lyrical Ballads* (1798)

The Rime of the Ancient Mariner (1797–8)   p. 207

1 Coleridge made a number of revisions after 1798, and added the
   marginal glosses to the text in *Sybilline Leaves* in 1817; the text here is
   that of 1912, which follows the text of 1834, the last edition of
   Coleridge's poems published in his lifetime. Coleridge's later version of
   the poem has been selected for a number of reasons: in it Coleridge
   tightened the narrative in places, revised a number of obscure expressions,
   abandoned many archaic spellings, and added the often beautiful
   marginal glosses in the style of a seventeenth-century editor of an older
   text. This version has become the standard one.

2 *Facile credo . . . distinguamus* (Latin) 'I can easily believe that there are
   more visible than invisible beings in the universe. But who will tell us of
   the family of all of them? And the ranks and relationships and
   differences and functions of each one? (What do they do? What places
   do they inhabit? [*added by Coleridge*]) The human mind has always
   circled around the knowledge of these things but has never reached it.
   Still, it is certainly desirable sometimes to contemplate in the mind, as it
   were in a picture, the image of a greater and better world: lest the mind,
   accustomed to the small details of daily life, become contracted, and
   sink entirely into trivial thoughts. But meanwhile we must be watchful
   of truth and must keep within suitable limits, in order that we may
   distinguish the certain from the uncertain, day from night.
       Thomas Burnet (?1635–1715), *Archaeologicae Philosophicae* (1692)

3 *How a Ship . . . country* This 'Argument' is from the 1800 edition of
   Lyrical Ballads.

4 *Eftsoons* (archaic) at once

5 *kirk* (Scottish) church

6 *ken*   (archaic) know

7 *swound*   (archaic) swoon, fainting-fit

8 *wist*   (archaic) knew

9 *Gramercy!*   (archaic) Great thanks! (from Old French, 'grant merci')

10 *gossameres*   (archaic spelling) gossamers

11 *clomb*   (archaic) climbed

12 *bemocked*   mocked at, flouted, deluded (*OED*)

13 *Mary Queen*   the Virgin Mary, mother of Christ

14 *sere*   (archaic) thin, worn; dried up, withered (*OED*)

15 *corses*   (archaic) corpses

16 *charnel-dungeon*   dungeon of bones or dead bodies

17 *seraph-man*   angel

18 *ivy-tod*   (archaic) ivy-bush

19 *shrieve me*   hear my confession and grant me absolution

20 *vesper bell*   bell for the evening church-service (vespers)

21 *forlorn*   forsaken

The Foster-Mother's Tale (1797)   p. 228
1 *A Dramatic Fragment*   This poem is an excerpt from Coleridge's tragic drama *Osorio* (1797). Cf. 'The Dungeon' (p. 234).

The Nightingale (1798)   p. 231
1 *Conversation Poem*   poem written in a conversational manner (but usually a monologue). C (who coined the term) was influenced by what he called the 'divine chit-chat' of several of the poems of William Cowper (1731–1800), particularly *The Task*. C's other major conversation poems are 'This Lime Tree Bower My Prison', 'Frost at Midnight' and other poems of the late 1790s.

2 *'Most musical ... melancholy'*   John Milton (1608–74), 'Il Penseroso' (line 62)

3 *conceit*   trope, figure of speech

4 *Philomela*   In classical mythology Philomela was raped by Tereus, who cut out her tongue to prevent her accusing him. She communicated the truth to her sister Procne by means of needlework. To save her from Tereus' subsequent wrath, the gods turned her (in Ovid's version, *Metamorphoses*, VI) into a nightingale.

5 *Friend ... Sister*   William and Dorothy Wordsworth

The Dungeon (1797)   p. 234
1 *The Dungeon* The whole poem is taken from Act V of C's play *Osorio* (1797). Cf. 'The Foster-Mother's Tale' (p. 228).

II Other Poems

The Eolian Harp (1795)   p. 235
1 *Eolian Harp* wind-harp or wind-lute: a rectangular box, with strings across an aperture in one of its sides, which produces a musical sound when the wind blows across it
2 *Cot* cottage
3 *Meet* fitting, suitable
4 *sequacious* following in coherent order
5 *Plastic* moulding, giving form or shape, creative
6 *Wilder'd* bewildered

Reflections on Having Left a Place of Retirement (1795)   p. 237
1 *Cot* cottage
2 *Bristowa's* Bristol's
3 *Howard's* John Howard (1726–90) was a prison reformer.

This Lime-Tree Bower My Prison (1797)   p. 239
1 *long-expected friends . . . accident* The friends were William and Dorothy Wordsworth, and Charles Lamb; the accident occurred when C's wife Sara 'accidentally emptied a skillet of boiling milk over my foot'.
2 *Charles* See Note 1.
3 *strange calamity* In 1796 Charles Lamb's sister, Mary, had stabbed their mother to death in a fit of madness.

Frost at Midnight (1798)   p. 242
1 *infant* C's two-year old son, Hartley (1796–1849)
2 *stranger* referring to the film of ash (line 15). C's note of 1798 commented: 'In all parts of the kingdom these films are called *strangers* and supposed to portend the arrival of some absent friend.'
3 *preceptor* schoolmaster: the Revd James Bowyer of Christ's Hospital, London, where C was at school

France: An Ode (1798)   p. 244.
1 *When France . . . upreared* referring to the outbreak of the French Revolution in 1789

2 *The Monarchs . . . And Britain* The kingdoms of Prussia and Austria declared war on France in 1792, England and Holland in 1793.

3 *Blasphemy's loud scream* a reference to the atheistic element in the French Revolution

4 *Helvetia's* Switzerland's. France invaded Switzerland in March 1798.

Fears in Solitude (1798)   p. 247

1 *Written . . . invasion* The poem was written at Nether Stowey (see line 221) in Somerset on 20 April 1798. Fear of a French invasion was felt particularly in the southern counties of England.

2 *all must swear* This refers to the swearing of oaths of loyalty to the church and the king, and perhaps also to the oaths sworn by members of radical political organisations, both of which became increasingly prevalent in this period of response to or reaction against the French Revolution. C argues here (lines 73–80) that these oaths have become mere blasphemous lip-service.

3 *my friend* Thomas Poole

Kubla Khan (1798)   p. 253

1 *Purchas's Pilgrimage* Samuel Purchas, *Purchas his Pilgrimage* (1613)

2 *Then . . . mirror* from Coleridge's poem 'The Picture; or, the Lover's Resolution'

3 *(Greek phrase)* 'I shall sing a sweeter song tomorrow' (recalling Theocritus' *Idylls*, I, l. 145)

4 *Kubla Khan* The Mongol Kublai Khan was the founder of the Yuan dynasty in China in the thirteenth century.

5 *Alph* probably from the Greek river Alpheus; in myth its waters are said to rise again as the fountain of Arethusa, the nymph who fled from the river god. The Alpheus flows in places underground.

6 *Mount Abora* probably an echo of Mount Amara in Milton's *Paradise Lost,* IV, l. 282, (' . . . where Abassin Kings their issue guard') – in legend one of the supposed locations of Paradise. (It is also relevant to C's poem that 'paradise', mentioned in the last line, comes from a Persian word meaning a walled garden.)

Christabel (1801)   p. 256

1 *Preface* The Preface was added for the edition of C's poems published in 1816.

2 *weal* (archaic) well-being

3 *Mary mother* the Virgin Mary, mother of Christ

4 *palfrey* (archaic) saddle-horse

5 *amain* (archaic) at full speed

6 *I wis* (archaic: a misunderstanding of Old English 'iwis', 'certainly') I know

7 *cincture* (archaic) belt or girdle

8 *bale* (archaic) sorrow

9 *I wis* See Note 6, above.

10 *plight* (archaic) plait

11 *presence-room* 'a room prepared for ceremonial presence or attendance' (OED)

12 *kenned* (archaic) knew

13 *I ween* (archaic) I suppose

14 *boon* (archaic) favour, reward

15 *descry* (archaic) see, discover

16 *askance* sideways

17 *The Conclusion to Part II* C pointed out (in a letter to Southey, 6 May 1801) that this conclusion was prompted by thoughts about his son Hartley. The lines have only a very oblique connection (the idea of words of bitterness arising from love) with Sir Leoline's anger in the preceding scene. As William Empson has pointed out, the connection is so oblique that C had to change line 639 from 'And did not work confusion there' (in the original MS) to 'And did but work confusion there', to make Sir Leoline's feelings fit in better with the conclusion (*Coleridge's Verse*, p. 245).

Dejection: An Ode (1802) p. 276

1 *Ballad of Sir Patrick Spence* an early Scottish ballad (usually spelled *Sir Patrick Spens*), included in Percy's *Reliques of Ancient English Poetry* (1765)

2 *Aeolian lute* See 'The Eolian Harp', Note 1, p. 304.

3 *Lady* In the original, longer version of the poem, composed on 4 April 1802, the lady was named as Sara Hutchinson (see 'Letter to Sara Hutchinson', in Coleridge, *Poems*, edited by John Beer, 1974). In other versions 'Lady' was replaced by 'Edmund' (a fictitious name) or 'William' (Wordsworth).

4 *Otway's self* Sir Thomas Otway (1652–85), author of *Venice Preserv'd* and other tragic dramas of the Restoration period

Hymn before Sunrise, in the Vale of Chamouni (1802)   p. 280

1 *Hymn ... Chamouni*   The poem is an expansion of a translation, 'Ode to Chamouny', of a twenty-line German poem by Friederika Brun. C's poem was revised from that of its first publication as 'Chamouni; the Hour before Sunrise. A Hymn' in the *Morning Post,* 11 September 1802. In this version the poem was preceded by the following headnote by Coleridge: 'Chamouni [modern spelling 'Chamonix'] is one of the highest mountain valleys of the Barony of Faucigny in the Savoy Alps; and it exhibits a kind of fairy world in which the wildest appearances (I had almost said horrors) of Nature alternate with the softest and most beautiful. The chain of Mont Blanc is its boundary; and besides the Arve it is filled with sounds from the Arveiron, which rushes down from the melted glaciers, like a giant, mad with joy, from a dungeon, and forms other torrents of snow-water, having their rise in the glaciers which slope down into the valley. The beautiful *Gentiana major,* or greater gentian, with blossoms of the brightest blue, grows in large companies a few steps from the never-melted ice of the glacier. I thought it an effecting emblem of the boldness of human hope, venturing near, and, as it were, leaning over the brink of the grave. Indeed, the whole vale, in its every light, its every sound, must needs impress every mind not utterly callous with the thought – Who *would* be, who *could* be an Atheist in this valley of wonders!'

2 *BLANC ... Arveiron*   See C's headnote. The mountain and the rivers are in Switzerland.

3 *Hierarch*   priest

Answer to a Child's Question (1802)   p. 283

The Pains of Sleep (1803)   p. 283

To William Wordsworth (1807)   p. 285

1 *a poem ... mind*   Wordsworth's autobiographical poem *The Prelude,* subtitled *The Growth of a Poet's Mind* (largely completed by 1805, but not published until 1850)

2 *Hyblean*   like the bees of Hybla, a city and mountain in Sicily, legendarily famous for its honey

3 *thou ... there*   Wordsworth travelled in France in 1791–2 during the early phase of the French Revolution

4 *An Orphic song*   an inspiring, creative poem. Orpheus was a poet in Greek myth who could move even inanimate things with the music of his lyre.

5 *Bard* poet (particularly one who celebrates mythical, national and historic events); originally the name given to a minstrel of the ancient Celtic peoples (Gauls, British, Welsh, Irish and Scots)

6 *Halcyon . . . hours* The ancient Sicilians believed that just before the winter solstice the *halcyon* (Greek, kingfisher) laid its eggs on the sea where they incubated for fourteen days, during which time the sea was completely calm.

7 *constellated foam* C added as a footnote his description of the sea viewed from a boat, from Satyrane's First Letter in his periodical magazine *The Friend,* No. 14: 'A beautiful white cloud of foam at momentary intervals coursed by the side of the Vessel with a roar, and little stars of flame danced and sparkled and went out in it: and every now and then light detachments of this cloud-like foam dashed off from the vessel's side, each with its own constellation, over the Sea, and scoured out of sight like a Tartar Troop over a wilderness.'

Work Without Hope (1825)   p. 288

1 *amaranths* flowers, in myth and literary tradition, which never fade (from Greek *amarantos*, everlasting)

Index of Poem Titles

Index of First Lines